Advance Praise for Howard Gardner's
Truth, Beauty, and Goodness Reframed

"This is a profound deepening of Gardner's earlier work on the various forms of intelligence. He now sees our ways of understanding the world as operating in, as it were, symphonic relations to each other, yielding the rich diversity that characterizes human thought in different cultural settings. This new book has a stunning freshness about it, a real leap forward. Bravo!"

> —Jerome Bruner, University Professor, New York University, and author of *The Process of Education*

"With this bravely imaginative book, fearlessly striking out in regularly contested terrain, Gardner has definitely established himself, along with his pantheon of mentors, Erikson, Bruner and Piaget, as one of the top social scientists of his age. Starting with his ground-breaking *Frames of Mind*, his genius has been marinating and is now fully manifest in this marvelous book."

> —Warren Bennis, Distinguished Professor of Business and University Professor, University of Southern California, and author of *Still Surprised: A Memoir of a Life in Leadership*

"This book is not merely informative, although it is surely that. It helps us understand and provokes us to think more deeply about some of the most important questions we face in trying to live a full and rewarding life."

> —Derek Bok, former president, Harvard University

ALSO BY HOWARD GARDNER

The Quest for Mind

The Arts and Human Development

The Shattered Mind

Developmental Psychology

Artful Scribbles

Art, Mind, and Brain

Frames of Mind

The Mind's New Science

To Open Minds

Art Education and Human Development

The Unschooled Mind

Creating Minds

Leading Minds *(with Emma Laskin)*

Multiple Intelligences: The Theory in Practice

The Disciplined Mind

Intelligence Reframed

Good Work
(with Mihaly Csikszentmihalyi and William Damon)

Changing Minds

Multiple Intelligences: New Horizons

The Development and Education of the Mind

Five Minds for the Future

TRUTH, *Beauty,* and **Goodness** Reframed

EDUCATING FOR THE VIRTUES
IN THE TWENTY-FIRST CENTURY

Howard Gardner

BASIC BOOKS

A Member of the Perseus Books Group
New York

Published by Basic Books,
A Member of the Perseus Books Group
387 Park Avenue South
New York, NY 10016

Books published by Basic Books are available at special discounts for bulk purchases in the United States by corporations, institutions, and other organizations. For more information, please contact the Special Markets Department at the Perseus Books Group, 2300 Chestnut Street, Suite 200, Philadelphia, PA 19103, or call (800) 255-1514, or e-mail special.markets@perseusbooks.com.

The Library of Congress has catalogued the printed edition as follows:
Gardner, Howard.
    Truth, beauty, and goodness reframed : educating for the virtues in the twenty-first century / Howard Gardner.
        p. cm.
    Includes bibliographical references and index.
    ISBN 978-0-465-02192-5 (alk. paper)
    1. Virtues—Study and teaching. I. Title.
BJ1531.G28 2011
179'.9—dc22
                                                              2010049055

E-book ISBN: 978-0-465-02337-0

10 9 8 7 6 5 4 3 2 1

To my colleagues at the Museum of Modern Art

Contents

Preface

In 1904 Henry Adams, notable historian and member of arguably the most distinguished family in American history, published privately a lengthy (close to two-hundred-page), convoluted essay called *Mont-Saint Michel and Chartres: A Study of Thirteenth-Century Unity*.* Adams felt inadequate to deal with the many transformations that had taken place since his birth in 1838—the growth of cities, the rise of mass transportation, the influx of immigrants, the political assassinations, scientific breakthroughs such as Darwinism, and, above all, the new technologies—X-rays, radio, the automobile. Unlike his contemporary, the novelist Henry James, Adams did not turn his back on these unwelcome developments and move to Europe. Instead, he looked with nostalgia to a much earlier time—indeed, to Europe of the medieval era.

As he saw it, life in France in the eleventh and twelfth centuries represented an ideal. And that ideal was most dramatically conveyed,

*All references can be found in the notes section, beginning on page 209.

indeed embodied, by the magnificent Gothic cathedrals—awe-inspiring buildings where individuals of various backgrounds and classes gathered to worship, to behold splendid works of art, to hear magnificent chorale works, and to be spiritually uplifted. These cathedrals testified to a precious unity in life. The abstract entity—the Church—and its physical realization—the cathedral—represented a world to which all should aspire. That world was *true*—directed by the word of God. It was *beautiful*—a magnificent construction made by man in the image of God. And it was *good*—with the inspiring light of the Church, and the examples of Christ and of the saints, people could and would live a good life. In a characteristic passage, Adams waxes rhapsodically:

> The whole Mount still kept the grand style; it expressed the unity of Church and State, God and Man, Peace and War, Life and Death, Good and Bad; it solved the whole problem of the universe . . . God reconciles all. The World is an evident, obvious, sacred harmony. . . . One looks back on it all as a picture; a symbol of unity; an assertion of God and Man in a bolder, stronger, closer union than ever was expressed by other art.

And as if the comparison with his own age was not sufficiently clear, Adams puts it into words: "All the centuries can do is to express the idea differently: a miracle or a dynamo; a dome or a coal pit; a cathedral or a world's fair."

Nearly a century later, in 2010, novelist-turned-essayist David Shields published a book entitled *Reality Hunger: A Manifesto*. This book proves more difficult to describe than Adams's. Presented in twenty-six chapters, each identified by an alphabet letter and a pithy title, the book actually consists of 618 squibs ranging from a few words to a page or so. The terrain of topics covered is very wide—

from writing to memory to communication to politics—and the ordering of the squibs seems arbitrary, even random.

What makes the book unique is that nearly all of it consists of quotations from other writers. The careful or informed reader gradually infers that much of the text comes from others; but in most cases it is not clear who is the "I" or "we" that is penning the words or what is the book or other literary work being referenced. Only at the end of his book does the ascribed author Shields state what he has done and why—and then, reluctantly, at the advice of lawyers at Random House, he supplies dozens and dozens of footnotes, indicating the sources of nearly all of the quotations.

But by this time, readers like me have become suspicious. If we have been led along a deceptive path for two hundred pages, why should we suddenly believe the author? And indeed, nearly all of the quotations call into question what truth is, whether it can be achieved, whether it matters. Consider just a few:

"The life span of a fact is shrinking, I don't think there's time to save it."

"All the best stories are true."

"Something can be true and untrue at the same time."

"It's difficult to separate what happened from what seemed to happen."

I am impelled to revisit Shields's book in light of the trinity that inspired Henry Adams. As a student of reality, I have to ask: "What, if anything, in Shields's book is *true*?" As a student of morality, I have to ask: "Is it *good* to publish a book that actually is a string of quotations, initially unacknowledged as such?" And as a student of the arts, I have to ask: "Is this work *beautiful*?"

In principle, David Shields's book could have been written at any time—certainly at the time of Henry Adams and perhaps even during the Middle Ages. Yet, it is unimpeachably a work of our time. It represents the sentiments of postmodernism—the unflinching challenge to any notion of impeccable virtues. And it self-consciously embodies the practices of collaging, mashing, and pastiching that are enabled by the new digital media.

The two books—and these two authors—exemplify the problematic of the present volume. No longer, if ever, can we accept such terms as *truth*, *beauty*, and *goodness* without scrutiny, if not skepticism. And yet, at least some of us, and perhaps most of us, want to preserve them in a valid form.

And so my goal in this book is twofold: to define truth, beauty, and goodness for our time and to explicate how we might nurture these virtues going forward.

| Chapter 1 | # The Virtues and the Challenges |

Here I am, sitting in my study in Cambridge, Massachusetts. It's a lovely, chilly January morning, with the sunlight streaming through the window to my left. In a box above my desk is a set of cards, each bearing a reproduction of a well-known Impressionist painting. The book on which I am now working—and that you are now reading—has two purposes. First, it's designed to help all of us think clearly about the current status of three crucial human virtues—truth, beauty, and goodness. In the light of this reframing, I offer suggestions to parents, teachers, and others, including ourselves, who ponder how we should educate across the generations.

I've just written a few sentences that would seem beyond objection, at least to anyone except a trained philosopher. Indeed, the sentences appear to exemplify what I'll term the *classical virtues*. The statements are *true*—it really is January, I am actually seated in my study, etc. I refer to paintings by artists like Claude Monet and Edgar

Degas, works of art that are widely considered to be *beautiful*. And I have cited the goals of my literary exercise—to discuss pivotal issues thoughtfully and to offer sound educational recommendations—both of which undertakings are widely considered to be *good*.

Let's suppose that statements like these, and the sentiments that they capture, were actually as unproblematic as I've just claimed. This book would be easy to complete—indeed, it could stop right here. And indeed, most of us do live our lives taking these virtues largely for granted: We assume that most of what we hear from others, pick up in the media, perceive with our own senses, is *true*. We could scarcely function if we devoted real time to doubting each and every input to our senses and our psyche. Likewise, whether or not we invoke the word *beauty*, our choices reflect our aesthetic sensibilities: We value certain sights and sounds above others, gravitate toward certain scenes and experiences even as we avoid others, and attend to our own appearances, as well as the looks of those humans (and pets and gardens and dining rooms and meals) for whose presentation we feel responsible. And then, there's the matter of our relations to other people, and our evaluations of the behaviors of others—those known to us personally as well as those drawn from the news, history, or literature. We rarely hesitate to judge some as good, some as bad, most others as an indeterminate amalgam. We could hardly survive—in fact we could scarcely make it through the day—if we did not, at least implicitly, navigate among the true (and what is not true), the beautiful (and what is not beautiful), and the good (and what is not good). Just try to do so!

Our classical virtues, however, have been pummeled by developments in our era. In the West, in recent decades, conceptions of the true, the beautiful, and the good have been subjected to considerable, perhaps unparalleled, strain from two unexpected quarters—both quite new: the ideas that we describe as postmodern and the ever-expanding, ever more powerful digital media.

From one angle—a *philosophical* one—postmodern critiques emanating from the humanities have questioned the legitimacy of this trio of concepts (hereafter, *the trio*). According to this skeptical account, assessments of what is true or beautiful or good reflect nothing more than the preferences of whoever holds power at a given moment; in a multicultural, relativistic world, the most to which we can aspire are civil conversations across often irreconcilable divides. And so, for example, the mild postmodernist might challenge my characterization of Impressionist art as beautiful, claiming that I am just yielding to an account of painting that, by an accidental set of circumstances, has come to dominate textbooks. The more aggressive postmodernists would throw out the term *beautiful* altogether—claiming either that the concept is meaningless or something even more venal: shorthand for stating that I have ascribed to myself the right to determine merit. So, too, my statements about truth and about goodness would be seen as arrogant, subjective, or meaningless.

From a quite different angle—a *technological* one—the new digital media have ushered in a chaotic state of affairs. Thanks to their predominance, we encounter a mélange of claims and counterclaims; an unparalleled mixture of creations, constantly being revised; and an ethical landscape that is unregulated, confusing, indeed largely unexamined. How to determine what is truth—when a statement on Wikipedia about who I am and what I am doing can be changed by anyone at any time? Or when we can all present ourselves on social network sites any way we want? Or when blogs can claim without evidence or consequence that the current American president was born in Kenya? How to ascertain what is beautiful—when a photograph by a once acknowledged master can be endlessly edited on Photoshop, or when judgments of works of art rendered by a majority vote are given more weight than those offered by experts? How to arrive at goodness—the right course of action—when it is so easy to circulate unsubstantiated rumors about another person's private life, or when nearly everyone downloads pirated music even though it is techni-cally illegal to do so.

The postmodern critiques and the digital media have independ-ent origins and histories, and yet they make strong and powerful bed-fellows. Either force alone should engender anxiety in those of us who value truth, beauty, and goodness; taken together, they should give pause even to the most confident among us. In this book, I unflinch-ingly defend the importance, indeed the essential vitality, of this trio. Without claiming that they are the sole unsettling agents, I seek to take seriously the threats posed by postmodernism and the digital media. I trust that the resulting analysis will tease out the "essential core" of these virtues, help us to preserve that core in our time, and suggest how best to pass these virtues on to succeeding generations.

Why *should* we care about the true, the beautiful, and the good? And why *do* we care? Why, indeed, do I care, so deeply? Such caring is fundamental to our condition as human beings, and has been so for thousands of years. Early humans displayed Machiavellian intelli-gence: They deceived one another through words or deeds, acts that are possible only if one person believes that a fellow member of the species does not have access to what the first person believes to be true. Such humans also decorated themselves, their graves, and, most dramatically, the interior walls of caves where they practiced rites—surely dawning (and perhaps crowning) manifestations of beauty. And even as statues were erected to commemorate human and di-vine heroes, swift and brutal punishments awaited those who bla-tantly violated the norms of the group—those who committed deeds deemed villainous. Indeed, since the dawn of history, every known civilization has developed a conception of which statements are true and which are false; which experiences are considered to be beautiful, ugly, or banal; and which human actions and relationships are deemed good, compromised, or frankly evil.

Human beings reached a crucial milestone when they began ex-plicitly to speak and write about these virtues and their lack: In the founding texts of the Hebrew Bible, the Confucian Analects, the Vedic Upanishads we find telling references to important truths, examples of beautiful language and images, and clear identification of good and evil. And a high point arrived when the philosophers of Athens—preeminently Socrates, Plato, and Aristotle—laid out explicitly their own definitions of truth, beauty, and goodness and what it means to lead lives guided by this set of virtues. (Philosopher Alfred North Whitehead was within acceptable hyperbolic limits when he wrote: "The safest general characterization of the European philosophical tradition is that it consists of a series of footnotes to Plato.")

At times, the definition and delineation of these virtues may not have been widely debated but rather simply dictated from on high. Totalitarian and authoritarian regimes pose fundamental challenges to the ongoing exploration of the three virtues—because despots like Stalin, Mao, or Hitler declare that these matters have been settled and insist on silencing all those who might dare to dissent. Writer George Orwell had such societies in mind when, in his dystopian novel *1984*, the Ministry of Truth declares, "War is peace, Freedom is slavery."

While concern with the virtues is always looming, vigorous debate about them has permeated the most vital societies. Is knowledge of truth innate, as suggested by Socrates' interrogation of a slave, or is it established by the kinds of observations and classifications arrived at by knowledgeable observers and detailed by Aristotle? Is beauty achieved by rigorous adherence to the golden mean and ratios, or is it a gift divinely offered by or seized from the gods or from God? Does goodness emerge from a single deity, from conflicts among those perched on the Olympian pantheon, or from laws chiseled on a tablet by a powerful leader or by representatives of the populace? Such discussion seems to have flourished during Hammurabi's reign in Babylon, the Greece of the fourth century, Republican-era Rome, the Sung Dynasty in China, the Moorish caliphate in Syria and Egypt, the Italian Renaissance, and the founding of the great constitutional democracies of the modern age. Armed with historical hindsight, we clearly discern the threats posed when a spirit of debate and inquiry collides with narrow delineations: the medieval Cordoba of Maimonides is overwhelmed by the Spain of the Inquisition; the Confucian China of poets, painters, and sages gives way over the centuries to the human massacres and cultural destructions of Maoist China.

But when conceptions within a society conflict too stridently with one another, epochal upheavals are likely. Consider the last gasps of czarist Russia in the first decades of the twentieth century, or the waning years of the German Weimar Republic in the late 1920s. In each case, civil debate waned, armed camps arose; to paraphrase the poet Yeats's phrase, "the center did not hold." The ultimate results were Stalinist Russia of the gulag and Nazi Germany of the concentration camps—societies in which *any* open discourse about the virtues became taboo.

In our own society and in our own time, both nationally and over much of the planet, unfettered inquiry and debate are manifest—and this state of affairs is certainly preferable to the alternative. Consider some examples. For every pro-virtue statement from one authority, one finds an objection from another. Nobel Prize winner Albert Camus declared: "Only one thing on earth seems to be a greater good than justice—that is, if not truth itself, the pursuit of truth." As if in response, Nobel Prize winner Harold Pinter claimed that "[t]here are no hard distinctions between what is true and what is false. A thing is not necessarily either true or false; it can be both true and false." Writer Gustav Flaubert tried to have it both ways: "Of all lies, art is the least untrue." A whole generation of artists and writers about art avoid discussions of beauty; and then, in short order, literary critic Elaine Scarry, philosopher Roger Scruton, and polymath Umberto Eco devote entire books to explorations of beauty. Clearly, these issues require, demand, reexamination. Conditions change, people change, and, in the absence of continuous dialogue, received wisdom evolves into unreflective orthodoxy. Still, we need constantly to steer a course between the papering over of differences, on the one hand, and outright hostility to those of contrasting viewpoints, on the other.

And so, we arrive at our current situation. Any society that hopes to endure must ensure that these concepts and values are passed on in viable form to succeeding generations. For, if we give up lives marked by truth, beauty, and goodness—or at least the perennial quest for them—to all intents and purposes, we resign ourselves to a world where nothing is of value, where anything goes. Lest we succumb to such a joyless or normless or pointless existence, it is vital to revisit the conceptions of the trio in clear light. Recalling the lively debates that marked earlier civilized eras, we need to determine what is essential, what cannot and should not be scuttled, what is no longer relevant or justifiable, and what ought to be reconceived going forward. Debate yes, dismissal no. Ultimately we must transcend the relativism and often concomitant cynicism of postmodernism; we must come to grips with the vast changes entailed in a digital universe; but we cannot simply revert to the simplicities or the absolutisms of past eras or of contemporary dictatorships. We also must reconsider how our young people should be introduced to these three virtues and how—and to what extent—older persons should periodically reconceptualize them.

Start with truth. Courtesy of the postmodern critique, we are insecure in stating that the truth is evident and consensual. Perhaps we are merely seeing the world through our own prejudices—be they those of Fox News or National Public Radio, of the BBC or Al Jazeera. Perhaps truth is too intertwined with power to have any validity at all—what, after all, was *actually* true in Orwellian Stalinist Russia or in Maoist China, or in the "truthiness" of Bush-Cheney-Rumsfeld Washington? And if we consider the welter of information and misinformation available on any search engine, how can we possibly determine what is true, or even whether the *search* for the truth has become a fool's errand?

Next, beauty. Perhaps we can gain universal assent—or at least a landslide majority of experts and art lovers—that a classical Greek vase or a Persian miniature or the seascape by Claude Monet above my desk are beautiful. But as you may remember from Art History 101, the works of Impressionist painters like Monet were widely repudiated by knowledgeable critics 140 years ago. And nowadays, in any comprehensive art museum, we see displayed numerous works that are valued and valuable, but that would not ordinarily merit the epithet *beautiful* (e.g., works by the British painters Francis Bacon and Lucien Freud). No wonder many writers about art now avoid altogether any assertions about beauty. Indeed, in much of the academy or among the chattering classes, it is considered unsophisticated to mention beauty because the purpose of art, as "enlightened opinion" now holds, is not to make stunning objects (that's passé or kitsch) but rather to shock us or make us think anew.

Or consider the options available with the new digital media. One can endlessly make and remake works of art through Photoshop; one can execute countless mash-ups of musical passages; one can string together dozens of verses by poets known and obscure, rewording them as much or little as one wishes. In so doing, one substitutes for an authoritative judgment of "beautiful" the vagaries of individual taste or the cumulative efforts of legions of anonymous creators whose work is never done, or always undone. When any image or sound pattern is evanescent, and when anyone in possession of a mouse can become a creator of art, the term *beauty* seems on thin ground or, if you prefer, floating aimlessly in cyberspace. In a textbook example of postmodern thought, the late critic Susan Sontag opined: "In the form of photographic images, things and events are put to new uses, assigned new meanings, which go beyond the distinction between the beautiful and the ugly, the true and the false, the useful and the useless, good taste and bad."

And finally the good. Within a particular historical era or geographical area, one can with some confidence identify what is good and what is evil. For example, in ancient Athens, valor in war and kindness to slaves qualified as good. Refusal to participate in battle or to condone slavery was a dubious stance—if not grounds for a forced shot of hemlock. But with knowledge of the twists and turns of human history, and growing familiarity with disparate cultures across time and space, we become tentative, timid, about assertions of good and evil. One group's terrorist is another group's freedom fighter: Who embodies good or evil—Athens or Sparta, Hamas or the Jewish Defense League?

Again, our technologically saturated era poses profound challenges to once relatively uncontroversial assertions of what is good, moral, ethical and what is not. How, in a digital era, do we think about a sense of privacy, the rights of authorship, the trustworthiness of an electronic correspondent whom one cannot look in the eye and who may reappear at any moment under a wholly different guise in a social network or on a blog? What is "goodness" in the virtual reality of Second Life? In multiple-user games like World of Warcraft, is it okay to bully and cheat because, after all, such a game is not *really* real? Are the plausible but unconfirmed rumors that circulate at warp speed on the Internet welcome wake-up calls, spurs to further investigation, or pernicious lies? In our fragmented, polyphonic digital age, the ideal of shared moral standards seems ever more elusive.

In my view, the three virtues are conceptually distinct from one another—each must be considered on its own merits (and demerits). As an example, we realize that something can be true (the fact that over fifty-seven thousand Americans lost their lives in the Vietnam War) without being beautiful or good. By the same token, something can be good without being beautiful—consider a gruesome documentary about prison life intended to shock people into embracing prison reform. And a scene of the natural world, after the demise of all human beings, can be cinematically beautiful, even though it is neither true historically nor good, at least for the species that has been annihilated—that is to say, us.

Yet it is important to recognize that what appears self-evident to contemporary informed adults has not always been so. A character in Bernhard Schlink's *Homecoming* muses, "Children hope against hope that what is good is true and beautiful and what is evil is false and ugly." Indeed, in many societies throughout most of history, the three virtues were seen as being integrally linked, if not identical to one another. Writer Margaret Atwood has suggested one such period, with reference to the ancient Egyptian concept of "ma-at." As she puts it, "'Ma-at' meant truth, justice, balance, the governing principles of nature and the universe, the stately progression of time . . . the true, just, and moral standards of behavior, the way things are supposed to be—all those notions rolled up into one short word. Its opposite was physical chaos, selfishness, falsehood, evil behavior—any sort of upset in the divinely ordained pattern of things."

And so, I must walk a fine line here. In what follows, I treat each virtue independently. I'll present its defining characteristics, its constant as well as its varying features, and the threats posed by postmodernism and the digital media. Indeed, as I see it, in our era each of the virtues has a different status and will have a distinctive fate. Yet I'll bear in mind the human tendency—across the ages and across the age range—to conflate the virtues. And I'll take care to point out times when we are in fact dealing with more than one virtue, as well as ways in which the virtues may impact one another.

Having laid out an admittedly grand scheme, I owe it to the reader to reflect on what has brought me to this point. I was trained as a psychologist in the specialized areas of developmental psychology, neuropsychology, and cognitive psychology. While I have wandered far and wide across disciplinary terrains, I still see the world through the lenses of a psychologist. The "far and wide" is captured in three successive thrusts of my work: I began as a psychologist of the arts, hence a researcher of the traditional terrain of *beauty*. Then, for many years, I investigated human cognition: through studies of intellect and understanding, focused on what is *true* and how we make such a determination. Most recently, for a decade and a half, I have collaborated on a study of ethics. Our team has been trying to determine what it means to be a *good* worker, a *good* citizen, a *good* person in the fast-paced, media-drenched, consumer-driven, global society of the twenty-first century. In the absence of a master plan (at least one that has been disclosed to me), my own scholarly life has in fact traced an arc from beauty through truth to goodness.

While I have long been interested in the issues addressed here, my own thinking has changed significantly in recent years. Courtesy of my psychological studies of intelligence—most notably, the theory of multiple intelligences—I became involved in educational efforts in the United States and abroad. This engagement ultimately stimulated me to put forth my own educational philosophy. In *The Disciplined Mind*, published in 1999, I contrived an entire curriculum around three topics: Darwinian evolution, the music of Mozart, and the Holocaust of World War II. These topics were not chosen casually. Rather, evolution was selected explicitly as an example of scientific truth; Mozart, as an example of artistic beauty; the Holocaust, as a historical instance of human evil (the sharpest contrast to good). With the benefit of hindsight, one could say that I wrote that book as a *naïf*—I simply accepted as unproblematic the trio of classical virtues. In this way, I probably resemble most readers—and most teachers—not versed in postmodernist thought.

But I now realize a peril in such naïveté. If we simply accept the virtues, we are unprepared for sophisticated (if not sophistic) arguments that attack notions of the truth, the beautiful, and the good. For example: Since the Impressionists were initially rejected by knowledgeable critics, how do we know we are right in revering their works and extolling their beauty? Are we smarter or more discerning than the "eyes" of 1870? How could slavery, or the inferior status of women, have been embraced in ancient Greece, the very society where philosophy and democracy were first forged? Why did people so long believe that the sun orbits around the earth and that the earth is flat, and why do so many still insist that man was created on the sixth day? (According to a recent poll carried out by the Barna group, 60 percent of Americans believe that God created the universe in six days.) Lack of satisfactory replies to such gadfly queries can lead even sophisticated adults to jettison notions of beauty, truth, and goodness. Restless youths, already primed to challenge conventional wisdom, will even more readily do the same.

In my naïveté, circa 1999, I also ignored rapid cultural changes, such as the emergence of the new digital media, which at the very least *problematize* these classical notions. If an entry in Wikipedia can be altered on a minute-by-minute basis, how can we establish what is true or, indeed, if truth even exists? If artist Damien Hirst's website consistently attracts attention and his art commands record-breaking prices, can we therefore conclude that his works—perhaps most notoriously, a dead shark floating in formaldehyde—must be beautiful or that beauty no longer matters? If a teenager commits suicide after being de-friended by a person on Facebook or photographed surreptitiously having sex, is there an evil person whom one can blame? I understand the feelings of a character in Daniel Kehlmann's novel *Fame*: "How strange that technology has brought us into a world where there are no fixed places anymore. You speak out of nowhere, you can be anywhere, and because nothing can be checked, anything you choose to imagine is, at the bottom, true. If no one can prove to me where I am, if I myself am not absolutely certain, where is the court that can adjudicate these things?"

While the idea for a book may appear in a memorable instant, its germs are invariably dispersed over space and time. Even when I wrote *The Disciplined Mind*, I was aware that I had chosen the most clear-cut examples, and that notions of truth, beauty, and goodness were by no means self-evident or beyond controversy. When I lecture, questioners frequently remind me of this point. Among my children, their friends, and my own students, I noticed ever more relativistic, if not nihilistic, views of the classical virtues: For those a generation or two younger, the virtues seemed highly problematic, if not anachronistic. I'd been aware of postmodernist accounts for many years, but because of my deepening involvement with New York's Museum of Modern Art, I began to pay more attention to them. Perhaps most important, I began to learn about the digital media. Very tentatively, I began to use them myself, and, with the help of talented colleagues, I undertook a systematic exploration of their use by young people. It gradually dawned on me that my most fundamental assumptions were being challenged. It was time for me to study, to reflect, and, as has been my wont, to present my conclusions in book form.

I can state these conclusions succinctly: Each of the virtues encompasses an abstract realm of experience—verbal propositions, evocative experiences, and relations among human beings, respectively. Each is best exemplified by certain specific human activities: Science and journalism traffic in truth; art and nature are the sphere of beauty; goodness concerns the quality of relations among human beings. The trio of virtues, while unquestionably in flux and under attack, remain essential to the human experience and, indeed, to human survival. They must not and will not be abandoned.

Turning to specifics: We can be ever more confident that truths exist in several spheres. We must strive to identify and affirm truths, while remaining open to revising them in the light of new knowledge. We must acknowledge the limitations of a canon of beauty and, equally, of a set of artistic attributes with beauty at the helm. Beauty now takes its place alongside other compelling aesthetic values, such as interestingness As compensation, we now each have an unequaled opportunity to attain an individualized sense of beauty. With respect to the good, we must recognize two spheres: the long-standing morality that obtains among neighbors, and the ethics associated with the ever-evolving roles of worker and of citizen. While cherishing their idiosyncratic customs, human societies embedded in a global matrix are now challenged to create and honor conceptions of the good that transcend particulars of time and place.

Every age has its predominant modes of explanation, ones that govern or even constitute the thinking of the era. Following the Newtonian revolution in physics, for instance, it became common to conceptualize people and the universe as mechanical devices. Likewise, the philosophers of the Enlightenment saw the world as marching steadily forward to the tunes of *progress*, *reason*, and *perfection*—and if a political revolution could help move things along, so much the better. Then, in reaction to the excesses of the dramatic political upheavals at the end of the eighteenth century, the nineteenth century ushered in beliefs in the distinctive practices of individual cultures, civilizations, regions, nations, and underscored the power of irrational forces and thoughts.

When I examine my own motivations for writing the present book, I realize that I have been stimulated, in significant measure, by the need to respond to two powerful analyses of the human condition—one emanating from biology, the other from economics. In my view, these accounts have gained undue ascendancy in recent decades. To be sure, nearly all of us have learned from concepts and findings in biology and economics—I freely cite their examples and arguments. Yet, taken as a whole, I take sharp issue with these lenses on the world. Those beholden to biological or economic accounts regularly give short shrift to the power of individual agents, and to the efficacy of individuals voluntarily and tirelessly working together to achieve desirable goals. In a sense, this book may be read as a sustained argument against the hegemonies of biological determinism and/or economic determinism.

First, the biological lens. As we learn more about the brain and about genetics, both scholars and laymen become curious about the extent to which various human characteristics are determined by neurobiology. Is there a gene for our aesthetic sense? Are certain parts of the brain dedicated to the detection of truth? Which? Can we identify the circuits that govern moral judgments? Such biologically specifiable sites may or may not be identified. But simply knowing that certain genes incline us toward preferring one graphic rendering over another, or that certain areas of the brain light up when we are making a difficult ethical decision, hardly constitutes the last words on our senses of beauty or morality. I am not even certain that such knowledge constitutes the first word: Just what is it that we now know that we did not know before?

Even more insidious is a two-step biological argument: (1) Human beings are what we are because of evolution—which is essentially a truism; (2) therefore, thanks to a slippery slope, evolution determines the nature and limits of our judgments of truth, our aesthetic preferences, our moral and ethical codes. On the contrary: I argue that what is distinctly human is our capacity to change, or to transcend, whatever traits and inclinations we may have as initial endowment, courtesy of evolution. Our prehistory, our recorded history, and our numerous diverse cultures testify to the flexibility of our species and the unfathomability of its future course.

Second, the economic lens. Without question, economics has become the privileged mode of social-scientific explanation for human behavior. In a way that seems particularly attractive to Americans, but has also proved alluring in other parts of the world, the application of mathematical or statistical models to real-world problems has become an intellectually privileged form of analysis. Let's count, let's rank, let's chart, let's correlate variables. Then we'll know what's what and, in all likelihood, what we should do. Put succinctly, we can and should quantify and rank—and we can trust the results of that quantification and the resulting ranking. The crowd is wise—and so we can rely on its determination of what is true. Equally, the market is unerring, and so the best works of art garner the highest prices. Finally, by a magnificent, if not miraculous process, society ends up better off because each of us pursues our self-interest in a lawful way.

Even before the financial meltdown of September 2008, many commentators pointed out flaws in this view of men and markets. We have had ample demonstrations that markets do not automatically adjust; that people do not know what is in their self-interest; indeed, that both individuals and markets are frequently irrational and not to be trusted; and that their combination can be toxic as well as tonic. Yet, especially in the United States, the economic lens remains the fallback position for much of the population. Even with the flaws and limitations of this perspective freshly recognized, a majority of people believe that societies should turn to economic analyses, whenever possible—a so-called accountability approach. If one mode of ranking does not work, we'll simply employ another. Currently, no alternative view of human nature has anywhere near the sway.

I enjoy the works of journalist Malcolm Gladwell, justly acclaimed for his books on the tipping point, intuitive judgments or "blink," and the often astounding performances that emerge when, for one reason or another, a person is an "outlier." In reading Gladwell, one is struck by the telling example—the expert who senses, in a blink, that the new acquisition by the museum is a fake; or the discovery that professional hockey players tend to be born in the first months of the year; or the phenomenon of the slow-selling book that abruptly leaps onto the best-seller list. On reflection, however, it is not difficult to identify cases that run counter to Gladwell's memorable examples. Intuitive judgments rendered in a blink turn out to be accurate except when they are not, indeed when they are disastrous. Professional hockey players turn out to be born early in the calendar years, except for the many born then who are nothing special, or the numerous talented hockey players who are born later in the year. And the vast majority of books register gradually changing sales, with no realistic chance of making any best-seller list.

In my view, the biological and economic lenses suffer from the same flaw, or, to be kinder, the *limitations* of predictability or explanation. There may be a gene or a brain section that lights up when we are altruistic; but there are all too many situations in which we nonetheless behave selfishly. Human beings may well make decisions rationally, particularly when playing an economics-generated game, except for all of those situations where personality or contextual or ideological factors induce nonrational reactions.

I yield to no person in my admiration for the work of Charles Darwin, and the importance of the evolutionary theory that he first proposed. And yet I believe that efforts to account for human behaviors, potentials, and limitations in Darwinian terms have gone way too far. What human beings come to value as beautiful owes far more to the vagaries of history, culture, and—indeed—pure chance than to the tastes that evolved tens of thousands of years ago on the savannahs of East Africa. By the same token, evolution establishes neither that humans are fundamentally altruistic, empathic, and good nor that human beings are fundamentally selfish, insensitive, and malevolent. Powerful proclivities exist in both directions. Look, rather, at the facts on the ground of history, culture, human development, and education. These facts determine *which* congeries of features comes to the core at a particular time and in a particular circumstance. Human agency matters enormously—indeed, it allows us to transcend the determinism alleged by theorists of the market and theorists of evolution.

In what follows, it is not my intention to whack the biological or economic perspectives, except when such disciplining seems warranted. Rather, I emphasize that biology or economics hardly ever provide the definitive account of human actions, decisions, and thoughts. Even when they work together, as through the new field of neuroeconomics, their explanatory power proves remarkably limited. I want to call attention instead to the importance of unique histories, distinctive cultural profiles, and happy—or unhappy—accidents. And I want to underscore the remarkable capacity of individuals to make their own decisions, even in the face of strong pressures to proceed in a certain direction; and of a few remarkable individuals, by dint of their mastery and their imaginations, to open up new possibilities that change the course of history. When economics and biology add to our understanding, fine; but when they keep us from searching in unexplored regions of the human landscape, as they so often have in recent decades, then these perspectives should be discarded.

One cannot understand the status of these virtues without taking a multidisciplinary perspective: Philosophy has its place, but so do psychology, history, and cultural studies, and, yes, even economics and biology. In the course of what follows, I will wander freely among these disciplinary terrains, while at the same time citing examples from current events and from daily experiences, including my own. But enough of generalities, summaries, promissory notes. It is time now to examine each of the virtues, first in its own terms, then in the light of challenges posed by new currents of thought and new forms of technology. Following the three surveys, I offer my considered views about how best to educate the young, and how those of us who are no longer young can remain engaged with these perennial topics. While not deluding ourselves that we can ever recapture them in idealized form, I believe we can nonetheless preserve central features of the classical virtues.

Chapter 2 | Truth

S ince this chapter is concerned with truth, it is reasonable to begin with a consideration of that virtue, and to make sure that I am committed to telling the truth—otherwise, why should you waste your time reading my words? So let me begin with a simple assertion: Truth is essentially a property of statements, of propositions—two plus two are four, True; two plus two are five, False. Statements can reference any topic—the past, the weather, one's aspirations, one's fears. And as the first sentence in this paragraph reveals, statements can even be about themselves.

In fact, this very situation—that statements can be self-referential—can get us, get me, in trouble. We encounter the famous liar's paradox. Suppose I make the statement "Howard Gardner lies all the time." If that statement, as spoken by me, is true, then I have contradicted myself, by stating a truth. Suppose, on the other hand, that the statement is false (I have been telling the truth about myself in what you've read thus far) and I have lied in characterizing myself as a chronic liar. The liar's paradox has amused many, while giving indigestion chiefly to philosophers. It reminds us that language is a supple resource; like a visual illusion, it can play odd tricks with our minds.

I've hinted that truth (and falsity) are tricky matters. The notion that truth and falseness are self-evident, matters of simple common sense, does not withstand scrutiny. And indeed, I do not believe that we can ever establish truth so reliably, that any statement, let alone any set of statements, can be ruled as inviolably true, for all time, and under all circumstances (though $2 + 2 = 4$ comes pretty close).

Yet it would be catastrophic to embrace the opposite stance—to give up the effort to approach and, when possible, to establish truths. Suppose we were to take postmodern views to an extreme—for example, to state that truth is but an expression of power, or that truth cannot be established with any validity, or that truth is a vacuous concept. Under such circumstances, we could scarcely function at all. Or if we were to cede all judgments to the digital media—if we posited that truth is nothing more than a majority vote on a webpage, or believed that the most recent edit of an online encyclopedia is more definitive than the accumulated judgments of experts—we would be relinquishing considered judgment to the whim of the crowd (or to the web-surfers with the most time on their hands).

It's important for us to salvage, indeed to valorize, the core idea of truth. I believe that human beings, working carefully and reflectively and cooperatively over time, can converge more and more closely to a determination of the actual state of affairs—to the way that things actually are. There is not just a single area of truth, however. There are different truths, in different scholarly spheres, as well as different truths in different practical spheres. These truths should not be confused or conflated with one another.

In what follows, I'll sketch the course of a sense of truth as it develops, note the many reasons why we cannot simply trust the evidence of our senses, consider the various spheres of truth, review the threats to a sense of truth posed by postmodernism and the digital media, and indicate what of value remains. It hardly needs to be stated that the establishment of the legitimacy of truth is important—not least, of course, for the rest of the inquiry into beauty, goodness, and education that I'm undertaking here. For while truth is not the same as beauty or goodness, its absence would preclude considered judgments of any and all virtues.

Truth has its natural home in human language, but the possibility for ascertaining the true state of affairs extends to the prelinguistic infant. From the opening days of life, our five senses tell us what the world is like and, by implication, what it is *not* like. A baby reaches for a cup and grabs it confidently—there really is a cup there. A baby reaches for a virtual cup, puts her fingers around it, discovers a simulacrum instead, and whimpers, acts frustrated, or even wails.

Fast-forward two years and a parallel event occurs on the verbal level. The child announces "There's daddy" and the mother nods her head and says, "That's right, that's daddy." But if the mother points to a picture of herself and says, "That's daddy," the child will be confused and taken aback. "No, no, not daddy," he exclaims. In some sense, as embodied in this simple verbal proposition, the two-year-old knows the difference between truth and falsity.

Our conception of truth arises initially from common sense, with an emphasis both on *common* and on *sense*. We rely in the first instance on our senses and, in the second instance, on what is commonly sensed—that is, what is seen or heard or smelled not just by us but by other representative members of the community, particularly those who are considered to be knowledgeable. And for much of life, as well as for the proverbial "man on the Clapham omnibus" or "the little old lady from Dubuque," that is enough.

Alas, common sense cannot get us very far. Misinformation or disinformation can spread readily through a community—becoming, in a sardonic phrase made famous by economist John Kenneth

Galbraith, the "conventional wisdom." After all, despite the evidence of our senses, the earth is not flat, the sun does not revolve around the earth, the earth and other celestial bodies do not float in the ether, time and space are not absolute, human beings were not created on the sixth day—the list of one-time widely acknowledged truths now rejected is endless. I can add that innumerable truths are of no interest. I could write that today is January 9, tomorrow is January 10, the day thereafter is January 11, etc.—none of which are false, but nothing is gained by amassing a mound of statements that are true but trivial. Even in the area of mathematics, caution is in order. Two and two may not equal five, but parallel lines *do* meet in non-Euclidean geometry.

Even when we *should* rely on our senses, we can easily be manipulated into ignoring the evidence that they willingly provide. Half a century ago, social psychologist Solomon Asch asked people seated around a table to indicate which of two lines was longer. The correct answer was perfectly clear—one line was perceptibly longer than the other. But then in a second round, respondents who were actually confederates of the experiment leader all selected the shorter line. Under these changed circumstances, the innocent subject-responder would usually conform to other members of the group, affirming what he believed to be false, perhaps even beginning to question his senses. This tendency to defer to others has been borne out in numerous experiments. If, for example, one group is led to believe that a certain tune is popular, and a matched group is not given that information, the first group will tend to rate the tune more highly and download it more often. We can readily be swayed against the evidence of our own senses or our own minds. Any defense of truth must be cognizant of such seductions.

Finally, it is important to bear in mind that not all statements can be accurately described as true or false. Many statements are indeterminate, either for the present or for all time. For example, the frequent assertion that "we use only 10 percent of our brains" is not something that can be determined by science. (Indeed, its validity depends on what is meant by the claim and whether it could in fact be ascertained.) And of course, many other statements are either exaggeratedly foolish ("I am the luckiest person on the planet") or poetic ("My love is a red red rose") or meaningless ("Colorless green ideas sleep furiously").

In reflecting on the human quest for truth, we can and should begin with the phenomenal experience of our senses. The possibility of a search for truth relies on the existence of our sense organs—our ways of coming to know the world beyond our skin and outside of our skull. But the search cannot and should not end there. The sphere of human knowledge represents a communal trek, over many centuries and many terrains, to place our senses of truth on firmer footing; to separate warranted truths from those statements that are perhaps equally seductive, at first encounter, but are ultimately judged as false or devoid of meaning; to valorize those statements that deserve to be repeated and perhaps even enshrined in a Hall of Strongly Supported and Significant Truths.

In the search for truth, our greatest allies are the scholarly disciplines and the professional crafts—in short, areas of expertise that have developed and deepened over the centuries. Each discipline, each craft explores a different sphere of reality and each attempts to establish truths—the truths of knowledge, the truths of practice. The firmest set of truths lies in mathematics: $2 + 2 = 4$, and so long as one remains within the realm of arithmetic, this truth will not change. The axioms discovered by Euclid also remain true; only when a new branch of mathematics arises, one called non-Euclidean (or hyperbolic) geometry, can Euclidean assumptions be called into question within that new sub-discipline. Other disciplines—such as physics or biology or history or psychology or economics—have their respective methods and criteria for ascertaining truths.

Even before there was mathematics, there were the practical pursuits—how to plant and harvest crops; how to slay, prepare, and devour an animal; how to smelt and cast bronze; how to lower a fever without harming the patient. I call these the *practical crafts*. The practical crafts range from the so-called learned professions—such as journalism, engineering, and architecture—to the making of objects, be they necklaces, aqueducts, or violins. It may seem that I've deviated from my definition of truth as a property of statements. But importantly, in principle, these practices can be—and often are—put into verbal propositions: "First you look all around you; then you lift your weapon; then you take careful aim, etc." It is usually easier to *demonstrate* how to slay and carve an animal than to *convert* the sequence of actions into a string of words or phrases. Still, the entire industry of self-help books, such as the enormously successful series of "Books for Dummies," assumes that much of what constitutes practice can be translated felicitously into verbal form, with perhaps an occasional illustration.

Undoubtedly there are powerful links between the practical crafts—some of which date back many centuries—and science as it came to be pursued, first in seventeenth-century Europe and now across much of the globe. Bear in mind that Albert Einstein, by anyone's definition a great scientist, began his work life as a patent officer who became intrigued by a practical problem: how one could synchronize the times on clocks at railroad stations strewn along a route. But the discipline of science is a fundamentally different enterprise from that entailed in effective craftsmanship. Science represents an effort to establish not the truths of practice but, rather, a model of how the world works—or perhaps more truly, though less elegantly, multiple models of how the world works. The models are initially descriptive (a caterpillar grows into a moth or butterfly) but ultimately they may be causal (Y occurs because of X) and predictive (If I enable X to happen, Y will result).

Ideally, scientists make scrupulous, disinterested observations and/or execute careful, transparent experiments. On the basis of these observations and experiments, scientists create such models—of the physical world, of the biological world, of humankind, etc. These models are never final. Indeed, what distinguishes science from faith or fiction or folklore is the possibility of altering, rectifying, or disproving the model. Typically this tweaking is done in gradual fashion. But as historians of science have taught us, there are sometimes abrupt and dramatic shifts in scientific paradigms—and then a whole new set of truths (e.g., those about evolution or relativity or plate tectonics) comes to the fore. We can probably order the sciences in terms of the relative security of the truths, with physics near the top of the hierarchy, psychology and economics closer to the bottom. But all sciences march—or at least attempt to march—to the same epistemological drummer.

History also seeks to establish truths, but the discipline of history, and its respective truths, operates in a fundamentally different way. History is an effort to establish what happened in the past—in our terms, to create true statements about the past. But unlike science, history cannot be subject to observation or experimentation; it happened once and that's it. Before the invention of writing, history and myth were to all intents and purposes indistinguishable. Preliterate groups had their "origin myths" but there was no way of establishing the validity of any such account. Once literacy had been devised, historians worked primarily from the written record; more recently, they have come to draw on recorded oral accounts and graphic records (photos, films, videos) and—then—on e-mail chains. But far more so than science, or at least in a different way, history involves an *imaginative leap*: The historian must try to understand how human beings—in some ways similar across time and space, in other ways fantastically, almost unfathomably different across those divides—came to think and act in the way that they did. (The kinds of leaps made by a biologist trying to understand how a caterpillar becomes a butterfly are not comparable.)

Also, and in dramatic contrast to the sciences, historians in each era rework the chronicles of the past. We may not know that much more about the Roman Empire today than we did eighty years ago. But it is inconceivable that contemporary American historians would write that history at the start of the twenty-first century as they would have in 1930; because in our lifetime, for better and worse, the United States *has become* the Roman Empire (a thought presumably far from the minds of American historians at work during the waning years of President Herbert Hoover's term in office). Any contemporary history of Rome will inevitably be colored by that knowledge. And yet despite these caveats, many historians share the faith that they can nonetheless get increasingly close—in the phrase of a famous nineteenth-century historian—to "how it actually was." Echoes contemporary historian Benny Morris: "I believe, and still believe, that there is such a thing as historical truth; that it exists independently of, and can be detached from, the subjectivities of scholars; that it is the historian's duty to try to reach it."

Now, in so characterizing history and science, I am well aware that not all scientists portray their endeavor in precisely the same way, and that there are numerous disputes among historians, historiographers, philosophers of history, and the like about the goals and methods of their profession. Both science and history are moving targets. Scholars in the twenty-first century are much more aware than those of earlier generations that scientists operate under the influence of powerful metaphors (science as exploration, discovery, documentation, thrust and counterthrust), and that both the scope and the tools of history undergo continual changes. Still, most scientists and most historians would concur that the broad strokes I've sketched, when viewed from sufficient distance, are accurately rendered—that is, that science and history are each in pursuit of statements that represent the truths ascertained by their respective disciplines. (Try getting tenure if you deny the difference between true and false accounts.) And probably more important, nearly all would agree that significant differences exist between the discipline (or disciplines) of science with its respective truths, on the one hand, and the discipline (or disciplines) of history with its respective truths, on the other. But not all: The committed postmodernist must knock *all* disciplines off of their pedestals; the postmodernist must arrive at the discouraging conclusion that science is as tenuous as history, that history is as tenuous as science, that any effort to arrive at or nail down scientific or historical truths is a fool's errand.

Other disciplines pursue truth in their own way, but I am not going to march through the course catalogue. (If you suspect that I am trying to avoid assessing the truth of psychology, well, you might just be right!) Instead, I turn to the other arena of truths: practical professions and crafts—what nineteenth-century American philosophers might have considered the spheres of pragmatic truth.

As a specimen craft, one that seeks explicitly to establish its own truths, let's consider journalism—sometimes dubbed the first draft of history. Reporters attempt to capture what is happening as it happens or shortly afterward—today and yesterday. In some ways, journalists operate like historians—they also read texts and try to establish context, motivation, perspective. But of course the journalists have little distance from the topic; their knowledge and vantage point is necessarily limited; they have to triangulate within hours; deadlines always loom. The journalist wants to get the story right, but it is also important that the story be reported promptly.

Journalists are made, not born or instantly created. In an ideal past, they began as apprentices. These cub reporters were sent out, along with established reporters, to cover local stories. They observed how the veterans asked questions, took notes, checked sources, wrote drafts, interacted with editors, conducted follow-ups, posted corrections. No one launched a career by covering the White House for the *New York Times*. Rather, the traditional reporter began with coverage of school board meetings or petty criminal cases in a small city. Only those who mastered the craft—who had done due diligence in Mahanoy City, Pennsylvania—eventually moved to the state house in Harrisburg, the financial district in Philadelphia, or, if they were among the most fortunate, to the Congress of the United States or a capital city in Europe.

This picture of "the making of a journalist" rang true in what one might consider the "golden age" of journalism—the period in mid-century America (and perhaps in other modern nations) when there were just a few major broadcast networks; when certain periodicals such as *Life*, *Look*, *Time*, and the *Saturday Evening Post* were widely read across the country; and when newspapers and magazines were sufficiently profitable to support reporting bureaus across the globe and to allow journalists the time they craved to write, photograph, and edit.

Though well within my own lifetime, that era now seems remote indeed. The proliferation of news outlets means that few, if any, are sampled as widely as the broadcast networks or the weekly publications of 1960. Profit margins are thinner, and many news organizations have either had to cut coverage drastically or go out of business altogether. Most dramatically, the advent of the Internet makes it possible for anyone to report observations as news, to create or spread rumors, to post photos or videos of breaking events, to beat or even to refute outlets of record, such as the *New York Times* or the BBC. And this situation has led to embarrassing situations: journalistic coups by bloggers such as Matt Drudge of the Drudge Report; and scandals of plagiarism or sheer invention by reporters such as Jayson Blair of the *New York Times*.

The pressures and the critiques that characterize the working lives of journalists today make them ready prey for those who dismiss the craft of journalism and/or challenge the ideal of journalistic truth. How indeed, they ask, does a reporter who calls herself a journalist actually differ from a conscientious citizen who tweets what she observes, posts footage of a crime on YouTube, or creates a widely read blog on City Hall or climate change? And, given that many items reported by the "establishment press" turn out to be false, and that the same establishment press misses many important stories altogether, why should we attribute any special status to journalists? Why should we hallow, or expect, journalistic truths?

I disagree sharply with those who would discard journalism-as-we-have-come-to-know-it. For all its flaws, and despite its deficient practitioners, journalism remains an essential and valuable craft—the optimal way that we have of establishing what is happening during *our* time, the time during which we must live, act, make decisions, and suffer or gain from their consequences. Moreover, at a time when ethical lapses and blatant crimes pervade the political and economic and clerical landscapes (and has there ever been a time when, or a place where, such malfeasance was absent?), well-trained investigative journalists are essential for the survival of democratic institutions. (The documents released by Wikileaks require context that should be provided by trained journalists.)

There is a fundamental difference between the effective journalist, on the one hand, and the propagandist, spin doctor, rumor monger, or even well-intentioned citizen blogger on the other. The creed of the journalist requires that she observe events carefully and impartially; assess the reliability of sources, shun (except under extraordinary circumstances) anonymous sources, confirm or ignore rumors, offer individuals who are criticized or charged with a crime an opportunity to rebut, and so on. As is the case with any profession, one gains the skills of reporting only through modeling by experts, careful training with feedback, learning from one's mistakes, interacting over time with experts, and benefiting from their evaluations—positive and critical. It may be hard to believe today, but for decades, many journalists in the United States even refused to vote—they did not want to undermine their disinterested status. Thomas Jefferson famously declared, "Were it left to me whether we should have a government without newspapers or newspapers without a government, I should not hesitate a moment to prefer the latter." He had a valid point, if not a truth to be held as self-evident! This, then, is the practical craft of journalism—a craft dedicated to the rapid ascertainment of facts.

To be sure, at first blush, determining journalistic truth has become much more challenging in the era of the Internet. I am old enough to remember a time when the CBS Evening News delivered what we the viewers believed was *the* authoritative truth about the world each evening, through the mellifluous tones of Douglas Edwards or Walter Cronkite. Cronkite even closed the evening news with the revealingly authoritative "That's the way it is." And each evening his somber and sober sidekick, commentator Eric Sevareid, told us what "it" all meant. Truths of the nightly news were confirmed by weekly issues of *Time* and *Life* magazines. While I would not defend those media as flawless, they did make our lives easier.

Nowadays, no news outlet carries anywhere near that much authority. Young people shun print newspapers, and many prefer not even to get their news from the online edition of the *New York Times* or *Time*. Rather, they read a few blogs, typically favoring those with which they are in agreement, watch satirists Jon Stewart and Stephen Colbert on the comedy channel, and decide what is true (if not beautiful and good) on the basis of these often eccentric sources. Or as young people have often said to me, "If it's important, I'll hear about it."

In my lifetime, there has been a seismic shift. Perhaps reflecting postmodern skepticism about the possibility of establishing truth, authority and objectivity have been supplemented—or even supplanted—by authenticity and transparency. Put differently, the young (and, increasingly, the not-so-young) do not believe individuals because of their status or their training or their expertise. Youths prefer to lend credence to those individuals who seem to be candid and who freely admit their biases.

But I cannot be satisfied with nostalgia. It's important to acknowledge that many "digerati" see the new media as a democratic nirvana—and at times I share their optimism. The online democrat scans dozens of sources regularly, discounts their individual biases, and arrives at his or her own truth or truths—and perhaps even The Truth. Recently I encountered a version of this stance. I bumped into a young man (I'll call him Ned) at one of those conferences where the briefing booklet contained a photo and a short canned bio of each participant. In a matter-of-fact manner, Ned said, "I never pay the slightest attention to these potted bios. Instead, I go to a search engine and read all about the participants so that I will know who they *really* are—the good, the bad, and the ugly." If this dispensation were truly followed, then in a sense we would all become our own best journalists and, in the extreme, our own best historians. And here, indeed, is the challenge for those of us who want to preserve the core notions of truth: Can we survey widely, synthesize wisely, and converge on what has actually happened? If we can do this, if we can take the proper leaf from the practices of Ned, then we are in a better position than ever before to ascertain the actual state of affairs.

Just as scholarly disciplines have their respective truths, professions and crafts have *theirs*, and these truths need to be honed. To be sure, these crafts are far more reliant today than in the past on the results of scholarly work in the disciplines. As appropriate, journalists make use of findings from science, economics, philosophy. Craftspeople make use of mathematics, natural sciences, social sciences—they draw on truths that arise from the disciplines and may be applicable across professions. Professionals such as lawyers or engineers no longer have to develop their own estimates—they can draw on expertise in statistics. Judges increasingly cite scientific findings, and juries must weigh the conflicting testimony of witnesses who exhibit expertise in various disciplines. Even clergy make use of surveys, and some of them conduct their own "institutional research." Yet these importations from the academy do not substitute for the core missions and methods of each profession, art, or craft. Professionals—lawyers, doctors, teachers—rely as well on the practical truths of their profession—"great cases make bad law," "listen carefully to the patient and then listen even more carefully," "over-prepare for class but be prepared to toss away your fifty-minute script if something important happens in the first few minutes." And that is as it should be, because we afford professionals a privileged status and then ask that they render complex, disinterested judgments under conditions of uncertainty.

Despite the example of the young man at the conference, we should not be so naïve as to believe that most individuals can become their own journalists or historians. By the same token, we should not expect that the average surfer of the web can become her own best lawyer, doctor, minister, or teacher. But the proliferation of sources on the web may well usher in a new situation: In the future we *can* expect more knowledge, better questions, and a refusal to accept authority, let alone stand in awe, just because a credentialing agency has placed a few additional letters before or after the professional's given name.

We should remain open to changes in professions, the emergence of new professions, and greater involvement on the part of laypersons. Yet, all who are concerned with the core values of professions must remain vigilant. In one of the most chilling media encounters in recent memory, journalist Ron Suskind was admonished by a senior adviser to President George W. Bush. Suskind was told that journalists live in "the reality-based community" and believe, mistakenly, that their job is to study discernible reality. The adviser went on to declare: "That's not the way the world really works anymore. We're an empire now, and when we act, we create our own reality. And while you're studying that reality—judiciously as you will—we'll act again, creating other new realities, which you can study too, and that's how things will sort out. We're history's actors . . . and you, all of you, will be left to just study what we do." Though the source of these sentiments may be improbable, a more succinct statement of the postmodern view of truth would be difficult to find. The only way to thwart it is to operate on the opposite assumption. Consider this commemoration of David Rosenbaum, a highly acclaimed journalist who was murdered: "He believed that there was, on most stories, something approximating truth out there if you were smart enough and hungry enough to find it."

Whether one considers a scholarly discipline, like history, or a craft like the fashioning of a violin, or a profession like journalism, it remains appropriate to speak about the pursuit of truth. Each of these spheres has its own methods and criteria; each has evolved over time; each must take into account new discoveries, fresh opportunities, unanticipated obstacles. History and journalism yield statements, and statements remain the home ground of truth. But even historians and journalists make various moves in daily practice, moves that could be verbalized but typically are not. The historian, for example, is ever alert to the analogies in the events of the day, while the journalist picks up hints for her craft in movies, television shows, conversations overheard at lunch or during jogs in the park. And when it comes to purely practical crafts, such as the fashioning of objects, then "putting the practices into words" becomes an option rather than a workaday principle. From a distance, then, we can observe a continuum of truth-seeking, ranging from systematic and self-conscious methods of academic scholars (such as scientists) to the less formal approaches of professionals (such as journalists) to the targeted variations of craftspeople (such as jewelers).

If one can speak about "truth" with respect to crafts, is it legitimate to speak about truth with reference to the arts? I've concluded that when it comes to the arts, application of the terms *true* and *false* constitutes a bridge too far. As I see it, the arts involve creations of the human imagination; the ways in which works of art are apprehended and interpreted also entail imaginative leaps. (Let me be clear: This does not mean that Shakespeare wrote *Julius Caesar* from scratch; nor does it mean that a reader could substitute an interpretation of *Moby Dick* for one of *Uncle Tom's Cabin* or vice versa.) Still, in the realm of human invention, as compared with the realm of understanding the world "as it is," or "as it was," assertions of truth and falsity seem to me to constitute a category error. It's as if we declared the weather to be true or false; it is neither, it just *is*.

Yet I can hardly ignore the reality: Many knowledgeable people speak of the truths of the arts, of a work of art as being true to life, or even of great art as laying bare the deepest truths of the universe. Returning once again to the realm of statements, some commentators have proposed a felicitous way of thinking about works of art—as "authentic" or "inauthentic." We should not think of plays or poetry or paintings as attempting to capture life in the manner of a physicist or a reporter. Rather, we should think of these works of art as capturing some aspect of life, the world, the human condition, in a way that is effective and powerful and (as I'll argue) beautiful—even if the particular vehicles happen to have been contrived or invented out of whole cloth. I resonate to the words of Pablo Picasso:

> We all know that art is not truth. Art is a lie that makes us realize truth, at least the truth that is given us to understand. The artist must know the manner whereby to convince others of the truthfulness of his lies.

Time to take stock. The notion of a single truth or a single standard of truth now seems hopelessly simpleminded. So, too, the notion that truth can be established simply by relying on one's senses, or by polling the neighbors, *especially* (in recalling the taunt of the late William F. Buckley) if they happen to be professors at an elite private university. Rather, over epochs, and with plenty of twists, turns, and setbacks, human beings have established expertise. Both scholarly disciplines and professional crafts allow the determination of truths—truths about how the world is *and* truths about how to act in the world in order to tackle challenges that are often quite complex.

Critiques by postmodernists have made us wary—properly wary, I would add—of glib claims to truth. New scientific paradigms, once they have been widely accepted, do not necessarily weaken or disconfirm old scientific truths; but they often rearrange the configuration of truths in new and unanticipated ways. After Einstein, after quantum mechanics, we acknowledge the spheres where Isaac Newton's laws of mechanics obtain as well as the spheres where other laws take over. Discoveries also alter professional practices—as when tested drugs are substituted for a long-standing herbal remedy or Google searches compensate for frailties of human memory—but such discoveries or inventions do not necessarily undermine wisdom that has been passed down through the ages. A single authoritative print or broadcast voice is replaced by numerous competing accounts, but the resulting chaos does not invalidate the search for a truthful account. As my young friend Ned could testify, the search may be initially more difficult but ultimately should be more reliable because it has been much more comprehensive, much more carefully vetted.

How best can we establish the status of truth in a postmodern, digital era? By showing the power but also the limitations of sensory knowledge. By explaining the methods whereby the several disciplines—mathematics, science, history—go about arriving at their accounts of the world and arriving at their respective truths. By demonstrating how we evaluate disciplinary evidence—and the evidence from multiple disciplines—in determining truth value. By illustrating the power of accumulated experience, of expertise, as well as the limits of rough rules of thumb, in the daily practices of reporters, physicians, lawyers, and other professionals pursuing their craft. By recognizing the ways in which humans may be irrational, prejudiced, or susceptible to propaganda but not allowing those proclivities to carry the day. By revealing the ways in which crowds can be wise (for example, making more accurate estimates than do individuals) as well as foolish (succumbing to the faddish and, more lamentably, to the Fascists). And by showing that the search for truth is fundamentally misplaced in the arts, but that the litmus test of authenticity, of feeling "right," may be appropriate.

Paradoxically, even—or perhaps especially—the most severe critics of authoritative truth confirm its importance. We pay attention to the blogger who challenges the assertion of newsman Dan Rather because we think that the blogger is onto a truth that was missed by the journalistic tradition. We disdain the college student Kaavya Viswanathan because a novel that she claimed to have authored has in fact been shown to be plagiarized from other works—a new truth about the work. Here (again, paradoxically), postmodern skepticism and the new digital media join forces to insist on a better-substantiated set of statements about what really happened.

To put it in the terms of my own discipline of psychology, the search for truth going forward must become ever more "metacognitive." That is, we can no longer just trust our eyes, or the spoken words of the nightly news, or the written summaries provided by *Time* magazine. There is no substitute for understanding the ways in which our senses are faithful and the ways in which they deceive; the ways in which a news reporter or commentator can struggle to get the story right, or, alternatively, pass on his bias, knowingly or unknowingly; the procedures used by scholars in the several disciplines, as well as those that are used, wittingly or unwittingly, by the most accomplished professionals and craftspeople. At the risk of being tantalizingly circular, we must try to understand the truths about truth.

Not a single truth any more, but a plurality of truths, each appropriate to its realm, each fallible, but each subject to continuing refinement and improvement. Never perhaps reaching the Promised Land of Pure Ultimate Truth, but over the centuries moving steadily in the right direction. In that limited but real sense, we can see that we have a truer picture—more properly, truer pictures—of the world than those who came before us, but also that we can never assume we have arrived at the ultimate destination: Our successors may well come to possess truer versions still.

Chapter 3 | # Beauty

Our survey of the concept of truth turned out to be complex but perhaps surprisingly upbeat. To be sure, there is no single truth and certainly no absolute truth. But despite the warnings of postmodernists, we can discern an encouraging development: a fairly steady march toward firmer and more widely accepted notions of truth. And while the new media generate storm clouds of competing and even contradictory truth claims, individuals with standards and stamina can arrive at confident judgments—perhaps judgments even more rigorously grounded than those that could have been reached in the predigital era.

But in certain realms, the notion of truth and falsity is misguided. The arts offer a prototypical example. It makes sense to think of works of art as products of the human imagination unconstrained by truths of the world as they are commonly understood. Instead, works of art can be subject to a test of *authenticity*: Such works are authentic to the extent that they capture or convey aspects of experience in a powerful and evocative manner. While they are not literally true, we can envision a world—a dream or a nightmare—in which they could be true. To put it another way, the arts represent ways of knowing about the world that are legitimate and yet fundamentally different from those that operate in the scholarly disciplines, such as science or history, or in the professions, such as law or medicine or journalism.

Of course, once one begins to speak about the arts, one enters a realm that has traditionally been far less concerned with truth, or with goodness, than it has been with beauty. Indeed, in the not-too-distant past, the primary standard applied to works of art—whether music, dance, literature, drama, or the graphic or plastic arts—was that of beauty. To take an example from the visual arts: Paintings, drawings, and pieces of sculpture were considered meritorious to the extent that they captured and exemplified widely held notions of what is beautiful—or, in the language of the eighteenth century, *sublime*. By the same token, in the past, viewers were disturbed by scenes or features that were deemed unbeautiful, ugly, or inexpertly wrought. Recall that works of Impressionism were initially rejected as ugly, particularly by those who cherished the picture-postcard aesthetics of the then prominent (but now less frequently touted) Barbizon School.

Today, particularly in the contemporary West, the status of beauty in relation to the arts could scarcely be more different. Some observers eschew the term *beauty* altogether, while others use it in ways quite different than in the past. In one respect such diverse stances are not surprising, since the appeal of the arts has long been considered a matter of taste—as far back as the Roman era, "de gustibus non est disputandum" (in matters of taste there is no dispute). But today we have to ask: Does the term, and indeed the concept, of beauty serve *any* purpose? And if so, how should we think about it?

In our pantheon of virtues, certain objects, experiences, events, or persons have been customarily denoted by the adjective *beautiful*. (Hereafter, for the most part, I'll use the single term *object* to encompass these disparate entities and phenomena.) In stipulating beauty, we indicate that we gain pleasure, a warm and positive feeling, a "tingle" if you will, from the beholding of the object—or, if you prefer, a neurophysiological reference, a rush of serotonin. Importantly, in apprehending the object as beautiful, we are satisfied to maintain a *distance* from the object; that is, we don't try to hug it, eat it, or slam it to the ground. The object projects and retains a definite power. We are inclined to *revisit* the beautiful object periodically (though perhaps not too frequently) in order to recreate or even amplify the pleasurable feeling.

Truth and beauty are fundamentally different: Whereas truth is a *property of statements*, beauty reveals itself in the course of an *experience with an object*. (To be sure, for communication purposes, we may declare "it's beautiful"—but this remark is an afterthought, not the essence of the experience.)

Another difference across virtues is more telling. Over time, our notion of the nature of truth has not changed—what has changed is merely the means by which truths are ascertained, and our determination of how firmly certain truth claims continue to hold. In contrast, I contend our views of which experiences are beautiful, and why they are beautiful, have changed quite a lot; moreover, they will continue to change in ways that cannot be predicted. And that is because beauty is continually affected by historical, cultural, and personal factors that by their nature resist precise determination and differ appreciably across individuals. Indeed, experiences regarded by many as beautiful today would have shocked our ancestors and continue to bewilder those who are not steeped in modern (or postmodern) civilization. And so, in what follows, I distinguish between "traditional beauty," on the one hand, and an "individualized sense of beauty," on the other.

If experiences of beauty resist definitive determination and explication, why concern ourselves with them? Above all, because the pursuit of experiences that are beautiful constitutes a crucial part of life,
particularly once basic needs—food, shelter, safety—have been satisfied. Indeed, speaking for myself, the opportunity to experience
beauty in the arts constitutes as important a part of my life as the
quest for truth in the scholarly or the practical disciplines. There is
another reason as well to explore the virtue of beauty: In the recent
past, courtesy of biologically or economically influenced scholars, ill-
considered statements have been made about beauty—and it is time
to set the record straight.

Before turning to these misconceptions, I should acknowledge one
point: The world of physical nature and, no less, the world of human
nature offer gradations of beauty and ugliness. Even across cultures
and epochs, certain scenes are traditionally seen as beautiful—verdant
land scenes, brilliant sunsets, imposing mountain peaks, still lakes,
and rushing rivers. Likewise, certain kinds of human faces and body
types are valorized. Even artifacts, such as vessels or weapons or jewelry, are likely to honor certain canons, such as balance, and to favor
certain geometric ratios like the golden mean.

In a revealing study, artists Alexander Melamid and Vitaly Komar
presented slides of works of art to inhabitants of different countries.
Considerable cross-cultural consensus emerged as to which works
were beautiful, and which were not. Moreover, the subject matter, so
to speak, of these preferences turns out to be predictable. Whether
slides are projected in the United States, China, or Kenya, respondents on the whole favor works that depict the aforementioned natural scenes (lakes, mountains) and give the lowest ratings to works
that consist of colored geometric forms (reminiscent of the paintings
of Nicolas de Staël). You can see the consensual preferences in the
pairs of images reproduced in Figure 3.1.

Where do these conceptions, these standards of beauty come from?
Of late, it has become fashionable—indeed, the highest fashion—to

Figure 3.1. *America's Most Wanted, 1994* (top left); *America's Most Unwanted, 1994* (top right). *China's Most Wanted, 1996* (middle row left); *China's Most Unwanted, 1996* (middle row right). *Kenya's Most Wanted, 1996* (bottom left); *Kenya's Most Unwanted, 1996* (bottom right). Images by Vitaly Komar and Alexander Melamid. Courtesy Ronald Feldman Fine Arts, New York. Reprinted with permission.

claim that the standards of beauty are built genetically into the human nervous system. Or perhaps slightly less boldly and less blatantly, that these standards emerge naturally, if not ineluctably, from the interaction of the human nervous system with expected environments of the planet. (There is even an evolutionary argument that these preferences have emerged because, in the past, certain environments proved more congenial to our ancestors. Attraction to such environments constituted an evolutionary advantage and, hence, was passed down by survivors through the generations.)

I would not be surprised if, at the broadest level, certain canons of natural beauty—for example, a body and face that are roughly symmetrical—could be proven to transcend the vagaries of history and culture and thus lay claim, as we now say, to universality. And perhaps we are all wired with a propensity to secrete certain neural transmitters when in the presence of certain sylvan scenes. I'm willing to concede that much to biologically oriented colleagues.

Yet I take the sharpest exception to the notion that these predispositions explain what is fundamental or profound about beauty in the arts across time. At most, they set very broad parameters for what the young, untutored organism will pay attention to—aurally, visually, or through other single- or poly-sensory modalities. Our common sensory experience may constitute the starting point for a determination of truth value; and yet, in and of itself, that shared experience captures surprisingly little about the fundamental truths of the world. By the same token I am firmly convinced that we will learn little of consequence about the realm of beauty—be it natural or manmade—by further probing the genes, the brain images, or the neurotransmitters of *Homo sapiens*.

Why do I take a position that seems epistemologically retrograde, in a scholarly world that is probing continuously for the gene for X, the neural network for Y, the evolutionary basis for Z? Because I believe that the realm of the human (I deliberately avoid the tendentious term *human nature*) is thoroughly suffused by accidents of history (and pre-history) and defined by extraordinarily wide differentiations within and among human cultures (and subcultures) and, indeed, across human beings within a single tribe or community. Our genes and brains do not differ materially from those of our ancestors fifteen thousand years ago, or even forty thousand years ago. And yet it is tremendously difficult for most of us, living in the twenty-first century, to place ourselves in the skin (or the minds) of our Paleolithic forebears, or of the population at the Athenian agora who voted to banish Socrates, or of the autocratic nobility overthrown in the French Revolution, or of our American forebears who insisted on the wisdom of slavery or the necessity for separation of the races, or of the mobs of young people in China during the Cultural Revolution of the 1960s who turned on (and turned in) their parents and teachers.

Just as these eras yielded very different kinds of human beings, they also valorized very different works of art, with contrasting notions of beauty, ugliness, sublimity, and bathos. Just compare public art such as Civil War monuments of the past (the solid and stolid military figure mounted on his favorite horse) with the Vietnam War Memorial (a list of over fifty-eight thousand names arranged on two rectilinear black-granite walls). It is as difficult to imagine nineteenth-century viewers being moved by the Vietnam memorial as it is to imagine contemporary viewers savoring an equestrian rendering. Likewise, in the eighteenth century, residents of France considered mountains to be repulsive. According to historian Graham Robb, "To those who gave the matter any thoughts, mountains—and the people who lived there—were remnants of the primitive world." Similarly, novelist Orhan Pamuk describes how differently tourists and residents of Istanbul experience the city: "A cascade of domes and rooftops, a row of houses with crooked window casings—these things don't look beautiful to the people who live among them; they speak instead of squalor, helpless hopeless neglect. Those who take pleasure in the accidental beauty of poverty and historical decay, those of us who see the picturesque in ruins—invariably were people from the outside." Clearly, many contemporaries cherish—and may label as beautiful—natural and man-rendered scenes that repel those who lived in their vicinity.

Biologically grounded accounts of aesthetic appeal exhibit a fundamental confusion. The reason for this confusion became clear when I encountered a trenchant distinction put forth by the renowned Viennese-American composer and sometime painter Arnold Schoenberg. This titan of the arts distinguished between *style* and *idea* (his terms, translated from the German). For Schoenberg, *style* is what distinguishes works of one era from those of another—say, in musical terms, the Classical era of Mozart, Haydn, and Johann Christian Bach from the Romantic era of Liszt, Schumann, and Berlioz. These distinctions are so vast that a child, perhaps even a pigeon or a rat, can hear (if not appreciate) the differences. (After all, it has been shown that pigeons can distinguish reliably between the paintings of impressionist Claude Monet and those of abstract expressionist Jackson Pollock.)

Untutored musical listeners lump all Classical composers together and all Romantic composers together, because compositions within each musical genre share stylistic features with one another. (Similarly, in the visual arts, unsophisticated viewers would lump together all impressionists, or all abstract expressionists, or all pop or all conceptual artists.) But what makes the arts interesting, intriguing, arresting are the *differences* between Mozart and Haydn (and between Schubert and Beethoven); the differences among Mozart piano sonatas and string quartets; even, perhaps especially, the differences between one musician's rendition of the C minor piano concerto (K 491) and that of another equally renowned musician (say, Glenn Gould as compared with Mitsuko Uchida). I see no way in which enhanced understanding of the nervous system or the human genome can begin to elucidate how we make these differentiations, let alone attach evaluations to them, some long-lasting, others quite transitory.

While biologically based explanations may give us insights into how we recognize certain gross stylistic differences, they fail utterly to elucidate judgments—including judgments of beauty—about particular works. Making this point, a British literary critic, Raymond Tallis, has taken to task A. S. Byatt, the well-known and deservedly lauded novelist. Byatt had sought to explain her attraction to the works of John Donne by invoking certain neuronal pathways and connections, such as those involved in the recently discovered mirror neurons. Tallis laments Byatt's intoxication with neuroliterary criticism—the application of findings from brain sciences to explain the appeal of certain themes and forms in literature. He playfully labels this stance *overstanding*:

> By adopting a neurophysiological approach, Byatt loses a rather large number of important distinctions: between reading one poem by John Donne and another; between successive reading of a particular poem; between reading Donne and other Metaphysical poets; between reading the Metaphysicals and reading William Carlos Williams; between reading great literature and trash; between reading and a vast number of activities—such as getting cross over missing toilet paper. That is an impressive number of distinctions for a literary critic to lose. But that is the price of overstanding.

The arts proceed along unpredictable historical, cultural, and individual tracks; we can marvel at works of art and revel in our experiences with them, but we will not be able to come up with an algorithm—mathematical, economical, biological, or psychological—that explains their meaning and accounts for their appeal. We may be able to explain why, on the whole, individuals across different cultures prefer sylvan scenes to geometric patterns. But we'll fail utterly to offer a general explanation for why individuals in one era value Bach or Donne or van Gogh while those in another era did not. To put the matter tendentiously, the predilections that *do* recur across disparate groups are tastes for kitsch.

We seem to have wandered far away from considerations of beauty as it is often conceptualized. But this wandering is appropriate because in the West, the arts themselves have meandered, or sometimes deliberately ventured, in directions distant from any traditional or even expansive notion of beauty. In the West and increasingly elsewhere, the high arts no longer try to document reality faithfully: That assignment has long since been assigned to the realms of photography and audio recording. The high arts no longer feature poems that neatly scan, or musical compositions that contain textbook harmony and regular beats; nor do they give pride of place to literary works with a classic "heroic" plot comprising a protagonist, an obstacle, the obstacle overcome, and an ending in which all—or at least the good guys—live happily ever after. Importantly, these artistic trends unfolded gradually, over many years. Far from being a consequence of postmodernism, they were catalytic in its emergence and its choice of name.

This state of affairs across the arts has led to a dismissal, on the part of many authorities, of the concept of beauty. Consider the testimony of fine-arts scholar Laurie Fendrich: "We who live in this speedy, diverse, more or less democratic society are, deep down, fairly suspicious of beauty. Beauty is based on a hierarchy that labels some things undeniably 'beautiful' and others irretrievably ugly. Most serious, inventive, and 'alive' contemporary artists do not want merely to reiterate elements of this established hierarchy." And indeed, postmodernist sympathizers like Fendrich are justified in challenging "beauty" as the sine qua non of all artistic experiences. But we should not dismiss the concept because of the particular powers that happened to invoke or to banish it. Instead we should examine the historical and cultural forces that have led to the marginalization of the traditional connotations of beauty and consider whether the concept might be reconceptualized for our era.

Let's submit that beauty—once defined by idealization, regularity, harmony, balance, fidelity to the appearance of the world—is no longer the exclusive or even the primary calling card of the arts. How can we characterize the state of affairs that has replaced that singular virtue? I nominate three antecedent features: The object is interesting; its form is memorable; it invites further encounters. When, as a result of these features, alone or jointly, the individual reports a pleasurable experience, it is appropriate (though obviously not obligatory) for him, for her, for us, to speak of beauty. That's what I, and so many others, do today.

"Uh, oh," the philosopher in me proclaims. "You are trying to define artistic beauty, and the arts have always defied definition." Indeed, as aesthetician Morris Weitz once argued, art is inherently an "open concept"—any effort to delineate its limits simply invites a challenge on the part of the next artist or art critic or philistine. A well-known case in point: the artistic couple Christo and Jeanne-Claude. It seems that every new work—ranging from wrapping the Reichstag to decorating Central Park with flag-shaped pieces of nylon—expanded our notion of what can be accepted as a work of art.

While one philosopher has posed a problem, another philosopher—my teacher Nelson Goodman—has proposed a path toward a solution. Just as a certain number or combination of symptoms suggests the presence of a disease, so, too, certain antecedent features prove "symptomatic" of artistic beauty. When these features are jointly absent, one cannot speak of artistic beauty. But when all or even most of the features are present, in all likelihood one is approaching the realm of artistic beauty.

And so I have proposed three symptoms antecedent to the experience of beauty, of which the first is *interestingness*. Increasingly, aficionados of the arts seek out material that is interesting, engaging, exciting, and unexpected, reacting positively when material that satisfies those desires is present. Many artists have responded to this demand—and perhaps they have helped to create it—by fashioning exotic objects or carrying out sensational activities and making sure that these activities are performed in galleries and observed by critics. At times, and for some people, the object or experience may be awful; at other times, for other persons, it is awe-inspiring. But at the very least it elicits interest.

Why create interesting objects, or perform interesting actions? A whole branch of experimental aesthetics documents how, whenever a sight or sound becomes familiar, individuals avert their eyes or tune out. And, as a contrast, when deviations from the "new norm" emerge, these attract attention instead, unless they have become so complex that they cannot be assimilated. But once the new stimuli become familiar, they too lose the capacity to command attention. Therefore, to maintain interest, one must continually raise the ante, though not always in the same direction. That is, when interest in A has piqued, one moves on to B, and then to C, but sometimes a return to A proves more attractive than a continuing movement in the direction of D, E, and F. In a version documented frequently by experimental psychology, over time individuals prefer to look at polygons with increasingly many sides (say, more than twelve or twenty) until a peak is reached, at which point preference reverts to simple, classic geometric forms having a small number of sides.

These "trajectories of interest" transcend the experimental laboratory and emerge across the range of art forms. Consider the evolution over the centuries of serious orchestral music. Following the classical works of the Mozart-Schubert era, romantic composers like Berlioz, Wagner, and Liszt began to challenge the supremacy of tonality. Then, in their respective ways, at the beginning of the twentieth century, Igor Stravinsky and Arnold Schoenberg created alternative systems of sound. Thereafter, as twelve-tone classical music became ever more complex and recondite, minimalist forms of music—constituting the sharpest possible contrast—gained in attractiveness. In the words of minimalist composer John Adams: "In comparison to the flamboyantly Baroque display at the New Complexionists [a self-styled intricate musical style of the middle of the twentieth century], the matter-of-fact notation of my own music was like a pup tent squatting next to the Chartres Cathedral. I had to move away from this setup and had to remind myself of how the notion of 'complexity as progress' is in fact a posture, an intellectual house of cards and always has been." Comparable forms of minimalism arose in the literary arts (Samuel Beckett) and in the graphic arts (Donald Judd), with much the same line of justification as that proposed by Adams.

Interestingness in itself, of course, is not particularly symptomatic of the arts—if it were, then mere newsworthiness would qualify an object or product as artistic. For me, this stretch does not compute— a single symptom signals neither a disease nor an objet d'art. But once the element of interest is embodied in a form or format *sufficiently powerful or evocative that it will be remembered in that form*, one has clearly moved toward the arts. In this way, we approach the possibility of experiences of beauty.

Conceptual art provides an intriguing example. It might seem that conceptual art is about an idea, and it suffices just to repeat or paraphrase that idea. But that is not the case. In *One and Three Chairs* Joseph Kosuth presents a chair and a photo of that chair alongside a dictionary definition of a third (see Figure 3.2). And in a whimsical version of a classroom punishment of earlier decades, John Baldessari has his wayward pupil repeatedly write: *I will not make any more boring art* (see Figure 3.3). In each case, a potentially interesting idea—

Figure 3.2. *One and Three Chairs.* Joseph Kosuth, 1965. Copyright © 2010 Joseph Kosuth/Artists Rights Society (ARS), New York. Digital image copyright © Museum of Modern Art/Licensed by SCALA/Art Resource, New York.

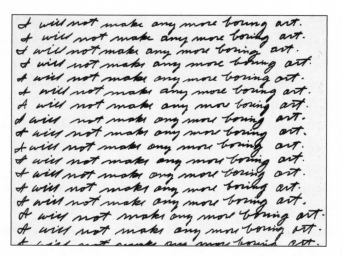

Figure 3.3. *I Will Not Make Any More Boring Art.* John Baldessari, 1971. Courtesy of John Baldessari. Digital image copyright © Museum of Modern Art/Licensed by SCALA/Art Resource, New York.

what is a chair, how to avoid boring art—is wedded to a form, or format, that is itself memorable, even unforgettable.

With *memorability of form*, the artist distinguishes herself from an epistemologist or an exhibitionist. An intriguing example comes from the contemporary performance artist Marina Abramovic. In one of her flagship performances, Abramovic sits motionless in a chair facing whichever visitor to the gallery chooses to sit in the second chair; the visitor can sit as long as he likes and the artist remains essentially immobile for seven hours. This unusual behavior certainly elicits interest. While anyone with fortitude could assume the Abramovic role, this artist takes consummate care in selecting the color and style of her costume, her head and hand positions, the expression on her face, her bodily posture. Not only does Abramovic stimulate us to reconsider what it means to attempt to have a relationship to a startlingly unreactive fellow human being; her appearance and behavior often remain unforgettably poignant for the participant and those who view the encounter. More casual, informal, or ill-considered choices could undermine the effectiveness of the artistic performance. Just as actor Laurence Olivier long "owned" the role of Hamlet, Marina Abramovic sets the parameters for others who would hope to emulate her seated performance.

The third antecedent of the experience of beauty is the impulse, the inclination, the desire to encounter again, to revisit the object, scene, or performance. What I'll term *the invitation to revisit* can arise from each of several factors: One likes the experience, one has curiosity to learn or to understand better, or one has a feeling of awe—which can derive from wonder, scintillation, overpowerment, or uncanniness. Absent a desire on the part of an audience to revisit, an experience does not qualify as beautiful—immediately or ultimately.

Why might one *not* revisit an experience that is interesting and memorable? Perhaps because one has gotten all that one wants to get out of it—there is no need to reexperience or to explore further. Perhaps because it raises no new questions and suggests no new answers. Or perhaps it is too awful or too awesome to allow the possibility of a productive further exploration. Either, like the Holocaust, the experience is too horrible to recontemplate. Or like an encounter with the gods, or a God, it is too terrifying to reexperience.

Yet at times, awe—a feeling that floods the perceiver in the presence of a powerfully affecting object—may invite further probing. The awe can arise from respect for achievement—How did the artist ever manage to carry off that work? It can arise as well from the effect on the perceiver—I feel myself in the presence of something extraordinary. Consider such telling examples as the Paleolithic renderings of animals, sketched on rock walls deep inside dark and damp caves scattered across southwestern Europe—art that twenty thousand years later continues to evoke *both* of the aforementioned connotations of the term *awe*. Or the pyramids of ancient Egypt, the cathedrals of medieval Europe, the impassive statues of Easter Island, the roughly hewn boulders of Stonehenge, the building and surrounds of the Taj Mahal or Versailles, the skyscrapers of East Asia—indeed, to be a tad irreverent, the sites that embellish the covers of travel brochures. In fact, quite a few audience members experience awe in the presence of performing artist Abramovic. No less an authority than the distinguished art critic Arthur Danto reported the experience of translucence: "the sort of magic that all our courses in art history and appreciation had encouraged us to hope for."

The feeling of awe is, importantly, not the same thing as the "tingle" that announces an experience of beauty. When an entity or experience is perceived as beautiful, one remains in control and maintains one's distance; when an entity or experience induces awe, one feels overpowered, overwhelmed, far less in command. And yet, as the result of further visits, the awe can be tamed and yield to the pleasurable sensation that announces or accompanies a feeling of beauty.

That we choose to revisit is a crucial ingredient for the experience of beauty. But *why* we choose to revisit turns out to be a personal, individual matter. And here we identify the key feature of beauty in our time—and perhaps for all time going forward. While the ascertainment of truth is a collective endeavor, in which many individuals are engaged, often over a considerable period of time, the experience of beauty has become a personal, an individualized, even—at times—an idiosyncratic matter.

Let's step back for a moment and revisit our central concept. One might argue, in a postmodern vein, that beauty is no longer a self-standing or self-evident attribute of an object or experience. Such a line of argument would posit beauty as simply an amalgam of interestingness, memorability of form, and inclination to reexperience. Yet I favor a slightly different formulation. Beauty merits a separate entry, in my view, because it entails the physiological and psychological "tingle" noted above—one distinct from the reactions of either mere interest or an inclination to revisit. An experience of beauty proclaims itself: The listener or viewer is conscious, as least from time to time, of the special nature of the experience. To adapt a formulation by the poet Coleridge, "beauty" characterizes a powerful experience that is recalled with tranquility.

Time to put this analytic apparatus to work. Recently I was powerfully affected by an exhibit fashioned by the Canadian artist Rodney Graham: a typewriter gradually covered by flakes of snow. Wandering around a junk shop in Germany, Graham had found an old, unopened case containing a manual typewriter dating from the 1930s. He fell in love with this antique object and decided to memorialize it. He then had the idea of filming the typewriter as it was removed from its case, set outside during a snowfall, and gradually allowed to accumulate flakes until its keyboard was completely covered. All of this was

Figure 3.4. *Rheinmetall/Victoria 8.* Rodney Graham, 2003. 35mm film, Cinemeccanica Victoria 8 35mm film projector and looper 10:50 minutes; continuous loop. Edition of five and one Artist's Proof. Courtesy Donald Young Gallery, Chicago. Digital image copyright © Museum of Modern Art/Licensed by SCALA/Art Resource, New York.

displayed courtesy of a ratchety old 35-millimeter projector (which transported me back to my grade-school classrooms of the 1950s). The film, about ten minutes in duration, is played and replayed (see Figure 3.4). At this point you might exclaim, "How ridiculous"—an old typewriter caught in a snowstorm sounds like a Laurel and Hardy movie, or a Monty Python skit. And indeed, neither the typewriter nor the projector nor the dark room in itself evoked much feeling. Yet I was not alone in gradually becoming enchanted by this exhibit and visiting it several times.

Now let's consider my experience in terms of the trio of antecedent symptoms and the judgment of beauty. First of all, with respect to interestingness, the idea of discovering an old typewriter and placing it under snowflakes intrigued me. Second, the appearance of the typewriter and the slowly falling snow were memorable—I kept thinking of them afterward in quite vivid form. Finally, I was drawn back to contemplate the work—I wanted to recapture such arresting and memorable imagery. At the same time, I retained distance from the display and was aware of my own pleasurable experience—it was natural to speak of my experience of beauty and to encourage others to visit the Graham display.

But wait! If, in the end, I experience the same "tingle" and utter the same "Ah!" that an earlier audience might have in the presence of a Greek vase or a Barbizon painting or one of Melamid and Komar's photographed displays, why go to the trouble of introducing new antecedent symptoms and a new terminology? Because Graham's work is a telling example of a contemporary artistic object that could not have been envisioned a hundred years ago—one that, although it does not satisfy classical canons of beauty, can readily be experienced and described as beautiful by viewers today. Other works—ranging from a John Adams composition to John Baldessari's writing exercise—elicit similar experiences and characterizations. (In fact, a 2010 exhibit of the works of Baldessari is entitled Pure Beauty!)

And so, in our time, once we are open to experiences that are interesting, memorable, and worthy of revisiting, we are likely to have the "tingle" that signals beauty. Anyone with a serious interest in the arts will have examples. To illustrate the highly individualized nature of these judgments, and how they change over time, I'll relate a few additional experiences: herewith, my "evolving portfolio" of beauty.

Exhibit A consists of the massive paintings of Anselm Kiefer (see Figure 3.5). Initially, I did not like them. I could not relate to these desiccated landscapes—I found them ugly, or, perhaps only slightly

Figure 3.5. *die Milchstrasse (Milky Way)*. Anselm Kiefer (German, born 1945), 1985–1987. Emulsion paint, oil, acrylic and shellac on canvas with applied wires and lead. Overall (diptych): 12 ½ feet x 18 ½ feet (381 x 563 cm); each panel: 150 x 111 x 8 inches (381 x 281.94 x 20.32 cm); each of two travel frames: 161 ¾ x 118 ½ x 10 inches (410.845 x 300.99 x 25.4 cm). Collection Albright-Knox Art Gallery, Buffalo, New York. In celebration of the 125th Anniversary of the Buffalo Fine Arts Academy, General and Restricted Purchase Funds, 1988.

better, a commentary on ugliness. The works may have evoked the descriptor *awe*, but more in the sense of *awe-ful* than of *awesome*. Yet something in the works impelled me—or perhaps even compelled me—to revisit them. And now, I cherish Kiefer's work. I would go—indeed, I have gone—out of my way to view an installation of his works. I consider them to be beautiful and I have the pleasurable tingles to prove it! Of course, *Kiefer* hasn't changed (any more than Picasso's portrait of Gertrude Stein changed)—*I* have.

The Kiefer experience underscores an important point. While few of us seek experiences that are initially repellent, such experiences can signal something important. At some level, I sensed that, in encountering a Kiefer canvas, I had more work to do. The work of art interested me and indeed stimulated awe. In that sense, ugliness is more revealing than blandness—and it may also signal a greater potential for ultimate apprehension as an object of beauty. And indeed, over time, my reactions shifted from repulsion to acceptance to an experience of pleasure—with the conclusion that many works by Kiefer merited the term *beautiful*.

For Exhibit B, let me turn to contemporary classical music. In 2008 the eminent American composer Elliott Carter celebrated his one hundredth birthday. To commemorate that milestone, the Contemporary Musical Festival at Tanglewood undertook an unprecedented program. On five consecutive days, festival organizers staged ten separate concerts, featuring nearly fifty works by Carter. The composer attended the entire event, as did numerous other enthusiasts of serious music, including my wife and me.

I have to admit that I did not know the work of Carter well and that I was drawn to the concerts as much by curiosity as by passion. I also found some of the pieces to be very challenging to listen to and comprehend. (I was reassured when I heard the following tidbit: The renowned composer-conductor Pierre Boulez said that he had to listen to Carter's pieces three or four times before he was able to grasp them.) But over the course of a week, the musical idioms became increasingly familiar to me, and by the end of the week I had become a devotee of Carter's music. I would have no hesitation in declaring the pieces interesting and memorable. And, attesting to the accompanying tingle, I happily characterize many passages as beautiful.

Our conceptions of beauty are a moving target. Anyone with a serious interest in the arts can document how his or her judgments of beauty have changed over time—constituting what I call the *individual portfolio* of experiences and judgments of beauty. Some additional Exhibits: I remember my initial enthusiasm for classical music, as a teenager, when I would listen over and over again to what I now consider tired "war horses." I admit, with a frisson of embarrassment, that my friends and I even timed different recordings (they were all long-playing 33's) of Tchaikovsky's first piano concerto, no doubt conferring first prize upon the speediest version. And I remember well my gradual transition from Tchaikovsky's bravura symphonies and concerti to Schubert's measured yet deep chamber music; and, later, my excitement at first encountering the modernist works of Stravinsky and Bartok; and my gradually dawning ability to apprehend even more challenging works, such as those by Boulez and Carter. Unlike the truths of science past, the beauties of the arts don't perish. I still cherish a good performance of Tchaikovsky's violin concerto or Schubert's *Death and the Maiden*. But just as I now honor the works of Anselm Kiefer or Rodney Graham or Joseph Kosuth, my musical mansion now includes rooms that would have been closed to me four or five decades ago.

Sometimes, one can even catch oneself in the midst of a shift from a feeling of distaste or confusion to the beginnings of a more positive reaction. At the end of 2008, the Museum of Modern Art devoted significant gallery space to a work of art by the highly acclaimed contemporary artist Matthew Barney. Called *The Deportment of the Host*, this gigantic installation features a large unkempt bed–like structure on the floor, with white braided wires emanating from the central structure (see Figure 3.6). When I first saw this work, I could make no sense of it; in fact, I was repelled by it, and might well have termed it *awe-ful* (I had no inkling that the work is actually supposed to be a Japanese teahouse that has been ruptured). A Matthew Barney lover (and there are many thousands) would have labeled me as a philistine.

If I had stopped at this point, the above example would reveal nothing about beauty. Yet, I could not help noting that both exhibit curator Constance Butler and my wife Ellen Winner, a trained artist, unhesitatingly termed the display *beautiful*. And when I pushed them on why, they described the lovely feel of the materials, their jelly-like texture, their brilliant white appearance, their enveloping shape—

Figure 3.6. *The Deportment of the Host.* Matthew Barney, 2006. Cast poly-caprolactone thermoplastic and self-lubricating plastic, 104 x 360 x 243 inches. Installation View: Gladstone Gallery, New York. Photo by David Regen. Copyright © Matthew Barney. Courtesy Gladstone Gallery, New York. Digital image copyright © Museum of Modern Art/Licensed by SCALA/Art Resource, New York.

for them, the work provoked admiration. In Ellen Winner's words, "I could eat it up with my eyes." This example makes an important point. One's impulse to revisit need not arise from within. Rather, the reactions of respected others prompt a reconsideration and, perhaps ultimately, a conclusion that the work is in fact beautiful.

So by no means has beauty disappeared from the arts, from museums, from collections of canonical and provocative objects. Rather, beauty serves as the culmination of a set of antecedent experiences, and is increasingly likely to arise at unexpected times in unanticipated venues.

I see the course of art history, as well as the trajectory of our own experiences of beauty, as inherently unpredictable, and resistant to explanation, even after the fact. Perhaps tonal music could not continue indefinitely into the classical terrain of the twentieth century. But who could have anticipated the emergence of Igor Stravinsky and his blend of Russian folk music and intricate rhythms and dissonant harmonies? Or of Arnold Schoenberg, his invention of twelve-tone serial music, and the predominant niche such music occupied for a generation? Perhaps representational art reached a point of no return in the heights of Impressionism, as captured in the works of Monet, Renoir, and Pissarro. But let's say that Cézanne had never been born, or Pablo Picasso and Georges Braque had never met, or Cubism had never been devised. Or that Mondrian had avoided geometric forms. Or that Miró had not decided to "assassinate" painting. Or that Jackson Pollock and Andy Warhol had never picked up a brush (or a camera or a goat's head). Who would dare say that our sense of art, beauty, or awe would have developed along lines that are now familiar?

These examples underscore the point that our judgments of beauty do not emanate from a preprogrammed interaction of mind/brain with object or performance. On the contrary: One must take into account the vagaries of history, the preferences and norms and taboos of cultures, and, most important, the unpredictable actions and experiences of individuals—artists who create as well as audience members who are inclined to revisit objects that are interesting and memorable and who in effect keep a portfolio of the continuities that they happen to find as well as the changes in their preferences. (In fact, our experiences with art works can be compared to our experiences with food over time. As cuisines evolve, and as we become exposed to the multiple cuisines of the world, we develop increasingly personalized preferences—our taste evolves, literally as well as figuratively.)

Until now, my discussion of beauty has focused almost entirely on our experiences of works of art. But of course, considerations of beauty arise in numerous other realms as well. Many scientists and mathematicians find beauty in the formulations of their disciplines. And indeed, these formulations may be interesting and memorable—and it's fine with me if enthusiasts speak of a "beautiful" formula or equation. And yet, these scholars are engaged in a pursuit that differs fundamentally from the work of artists. Maybe Poincaré would have discovered the theory of relativity if Einstein had not (certainly, sooner or later, *someone* would have). Maybe people would today be referring to Alfred Russel Wallace's theory of evolution, had Darwin not journeyed on the *Beagle* and reflected for decades on what he had observed. While the terminology we now use might be different, the concepts of the scientist or the mathematician transcend the particular formulation by a specific scholar. However egotistical they may be as persons, these scholars are engaged in an inherently communitarian exercise.

Scientists are modeling the actual world; mathematicians are describing the variable or invariable orders and relations found in symbolic realms of their or others' devising. To practice their disciplines, these scholars need to observe the rules of their respective fields. In contrast, artists—and most especially contemporary artists—are not modeling the world of Nature. Artists are presenting visions and revisions of well-honed imaginations, and these imaginative powers can and will evolve in ways and directions that are inherently unpredictable. No one—neither scientists nor historians nor economists nor psychologists—can anticipate how art forms will evolve and what seasoned connoisseurs or rebellious youths or ordinary folk will cherish a decade from now. Nor, for that matter, can curators, dealers, or collectors. That is why we may flock to the works of artists X, Y, and Z in one season and then find ourselves de-accessioning them or hiding them in the bowels of the acquiring home or institution.

For such reasons, approaches to beauty based on considerations of economic factors can be dismissed—even more quickly and more decisively than approaches derived from biological considerations. One can, if one chooses, decide to judge beauty on the basis of the financial value of a work of art—how much it will bring on the open market or in an auction. But these judgments are entirely ex post facto. This season's triumph is the subject of a garage sale a decade later, while works of art that were at one time of no interest are now worth thousands, millions, even tens of millions of dollars. Moreover, the mere fact that a work commands millions should not affect any individual's judgment of whether the work actually engenders the experience of beauty.

Over time, it has not been possible to predict which experiences will be deemed beautiful—and that will certainly be true going forward. Yet it is possible to ponder how two contemporary forces—the digital media and postmodern thought—affect the experience and judgment of beauty. I've already argued that our judgments of beauty have been fundamentally altered in recent times. I should reiterate that these changes were under way a century ago and are not, in any strict sense, a direct consequence of our two contemporary forces. But trends already begun have been enormously intensified by the ubiquity of new media and by arguments couched in postmodern terms. What may have once been evident to a small minority of art aficionados has now become a widespread and widely felt experience throughout the contemporary world.

With reference to the postmodern critique, I can be quite summary. During much of the twentieth century it appeared that the notion of beauty and the epithet of *beautiful* were no longer relevant, at least among those who consider themselves artistic connoisseurs. Trends in art had overthrown traditional notions of beauty. Modernism—as embodied by James Joyce in literature, Pablo Picasso in painting, and Igor Stravinsky in music—may have sought to retain a link to earlier genres and sensibilities but soon stretched conventional notions of beauty to a breaking point. Then along came artists who were literally postmodern—minimalists, pop artists, mixers of media, conceptualists—who did not even make gestures to the realm of beauty—unless those gestures were ones of ridicule of traditional icons.

In view of these powerful trends, it is not surprising that reference to beauty was suspended. But in my view, this exclusionary move has proved unsustainable—a prototypical case of throwing out the baby with the bathwater. What is needed is not banishment or exorcism of talk about beauty. Rather, we crave a deployment of the word, and the concept, that is adequate to the current artistic situation. We can—and should—each develop our own portfolio of beautiful objects and experiences—as it were, a record of our own perhaps idiosyncratic but deeply felt tastes.

The new digital media invite more discussion. Artists have always been alert to new media of expression; indeed, they have been among the first workers to convey their visions in new technologies such as cinema, radio, lasers, holograms, virtual realities, and many other computer-aided or -inflected devices. And, as Marshall McLuhan persuasively argued, human beings almost always inaugurate new technologies of communication by presenting the familiar content of the old media in the form of the new media. Thus we find composers like John Adams creating easily recognizable pieces on electronic rather than manual instruments, painters like Salvador Dali contriving filmic scenes that are reminiscent of their drawings and paintings, and media artists like Nam Jum Paik presenting movie-style close-ups of faces on television screens.

But soon enough, artists begin to understand and use a new medium on its own terms. It is exciting to contemplate artistic works and experiences that could hardly have been imagined in a predigital era. In this context I think immediately of *Design and the Elastic Mind*, an exhibit curated by Paola Antonelli of the Museum of Modern Art. This exhibit deliberately and successfully challenged many distinctions that would once have been seen as unproblematic, if not self-evidently

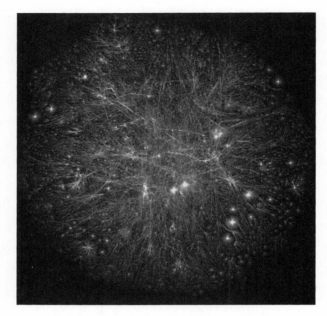

Figure 3.7. *Map of the Internet from 2003.* Barrett Lyon, 2003. Courtesy of Barrett Lyon/The Opte Project.

valid: art or science, art or design, natural or man-made, real or virtual, microscopic or macroscopic. Not surprisingly, the most striking works draw on digital technology, concepts, and sensibility.

Let me characterize this new state of affairs. To begin with, computers (or, more precisely, their programmers) are now able to create works of art. Whereas experiences of beauty were once the result of creations by God or by a single artist, computer programs now create works and experiences that—for many audience members—are indistinguishable from, preferable to, and perhaps even experienced as more beautiful than those made by human beings. Consider, courtesy of Barrett Lyon, the rhapsodic stellar patterns made by a simple record of the number of Internet users in a given geographical space (see Figure 3.7). Or William Ngan's beautiful floral configurations, courtesy of Java and processing software (see Figure 3.8). Or Alex Adai and Edward Mar-

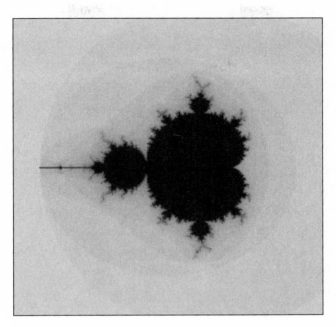

Figure 3.8. *Mandelbrot Set.* William Ngan. Courtesy of William Ngan. http://metaphorical.net.

cotte's use of Large Graph Layout software to represent how genes are related to one another (see Figure 3.9). (They looked at sequences of proteins in 140,000 known genes, did 21 billion comparisons, and established which ones had homologous relations to one another.)

Computers can also serve as literal handmaidens to human activities. Members of The Front Design team make freehand sketches in the air. Their motions are recorded and then digitized into a computer model. A rapid manufacturing machine "prints" the objects into attractive plastic furniture (see Figure 3.10). In the Celestial Mechanics Project, software designer Aaron Koblin uses FAA aircraft data to plot the changing dynamics of aircraft in the sky. The resulting patterns can then be displayed in a planetarium (see Figure 3.11).

Traditionally, museums exhibit works of art at a single moment in time. Now, of course, it is possible to display digital works that change continually. In the *Design and the Elastic Mind* exhibit, one is able to watch the constantly changing patterns of Internet use in locales of different scope. Moreover, once a work has been posted, it can be re-worked continually by the same artist, or by other would-be artists, known or unknown, gifted or bereft of talent. The notion of a com-pleted work of art—which remains the same for all time—is no longer unchallenged. Indeed, works made by individual artists, works fash-ioned by collectivities, and works produced simply by computers are subject to endless variation.

The possibility of creating works out of other, preexisting works— wholly or in part—has been extended immeasurably. With mere clicks of a mouse, one can concatenate as many still, moving, linguis-tic, and musical patterns as one likes and create a new work. As sig-naled in my opening example of David Shields's compilation *Reality Hunger*, considerable controversy surrounds whether such activity deserves to be considered an original work of art or simply a borrow-ing or even theft of the creations of others. One's own reactions to an

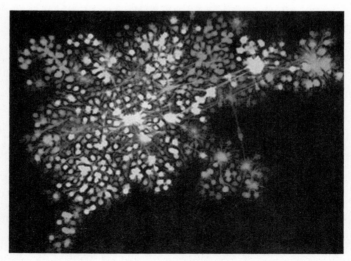

Figure 3.9. *Protein Homology Graph.* Alex Adai and Edward Marcotte. Image courtesy of Alex Adai and Edward Marcotte.

Figure 3.10. *Sketch Furniture.* Sofia Langerkvist, Charlotte von der Lancken, Anna Lindgren, and Katja Savstrom. Courtesy of Friedman Benda and Front Design.

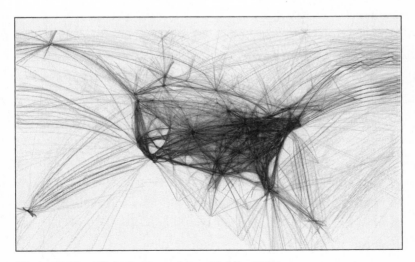

Figure 3.11. *Flight Patterns.* Aaron Koblin, 2005.

object may well reflect one's knowledge or ignorance of the actual means of production.

I am grateful to the artists and designers who have allowed me to reproduce admittedly inadequate photographs of their works. At the same time, I must confess to a certain frustration. Existing words, concepts, frameworks, reproductions do not suffice to characterize the current state of affairs within and across the traditional art forms. (Indeed, it is hard to describe these images, and even harder to convey their significance when the size and color cannot be presented faithfully.) Artists, designers, curators, and scholars in various disciplines are provoked to develop the framework in which to analyze such "works"—making the uncanny a little more canny, dissolving a bit of the awe around awesome, but also problematizing distinctions that had once seemed clear. Contemporary artists, designers, scientists, engineers want to make things, try them out, futz with them; they don't care about boundaries, they don't even think to specify the "bucket" in which their creations belong. The divisions among disciplines, arts, and crafts, real and virtual, digital and analog, are melting more rapidly than the polar ice caps.

To be sure, intimations of these trends could be discerned in earlier times. We could argue about whether the nature of artistry, and our senses of beauty, have changed qualitatively, or only quantitatively. We could debate whether, and to what extent, these changes depend on postmodernism and the digital media. But note well: One hundred years ago, perhaps even fifty years ago, an exhibit like *Design and the Elastic Mind* would have been regarded as inappropriate for an art museum, for an institution that displays objects of beauty designed by practicing artists, mostly from the distant past. By the same token: One hundred years ago, perhaps even fifty years ago, an old typewriter caught in a snowstorm would have shocked the nervous system of a major museum, and would have seemed more appropriate "on the fringe" of off-off Fifth Avenue. Now such works and exhibitions are commonplace. Beauty is by no means discounted. Rather, it accompanies new sets of objects and experiences that—in defiance of geometric ratios or golden means or photographic realism—provoke interest, are memorable, and invite further exploration.

Eventually, the inherent powers, as well as the limitations of the new media, will become clear. The emerging profile is almost always a surprise, especially to those who are not "native" to the new media. I managed to be born well before personal computers, virtual realities, and the blogosphere could have been envisioned—even by visionaries. And so my mind is boggled, bloggled(!), by the various possibilities that only a few years ago seemed impossibilities: that favorite works of art can instantly be transmitted all around the world; that a museum can display all of its works online; that ARTstor has made available online countless works of art that the world values (and will change its offerings as new valuations emerge); that individuals can mix and match the contents of songs already composed and easily add their own blends to the amalgam; that, via Guitar Hero, adolescents can emulate any guitar rock star that they choose; that even young children can assemble portfolios of their own work online; that videos created by rank amateurs can now be received and critiqued on YouTube by dozens, hundreds, or even thousands of viewers; that the good and the bad, the beautiful and the ugly, the true and the false can be sent readily and powerfully all around the world, if not into outer space.

No doubt, in next Monday's *New York Times* (assuming that the publication still exists), I will learn about yet another medium that can play with sounds, images, and personae in an original way.

In surveying this state of affairs, I draw on an idea introduced some decades ago by André Malraux, one of the preeminent French intellectuals of the last century. To describe the accessibility of works of art in the photographic age, Malraux coined the phrase "the museum without walls." Even in Malraux's time, thanks to reproductions, it was possible for an art lover to have at least some exposure to works of art drawn from the range of cultures. And now, of course, thanks to the Internet and to sources like ARTstor, we can actually have access— instant access—to just about any work ever created, as well as to close-ups, mash-ups, cut-ups, or virtually any other version thereof.

Two sequels. As I've noted, first of all, anyone can now develop his or her own aesthetic, including a sense of beauty, and monitor the course of that individualized portfolio over time. The multifarious changes that are wrought by new media will influence how I, and countless others, perceive works of art, what we consider to be beautiful, and what forms our individualized portfolio assume, going forward. Second, access to the actual "original" work might become less important, since simulacra of the work have become so accessible. And more than a few persons have therefore been led to ask: Why bother to go to an expensive concert when I can hear flawless performances on my home speakers or at a specially equipped theater near my home?

One possibility is that the work of art itself will move off center stage, becoming just part of a much broader experience. Artistic experiences could become, perhaps they are already becoming, about the person(s) connected to the production or dissemination of that work. How much of today's visual art world is about Jeff Koons, or Matthew Barney, or Jenny Holzer, or Cindy Sherman as celebrity artists rather than about their works alone, or perhaps even about their works per se? Or about the Chelsea gallery that displays their works, the Hollywood celebrity who has purchased their works (and for how much), the auction house that handles their sale, the ways in which the works themselves have been transmogrified, perhaps digitally or perhaps virally?

In this context, the changing roles of museums may be particularly revealing. At one time, art museums were sanctuaries where individuals went, often alone, in order to have direct, unmediated experiences with original works of art. Nowadays, however, for many visitors, museums are alluring because of the overall experience of the visit. To be sure, the overt pretext remains the experience of objects: ones that interest, have memorable form, invite additional visits, and that, with any luck, will evoke frequent though not entirely predictable experiences of beauty. Yet in practice, individuals visit museums with family or friends, to behold them as well as other visitors, to browse the bookshop, eat in the café, surf the Internet on the kiosk or in one's handheld devices, perhaps asking questions about the works but perhaps not. Paramount may be the conviction that the time at the museum is well spent.

Just possibly, museums will one day be supplanted by live performances by artists, against a digital backdrop of their ever-changing work. And just as the arts may have become about the artist, or the artist and her work, art may also become about the group, in a digital era. No longer is choreography focused on the idiosyncratic style of a specific "star" choreographer. Rather, according to Carla Peterson, artistic director of Dance Theater Workshop, "We're seeing surfacing in American contemporary dance work in recent years the deliberate use of strategies that have long been common artistic practice in other art forms. . . . Appropriation, sampling, referencing, and dialoguing with other artists' works, notions of authorship, dissolving of genres, the rethinking of dance's relationship with movement, and with audiences, etc., are all in play." Distinctions and borders that would have been assumed in decades past have become blurred and may be disappearing. And perhaps beauty will have to be reconceived yet again, with reference to new institutions and novel modes of production and connoisseurship.

Time for some reassurance. Despite the unsettling, if not dystopic possibilities that I've just contemplated, I do not expect that we will reject works of art that have been hallowed in the past. Spectators will still want to view Greek vases, Chinese landscape paintings, the sculptures of Michelangelo—if at all possible, in original form and at their original venue. Audiences will still attend performances of plays by Euripides, Shakespeare, and Molière. There are reasons why certain works endure over the long haul—and that is because they continue to invite further and deeper exploration. Earlier notions of beauty are not deleted; rather, they are expanded and individualized along the lines I've suggested.

I am even so bold as to predict that there will continue to be concerts of Classical and Romantic music—embodying changing conceptions of beauty in music—and I will continue to attend them. Perhaps there is a musical version of Zeno's paradox: At concerts (and only at concerts), no matter how old I get, I may never catch up to the mean age of the audience! And I think that museums are likely to endure, offline as well as online, and that audiences will still flock to an exhibition of the works of Renoir and van Gogh, of Mark Rothko or Jackson Pollock, even if the artists themselves are not present to hawk their works, or to be featured on the cover of *Time* magazine. There may be fewer solitary visits, attendees may be more often accompanied by handheld devices, the audience may even care more about the experience as a whole than about the specific work(s) encountered: But the encounter with the work of art itself—*Das Ding an Sich* (in Kantian terms)—will never disappear. By the same token, individuals will continue to cherish nature—though, as the example of mountains in the eyes of eighteenth-century French dwellers reminds us, *which* aspects of nature are cherished may well change.

Were Immanuel Kant to return today to his home in Konigsberg, Germany, he would be bewildered. He would have to rework his treatise on judgment and his reflections on the beautiful and the sublime—and perhaps agree to sign books at the nearest bookstore. If he had no publicist, he might have to wait in obscurity. But I also believe that, once it could be discerned despite the competing din, the merit of his work—indeed, its powerfully valid points—would ultimately be discovered and confirmed.

Still, if my line of argument has validity, traditional notions of beauty will cease to be dominant. We will devote more physical space, more psychic space, perhaps even more neural space, to other symptoms of the arts: to works and experiences and "performance art" that are better characterized as interesting, perhaps awe-inspiring, and, I would suggest, sometimes even awful but also memorable in their mode of presentation and inviting further exploration.

Equally dramatically, the notion of the single solitary artist, slaving in the garret to produce an unknown masterpiece, will seem increasingly anachronistic (just as individual scientists are increasingly giving way to large teams of often anonymous researchers at one or more huge facilities). Artists will continue to be known—and perhaps become famous for even more than fifteen minutes—but this fame may be increasingly difficult to separate from a cult of personality, a history of acquisition, and a niche within a broader narrative. And the works, processes, experiences that are shared widely may often have a communal origin and a communal reaction. The once-firm lines between art and science, real and virtual, individual and collective, nature and culture will be so sharply challenged that the earlier delineations—including ones evoked here—may come to be seen as anachronistic.

And so, as promised, we encounter a complex state of affairs, but one that in the end is reasonably reassuring. Individuals will continue to seek and cherish objects and experiences that elicit experiences and judgments of beauty. After the fact, we may be able to give a coherent account of how these experiences and judgments came about. But the examples I've given, from the history of the arts, and from my own experience, are telling. Such examples give the lie to any attempt to predict what will be beautiful—on the basis of either knowledge of the nervous system, on the one hand, or of current market values, on the other. Indeed, explanations that rely heavily on biology or economics are doomed to be trivial or wrong. Rather, only on the basis of detailed, contextualized knowledge of history, culture, and individual human nature can we explain specific experiences of the beautiful—those cherished by an individual and those that reverberate across groups or even across cultures.

In the end, our "story" of beauty turns out rather differently from our "story" of truth. Despite the postmodern and digital complexifiers, the trend toward firmer established truths is solid. In contrast, traditional conceptions of beautiful objects and experiences no longer suffice. The experience of beauty is ever more dependent on the creation of objects and experiences that, whatever their provenance, engender interest, are memorable, and invite further exploration. Moreover, and importantly, what will be judged as beautiful cannot be predicted in advance; historical, cultural, and accidental factors overwhelm any brain-based or economic considerations. Instead of pondering the evolutionary predilections of premodern women and men or the allegedly inexorable laws of supply and demand, we have to focus on the variations that emerge—by accident or design—and wait to see which ones of them come to enchant or haunt each person who is immersed in the world of the arts. We may converge ever closer to truth, but our own experiences of beauty will increasingly diverge from the experiences of others.

Chapter 4 | Goodness

Wen I began to ponder the themes of this book, Immanuel Kant was not on my mind. And yet it did not take long until I realized that, at least in a general way, my three virtues recall the foci of Kant's seminal philosophical trilogy: Pure Reason dealing with the true, Judgment with the beautiful, and Practical Reason with the moral sphere, the good. According to economist John Maynard Keynes, an equally influential thinker, we are all slaves to the theories of some dead economist, though we are unlikely to be aware of it. That is, the ideas that we *think* are our own, or that we believe have *always* existed, almost always came from a thinker whose ideas have been absorbed, knowingly or not, into the culture. Just note the way psychoanalytic explanations pervade our culture, even among those who explicitly reject Freud's ideas or those who have hardly heard his name.

But much as we might like, we should not simply rest on the problematics or the conclusions of our illustrious forebears. Were Immanuel Kant somehow to arrive on the scene today, he would doubtless be perplexed by the postmodern critique that challenges any serious effort to delineate—let alone glorify—the true, the beautiful, and the good. Moreover, like so-called digital immigrants of our own era, he would not know what to make of social networks like Facebook, virtual realities, multiple-user games with many thousands of players, and the millions of postings of motley quality available on the Internet. He would have to rethink and, perhaps, revise his enterprise. In his absence, lesser mortals must pick up the Kantian gauntlet; each generation must revisit the true, the beautiful, and the good. However tempting, we cannot simply sanctify or brutally banish these concepts.

When it came to truth, I reached a reassuring conclusion. While there is no single truth, various disciplines and professions have allowed us to delineate different spheres of truth, with some confidence; and, over time, we should be able to establish truth (and truths), and to distinguish it (and them) from falsity and from "truthiness." I also preserved a role for the experience of beauty in our appreciation of the arts—and of the intriguing hybrids and amalgams of art and science, and art and the natural world—that have become prevalent in recent years. But I stressed the importance of complementary "symptoms of the arts"—specifically the trio of interestingness, memorability, and invitation to revisit—that can give rise to experiences of beauty. I concluded that senses of beauty are becoming increasingly individualized in our time and applauded this trend.

We now arrive at our remaining topic—the good. Or, to be more precise, the Fate of the Concept of the Good in a Postmodern, Digital Era. (It has an almost Kantian sound to it!—Das Schicksal von der Konzept. . . .) I've come to see "the good" as a property of our relations with other human beings—individuals whom we know well and also those who are unfamiliar; groups, both close and remote; and, less directly though equally importantly, individuals with whom we have relations as a result of our work or our membership in a profession. Accordingly, in what follows I speak of *good persons, good citizens*, and *good workers*. In some ways, our notion of what constitutes good relations with others has changed little over the millennia—and here I speak of "neighborly morality." But in important ways, what it means to be a good worker or a good citizen has emerged gradually in recent times—and here I speak of "the ethics of roles."

I'll then turn to the topic of greatest importance: the ways our sense of "the good" has to be rethought in our era. I'll suggest that, in the wake of pervasive digital media, we need to create anew the ways in which we deal, online, with persons known and unknown. Moreover, in the face of pressures to embrace relativism or succumb to absolutism in a world wafted with postmodern sentiments, the co-construction by disparate cultures of a global set of ethics has become crucial.

If you are like me, you remember the Ten Commandments from the earliest years of your conscious life. Until recently, however, I had not realized that the commandments actually fall into two categories. The first four commandments remind us that we are in the presence of God, and that we owe Him ceaseless, unquestioned respect and obedience. That takes care of the Super-Natural. The remaining commandments are strikingly local. Honor thy parents, and treat thy neighbors well—specifically, don't kill them, steal from them, lie to them, or sleep with them. One can easily envision these commandments at work in the primitive clans in which humans once lived—communities of at most a few hundred people, where you knew just about everyone, at least by face (and that face might well belong to a close relative), and everyone knew you. If you committed a sin, it would likely be common knowledge soon, and, unless you were extremely powerful, you were likely to face retribution on the part of offended individuals, or their relatives, or the broader community. The Ten Commandments enshrined these moral precepts; it is doubtful that any community could have long survived, or, indeed, that any community *did* survive, in which stealing, adultery, and murder were the order of the day or the pattern of the night.

In many societies, we encounter an even simpler adage: the Golden Rule—"Do unto others. . . . " Or, if you incline toward the pessimistic, you can invoke the less positive version: "Do not do unto others. . . . " Again, I see this as a statement about one's relationship to the local sphere, with respect to those whom one knows and encounters on a regular basis. The Golden Rule was presumably present and operating long before it was captured in a succinct oral or written phrase—Hammurabi's "An eye for an eye" seems to have lexicalized a well-entrenched principle. Long-term survival of a community presupposes some kind of benevolent reciprocity.

Now, you may be thinking that my appeal to universals presages an evolutionary account of morality. The very author who scorned a biological account of beauty in art is about to embrace a biological account of morality. And I do believe that, courtesy of evolution, we higher primates have a very keen sensitivity to fairness and, equally, as the pessimist might have it, an acute alertness to those who cheat or who "freeload."

But important considerations undermine any attempt to reduce human morality—let alone ethics—to a strictly biological account. First of all: the definition and size of the relevant group. I doubt that there is any society in which murdering, stealing, or adultery is condoned within the nuclear family. Indeed, we are especially repelled when tyrants like Saddam Hussein or Josef Stalin abuse or annihilate members of their own families. But as those horrific examples remind us, the size of the relevant group can be quite small and subject to rapid change. Woe be it to anyone in the Communist party of the

1930s or the Baathist party of the 1980s—even those in the "inner circle"—who dared to question anything that the Supreme Leader ordered, or even intimated!

Once one goes beyond the neighborhood, all bets are off. The Bible is hardly a handbook of kindness and grace; genocide with respect to "the other" is a leitmotif of the Five Books of Moses. And in the days of modern warfare, when our enemies are remote and anonymous, when drones can do the warrior's bidding, the ethological restraints on killing—a human enemy who raises both arms up high or lies prostrate on the ground—are sharply reduced. I'll paraphrase a remark attributed to Freud: "If one could get a coin by pushing a button and killing a person on the other side of the world, by the end of the week everyone in Vienna would be a millionaire." To put the point succinctly: Our morality can be frighteningly, parochially local.

Yet—and this is the crucial point—our neighborly morality need not be applied only to those on our street. The most impressive human beings behave in equally moral fashion toward *all* other persons, irrespective of their appearance, background, and distance. The size of the group whom we choose to include in our "neighborhood" is a product of history, culture, and individual agency—not of brains or of genes.

A biological account of the good is inadequate in another respect: It cannot deal with the emergence and continuing evolution of large societies. Such societies become socially complex. To use a term of art drawn from Émile Durkheim's sociology of a century ago, they are marked by an increasing "division of labor." In a small agrarian, hunting, or fishing clan, from one year to the next, all the men do pretty much the same things (e.g., search for food) and all the women do pretty much the same things (e.g., prepare and serve the food). And so the rules of society—including the do's and the don'ts—apply across the board. The Ten Commandments and the Golden Rule—or, in a more vengeful version, Hammurabi's "An eye for an eye"—suffice, with respect both to the sphere of work and to membership in the community.

It is possible for a society to grow in size without appreciable division of labor. Perhaps such ballooning happened over the centuries in large regions of agrarian China and India. But by and large, as societies grow larger, and civilization as we know it emerges, division of labor beyond sex-linked roles inevitably follows. A select few rule and many are ruled. A privileged few become literate. They write regulations; compose, recite, and interpret texts about the society past and present; handle complex mercantile exchanges; maintain the financial records of the household or the kingdom. The rest continue to cope with life's trials and tribulations without the benefit of these literate skills. Eventually, quite specialized arts, crafts, and professions emerge. And so, by the summit of the medieval era, say, by the year 1200 A.D., whether in the centers of power in China, India, Mexico, Peru, or Western or Byzantine Europe, societies encompassed military leaders, political potentates, serfs, artisans, jewelers, healers, judges, and builders, along with other highly differentiated roles.

Under such circumstances, the Golden Rule and the Ten Commandments fall short, sometimes woefully so. Not that one should avoid kindness or reciprocity. But rather, the roles that are part and parcel of any complex society regularly produce quandaries that could not have been anticipated in earlier times, dilemmas whose solution may elude even the best of intentions or the most memorable antecedents.

Let me elaborate on a distinction and an accompanying vocabulary that have clarified my own thinking—the distinction between morality and ethics. I propose that we reserve the term *moral* for those interactions that exist between or among human beings by virtue of their common humanity, their mutual recognition of this fact, and their membership in some kind of a designated tribe, clan, or local community. In an effort to avoid confusion with ordinary usage, I have coined the phrase "neighborly morality." We are in the territory of the Ten Commandments, the Golden Rule, the Code of Hammurabi. When Sigmund Freud remarked that "morality is self-evident," he was presumably referring to what is considered good and what is considered bad at the local level. Courtesy of our genes and our brains, we are predisposed to adopt neighborly morality.

As young as the age of two or three, most children have come to use, to articulate, indeed to rely on, the distinction between good and bad. To be sure, the initial sense of good largely centers on what is good for Ego—namely, what makes one happy, well fed, and stocked with possessions as opposed to being browbeaten, bullied, hungry, or worse. Within a few years, "good" comes to encompass a sense of fairness—perhaps one is not always fair to others, but one certainly expects to be treated equitably by relatives, neighbors, and, above all, peers. Socialization by the community—whether carried out in a harsh or benign fashion—entails broadening and leavening the sense of the good, so that it becomes less self-centered, less egocentric, more cognizant of the welfare of other members of the group, and more alert to the "common good." This socialization can be executed poorly or well, consistently or inconsistently. Within a few years, the results—be they admirable, lamentable, or an amalgam of both conditions—can be seen at home, on the street, on the playing fields, in initiation rites, and in organized institutions like schools and churches. If all has gone well, if she follows the Golden Rule and some variant of the Ten Commandments, Sally is seen as a good girl, a good person.

I contrast *morality*, a neighborhood concept, with *ethics*, a concept appropriate to complex societies. Such societies, being highly differentiated, have over time created sets of principles and practices that mark and regulate a particular profession. Ethics involves an abstract capacity, an abstract attitude. When in the sphere of neighborly morality, one thinks of oneself as simply an individual (I am Howard) and one thinks of others by name (my wife Ellen, my sister Marion, my children, more distant relatives, friends, neighbors, touters and taunters). In the sphere of ethics, by contrast, one thinks of oneself in terms of roles. Thinking of oneself as the occupant of a role requires the capacity to step *outside* of one's skin and one's quotidian interactions, so to speak, and instead to conceptualize oneself as a Worker and as a Citizen. And so, complementing "neighborly morality," I've coined the phrase "the ethics of roles."

In my own case, as I don the ethical hat in the sphere of work, I think of myself as occupying the roles of teacher, scholar, social science researcher, author, and public speaker, if not public intellectual. Each of these professions has its own ethical presuppositions, sometimes captured in explicit codes. Turning my attention to citizenship, I think of myself in my roles at the workplace (Harvard University), my community (Cambridge, Massachusetts), my organizational affiliations (board memberships), my state, region, nation, and, increasingly, the planet (I stop there, though the more far-sighted or grandiose among us may construe themselves as citizens of the galaxy or even the multi-galactic universe). Once again, with respect to each of these spheres, there are ethical expectations, sometimes captured in regulations or laws.

Note that, according to this line of argument, citizenship is not a natural or self-evident category. Since time immemorial, individuals have been members of a clan and tribe; in that capacity, they have expected others to behave morally toward them, have minded their own mores, and may have assumed some broader-based responsibilities to the collectivity (e.g., be on the lookout for intruders, leave some crops for others to harvest). But, on my account, the idea of being a citizen of a polity—be it the Greek city-state, the Roman Republic, the United States, or France after 1789—makes sense only within a larger society, where one has relations even with individuals whom one has not met and may never know personally.

The ethics of roles entails a crucial additional component, beyond the capacity to adopt an abstract attitude per se. That feature is the concept of *responsibility*. Nowadays, particularly in the United States, no group, whether social or professional, has any trouble stating its rights. (I sometimes quip that the first nonphysical verb mastered by American toddlers is the verb *to sue*.) From my perspective, the cardinal feature of a genuinely ethical stance is a sense of responsibility. To be sure, the worker or citizen is entitled to certain rights. But the ethical worker does not get up each morning and thunder: "What is owed to me? What are my rights?" Rather, she asks: "Insofar as I am a professional, and am thereby accorded a certain amount of resources, respect, and autonomy, what are my responsibilities?" The ethical citizen, too, does not perseverate on her rights—though they are important and may have been attained only after struggle. Rather, she asks: "Insofar as I have attained the status of citizen, what are my responsibilities?"

An important proviso: It is easy to be ethical when one's self-interest is advanced—no problem, proceed directly to Go, and collect two hundred or two trillion dollars. The acid test for ethics occurs when one's self-interest is pitted against the right thing to do in one's role. The physician is all set to go on holiday with his family, but a patient shows up with a condition that requires immediate care. What should the doctor do? The affluent citizen may oppose a sharply progressive tax hike as much as his neighbor ("Oh, for another yacht"), but he realizes that an increase in his tax payments will disproportionately help those who are less fortunate by providing needed medical or educational services. How does he vote on the proposed tax hike? The test of ethics is responsibility, independent of one's own particular niche or stake in the outcome. I think here of philosopher John Rawls's view of the "just community," established through a veil of ignorance. On Rawls's account, the rules governing a society should be crafted without foreknowledge of one's own capacities and niche within that society.

I have sought to demonstrate why, in our time, the short and simple word *good* harbors considerable complexity. In any differentiated society, neighborly morality can get one only so far. What it means to behave properly in one's role as a lawyer, physician, engineer, accountant, teacher, merchant, and so on—or to be a responsible citizen of one's workplace, the organizations to which one belongs, and the successively larger polities of which one is a member—is simply not clear, let alone transparent. Neighborly morality is self-evident, to be sure—"love thy neighbor as thyself." But each of the aforementioned professional domains involves technical knowledge. There is no legitimate way in which nonexperts can dictate to a lawyer, for example, what evidence should be included, and how it can be secured; or to an architect how to create and implement plans that are at once attractive, practical, safe, and legal; or to a physician which treatment manual or website to consult and under which circumstances to ignore the recommended "best practices." Nor will the Ten Commandments instruct me on how to vote on a faculty appointment, whether to support the de-accession of a famous work of art, or how to choose among political candidates who favor contrasting approaches to global warming.

Yet, with respect to the distinction between neighborly morality and the ethics of roles, one should bear in mind some cautionary notes. First, writers use the terms *morality* and *ethics* in many ways—sometimes, for example, *morality* is the umbrella term, with *ethics* considered to be a subset. Second, some authorities believe that the precepts I have located in local clans are actually universal rights and obligations, which suffice to govern our actions as workers and citizens. Much as one might wish this were so, I believe that it is an aspiration rather than a reality.

It's important to stipulate that the distinction between morality and ethics is anything but absolute. Much of what we have considered moral leaks over into the ethical: We should not harm those who are far from us, any more than we should harm those whom we see every day. And much of the ethical is relevant to the moral: We may see ourselves as workers and citizens even with respect to those who inhabit our school classroom, the house down the block, or, indeed, our own home. The lines between person, family member, neighbor, worker, and citizen are porous, not absolute.

Bearing in mind these cautionary notes, how should one think of "the good"?

On the definition I've introduced here, assessments of what is "good" (or "not good") apply to *human relations*: the relations that govern how we human beings act toward one another, locally and globally. The first and primary sense of "good" (or "bad") has been with us over the millennia: It refers to how we treat our relatives, friends, neighbors—Are we cruel or kind, generous or selfish, fair or unfair? In a word, it characterizes us as persons who are "good" or who fall short in various ways. But because of the evolving complexity of societies in more recent times, we need to add an additional sense of "good": Do we live up to our principal responsibilities as workers and as citizens, or do we fall short in significant ways?

As it happens, my own research has come to focus on these issues. The research has suggested ways in which to conceptualize these newer instantiations of "the good" as well as the ways in which work and citizenship are newly challenged by postmodern views and by the digital media.

Since the mid-1990s, with valued colleagues Mihaly Csikszentmihalyi, William Damon, and many other fine researchers, I've been studying the concept of "good work." (More recently, this study has been extended to include consideration of "good citizenship.") Our work was stimulated primarily by two events. On a personal level, we had on occasion seen the findings from our earlier research applied in ways that were disturbing. This unexpected abuse led us to consider the ways in which, as professionals, we had broader responsibility for the impact of our work. On a societal level, we noted a growing belief that all sectors of society were best regulated by market forces. To be sure, we ourselves were beneficiaries of the market in many ways and had no reason to be critical of the operation of markets "across the board." But we felt strongly that the realm of work—and particularly work in the professions—would be vulnerable to abuse if its defining facets were simply left to the forces of supply and demand. Each profession is organized around a central set of values, and it is essential to preserve and realize those central values whether or not the profession-in-question passes a "market test," in a strict sense of that term.

In executing the Good Work Project, we conducted in-depth interviews of more than 1,200 professionals in nine different spheres of work. Reflection on our findings has led us to conceptualize good work as exhibiting three components, each exemplified by the letter E. Good work is *excellent*—it meets the technical standards of the relevant profession or craft. It is personally meaningful or *engaging*. Carrying out good work over the long haul proves too difficult unless that work remains inviting and meaningful to the practitioner. The third E is *ethical*. Good work is carried out in a responsible, ethical manner. The good worker constantly interrogates herself about what it means to be responsible; seeks to behave in that way; and attempts, as we all should, to admit her failings and thereafter to correct course.

The distinction that I've drawn between "neighborly morality" and "the ethics of roles" emerged from this research. As human beings living in neighborhoods, we are expected, and expect others, to behave in a moral way. That's what it means to be a good person. As professionals, we are expected, and we expect others who occupy professional roles, to behave in an ethical way. These two "flavors of goodness" reflect mechanisms that are now thought to underlie the gamut of moral behavior: One, more automatic and intuitive, may govern neighborly morality; the other, subject to conscious reflection, is more relevant to our roles as workers and citizens.

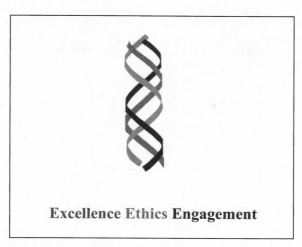

Excellence Ethics Engagement

Figure 4.1. The Three Intertwined Strands of Good Work.

Through a convenient analogy, we can conceive of good work as the DNA of the good professional (see Figure 4.1). Just as our genetic DNA allows us to develop as a flesh-and-blood surviving member of *Homo sapiens*, our professional DNA—or, if you prefer, ENA—allows us to be good workers. And our professional triple helix opens up the possibility of passing on the relevant "memes," or units of meaning, to future generations of workers.

Though it stretches the point a bit, we might think of the three Es of good work as the current instantiation of the classical virtues. Excellence lies in the realm of pure reason and truth. Scientists and scholars pursue the truth. Engagement reminds us of the arts and of nature—we are engaged by what is interesting, memorable, and inviting. (Indeed, when engaged, we may even feel a "tingle.") And ethics takes us into the realms of justice, the good life, and the good society.

As I mentioned, the analysis of good work can be applied readily and appropriately to the realm of citizenship. Put succinctly, the good citizen is technically *excellent*—she knows the rules and procedures of the polity or polities to which she belongs. The good citizen is *engaged*—she cares about what happens and rises to the occasion as needed, or even proactively. Third, and of particular importance, the good citizen is *ethical*. She tries to do the right thing—even when, indeed especially when, the proper course of action does not promote her self-interest.

Ideally, individuals can and should be "good" across the board. But in applying this framework, we should realize that an individual might be a good person without being a good worker or a good citizen; and all other combinations of "good" and "not good" are possible as well. Failure to make these distinctions leads to frequent surprises—as when one discovers, for example, that the exemplary worker beats his spouse, or that the most helpful neighbor on one's street never bothers to stay informed or to vote.

Doing good work is never easy; conflicting demands and opposing opportunities abound. Good work is most easily achieved when all of the stakeholders in a particular line of work want the same things, roughly speaking. We call this condition *alignment*. In concrete terms, a profession is aligned when the classical values of the profession, the goals of the current practitioners, the demands of the marketplace, the leaders (and, in for-profit contexts, the share-owners) of the institution, and the stakeholders in the broader society all want roughly the same thing. As an example, in the last two decades in the United States, it has been relatively easy to carry out good work as a genetics researcher, because the society supports this work in a nonjudgmental manner. We all want to live longer and be healthier; we look to geneticists and other biologically oriented scientists to help us achieve these goals; and we facilitate—rather than obstruct—their enterprises. (When issues like the appropriateness of stem cell research start to generate controversy, alignment may weaken or even dissolve.)

In sharp contrast, over the same period it has become increasingly difficult to carry out good work in journalism—work that is objective, fair-minded, and devoid of sensationalism or of unwarranted reliance on rumor and anonymity. And that is because the various stakehold-ers—the owner(s), the publisher, the editor, the reporters, the general public—seem to want quite different things in their news diet: Ac-cordingly, alignment is essentially absent. Indeed, it is questionable whether print journalism will even survive, at least in a form that old-timers could recognize.

In general, alignment helps the profession as a whole stay on track. In the end, however, it is individuals, and individuals alone, who decide whether or not to carry out good work. You can be a good worker in bad, unaligned times; indeed, some workers are stimulated by nonalignment to create new institutions that embody and confirm the highest values of the profession. In the United States, the dearth of high-quality radio news and cultural programs (of the sort associ-ated with the British Broadcasting Corporation) led to the founding of National Public Radio; in the Middle East, the absence of news cov-erage in a moderate, multiple-perspective vein led to the launch of Al Jazeera. And of course, one can be a bad worker even when the pro-fession is highly aligned. There are rotten apples in well-aligned do-mains such as genetics, as well as freeloaders who take advantage of the high ethical standards of their peers.

Nor is good work restricted to card-carrying members of a desig-nated profession. Blue-collar and white-collar workers encounter their share of ethical dilemmas as well. The bus driver has to decide whether to delay the route and antagonize those in a hurry in order to come to the aid of a passenger who seems distressed; the factory worker has to decide whether to finish an important job, even though he will not be paid overtime, or to leave it unfinished for someone else or for another day. But because the nonprofessional worker often has less power, less of a sense of agency, I'll suggest the aptness of a forth E. The "ordinary worker" is more likely to aspire to good work in a workplace that is *equitable*. In such a work environment, everyone is treated fairly; privileges for management, as opposed to the rank and file, are modest in amount rather than excessive.

Given a choice, few would opt for a "bad" or "compromised" work environment. Yet, as a matter of fact, in most places good work is difficult to achieve and difficult to maintain over the long haul. Our research has revealed three factors that increase the likelihood of good work:

1. *Vertical support*—the values and operating principles of those persons who are at or near the top of the work pyramid. If your boss is a good worker, models good work, expects the same of you, and imposes increasingly severe sanctions in cases of compromised or bad work, her example will exercise a powerful influence on your work ethic.

2. *Horizontal support*—the values and customary modes of behavior of peers and colleagues. Those at your level in the workplace who are good workers, and who send out warning signals in the event that you (or others) deviate from that norm, also set examples that matter.

3. *Periodic booster shots*—in any profession, there will be occasional acts of heroism, as well as wake-up calls consequent upon the discovery of compromised or frankly bad work. Workers can be strongly affected by these benevolent or malevolent events and, in particular, by the way others react to them.

Thanks to gutsy reporters, editors, and publishers, print journalism received such a boost during the era of the Pentagon Papers and the Watergate burglary. On the other hand, shortly after the start of the first decade of the century, the storied reputation of the *New York Times* suffered because of a double whammy: the irresponsible reporting and plagiarism of rogue reporter Jayson Blair, and the failure of reporters and editors to challenge unfounded claims by sources in the U.S. executive branch that Iraq possessed weapons of mass destruction.

The reaction to a wake-up call is as important as the call itself. When the *New York Times* instituted various measures of quality control, including the hiring of an independent "public editor" and a prominently featured daily report of errors and corrections, these acts tipped toward the positive side of the good work scales. In contrast, consider the behaviors of auditing, financial, banking, and regulating professionals at the start of the first decade of the twenty-first century. Despite the massive irregularities that led to bankruptcies in Enron, Global Crossing, WorldCom, and Arthur Andersen, professionals failed to attend to warnings and thereupon to institute and then rigorously apply appropriate regulations. The result: the worldwide financial meltdown toward the end of the decade.

Readers may be surprised that I have not discussed a fourth, and possibly primary, facilitator of good work: adherence to a religious credo. Without question, throughout history, many individuals have been stimulated to be good neighbors, citizens, and workers as a consequence of their religious beliefs and/or their membership in a religious group. Indeed, it can be argued that religion itself arose as a means of encouraging neighborly morality and, later on, as a means of promoting ethical behavior in various roles—and that in the absence of religion, many would have little reason to pursue a moral or ethical life.

Though not a religious person myself, I have no desire whatever to belittle religion or to challenge those who believe in a deity. (Indeed, I think that those commentators who frontally attack religious believers are engaged in an undesirable and counterproductive activity.) Over the course of human history, religions have often played a constitutive role not only in the promotion of the good but also in the provision of various forms of beauty.

Yet my decision not to dwell on religion is deliberate. I don't believe for a minute that pursuit of goodness is dependent on any particular religion, or, indeed, on religious beliefs altogether. Indeed, considerable empirical evidence documents that various kinds of misdeeds are as likely, or more likely, to be committed by religious believers than by atheists or agnostics. And crime rates are actually lowest in the northern European countries that have the lowest percentages of believers and the lowest attendance in church. In spite of some recent trends to the contrary, I anticipate that belief in God, and religious beliefs more generally, are likely to wane in the period ahead. Whatever the case, I do not want to tie the moral or the ethical life to any particular institution, including religious ones. That said, I would be thrilled if a new, truly universal belief system, which could be religious or spiritual in tone, were to emerge and to help individuals carry out various roles in a more ethical manner.

I could simply assert that our conceptions of goodness in neighborly morality and ethics have been set for all time—and then this chapter could draw rapidly to a close. But the pair of novel forces we've been examining have clearly complicated the status of "the good" today. Particularly among the young, postmodern modes of thought have come to permeate the ways in which we think about human affairs. Even more dramatically, our entire conception of "the good" is being continually and radically altered by the digital media. Let's consider each of these forces in turn.

First, postmodernism. There is no sphere of life in which the relativist critique has had more potency than in the domains of morality and ethics. To be sure, ordinary citizens may be more reluctant than in the past to talk about beauty as if it were self-evident; and most citizens do recognize biases in the media, if not in our senses, that, at least initially, make the determination of truth problematic. But fundamental threats to conceptions of truth and beauty are more apparent to those in the academy and to members of the chattering classes than to the majority of women or men in Peoria, Pisa, or the Punjab.

Not so with the realm of morality and ethics. As suggested by political scientist Alan Wolfe, Americans may be the first group in the history of the world to adopt a code of moral freedom. According to Wolfe, if they are to endure, societies need a consensually shared code of morals and values—in a sense, the society needs to act as if it were one large clan. In the abstract, Americans may agree with this proposition—essentially, it is an endorsement of neighborly morality on a broad scale. But in our time, Americans then take the unprecedented step of asserting that each person can and should be trusted to develop her own moral code and to lead her life consistently with it. And, equally, most Americans are extremely reluctant to judge harshly the moral codes of others, unless these codes sanction frankly and unambiguously destructive behavior.

Wolfe's findings raise questions. First of all, we must ask whether the claims for a belief in moral freedom are accurate. With respect to a tolerance for drugs and alcohol, for different sexual preferences and lifestyles, for a range of artistic preferences, for diverse ethnic and racial groups, the trends over time are unmistakably in the direction of greater acceptance. To be sure, those who watch the cable news networks may infer that Americans are hyper-judgmental about the morality of their fellow citizens. But several lines of research document that this sensationalist picture is wrong. Most of us are not fundamentalists of the left or the right—rather, we tend toward moral relativism: "Live and let live."

Other questions center on the reasons for this reluctance to judge others. Without a doubt, one can find roots for tolerance in various strands of American life, dating back to the Quakers of the prerevolutionary era. By the same token, one can find plenty of evidence for harsh judgments—for example, on the part of the Puritans of prerevolutionary times. But our own research suggests that the perspective documented by Wolfe is of more recent origins and that in fact it reflects a postmodern perspective on life.

In the first years of the new millennium, toward the end of our formal study of good work in the most prominent professions, we extended our research enterprise to young people (professionals and preprofessionals ranging from teenagers to workers in their early thirties). All of our subjects were already accomplished workers in their respective spheres. We encountered a surprising and deeply troubling state of affairs.

Over and over again, young workers in the United States told us that they knew and admired good work. But too many of them told us that good work was for "later." As they saw it, good work requires an ethical stance that they were unprepared to assume at the moment. To be sure, they might evince neighborly morality with reference to those in their intimate circle. But they craved success, they wanted it now, and they did not trust their peers to behave ethically. And so, essentially, these young workers asked for a pass. They said, "Allow us to cut corners, compromise now. *Someday* we will be good workers when we can afford to be, we will embody good work, we will hire and encourage good work in others." Of course, this is the classical "end justifies the means" argument, repugnant to Immanuel Kant (and not just to Kant)—the slippery road emanating from Good Intentions but headed straight toward Hell. Hearing the words of many American youths, I am reminded of St. Augustine's famous plea: "Oh, Lord, make me chaste and continent, but not quite yet."

Alas, our discovery has been confirmed by other researchers and reporters, who document the thin ethical dossier of many young people in the United States (and not just in the United States) today. Of course young people (and not a few old people) have always cut corners, but, to paraphrase Alan Greenspan's famous comment on contemporary human greed, "there have never been so many ways to cut corners." Moreover, the ways in which young people reflect on their judgments has indicated to me that—consciously or not—they have adopted postmodern ways of thinking.

In the past decade, I have conducted numerous informal "reflection" sessions with young people at various secondary schools and colleges in the United States. Certain themes and attitudes have recurred. Asked to list people whom they admire, students are reluctant to mention well-known figures, preferring to defer a response altogether or to mention only persons known personally to them. Moreover, when students are asked to mention those whom they do *not* admire, they are strangely reluctant to do so. Indeed, in one session I could not even get students to state that Hitler should be featured on a "not-to-be-admired" list. As one student murmured, "He *did* do some good things for Germany."

Turning to the sphere of work, we find that many students are reluctant to judge compromised work as unethical. Many of my contemporaries were stunned by the contemptuous behavior on the part of energy traders portrayed in *The Smartest Guys in the Room*, a docudrama about the now-defunct energy giant Enron. In one vivid scene, traders laugh aloud as they gratuitously deprive hundreds of thousands of Californians of electric power and toy frivolously with the price of energy. But our students hesitated to censure the traders. One said, "It was the fault of Governor [Gray] Davis, he should have known what they were doing." Another opined, "The legislature should not have deregulated the cost of energy, the Enron traders were simply exercising their rights in the marketplace."

In another "reflection" session we discussed the case of a highly respected dean of admissions at MIT. The dean, it had recently been discovered, had repeatedly misrepresented her own educational credentials and was summarily fired as a result. No student spoke up in support of the decision to fire the dean. Students divided equally between two sentiments: (1) "She was doing her job well, what was the problem?" and (2) "Well, after all, everyone lies on his/her résumé."

In analyzing these conversations, I've been struck by two things: the perspectives adopted by the young people and the affect with which they convey them. Over and over again, when asked about a particular person or action, these youths exhibit a reluctance to pass judgment, even at times to voice a personal preference. Equally, there is a subdued quality to their mien—the affect that might follow upon a personal slight seems absent with respect to broader ethical violations. As someone who engaged in discussions with my peers decades ago, and has conversed, at least informally, over the years with generations of students, I feel in the presence of a new state of affairs.

Specifically, I believe that the lines of argument put forth by post-modern thinkers over the last half-century have now entered into common parlance, at least among educated youth in the United States. These students may not have read key texts by French and American intellectuals, but they have picked up some of their ways of thinking and expression. And so, over and over again, one hears that one person's truth may not be the same as another's; that two perspectives can be equally valid or equally right; that one has no right to judge people from another background or culture; that everyone has both good and bad properties.

We'll never know for sure whether these trends could have occurred in the absence of postmodernism—counterfactuals can't be tested. But in any event, those of us interested in "the good" face a troubling situation. Americans increasingly assert their right to formulate their own moral principles and are surprisingly reluctant to pass judgment on the morality of their peers. No more placing of miscreants in stockades on the village commons!

Still another trend is equally disturbing: Young Americans seem to lack an ethical compass that governs their own behavior. A poll of thirty thousand students conducted in 2008 revealed that almost two-thirds had cheated in class in the past year and almost one-third had stolen goods from a store. (We can safely assume that the students were not exaggerating their misdeeds—if, indeed, they saw them as misdeeds.) No wonder such young people prove surprisingly insensitive to the violation of ethics by workers in the professions. Before we look askance at these young people, however, we adults need to examine ourselves in the mirror. If the standards of behavior have become lax, it is because *we* served as inadequate role models of admirable behavior, as well as inconstant, reluctant, or absent sanctioners of unacceptable actions. And it may be, as well, that we elders have failed to provide convincing responses to critiques that embody a postmodern perspective.

Perhaps, as psychologist Lawrence Kohlberg suggested several decades ago, one can expect a temporary dip in a sense of responsibility during the adolescent years. Yet, I think that the general tenets of postmodernism have raised the ante—threatening to undermine *any* set of ethical or moral absolutes. And while the postmodern critique has had its sobering and perhaps even its positive aspects, it leads to an unacceptably normless situation, a classic example of anomie, whereby young people—and people who are not so young—are reluctant to judge *any* behavior, action, or attitude as immoral, unethical, just plain wrong. Where anything goes, nothing will endure.

As if the postmodern critique were not enough, along came the new digital media. Many have wondered how young people's minds and behaviors have been affected by the web, social networks, instant messaging, multiple-user games, virtual reality, and the like. As an observer of their ranks for some time, I've come to a strong conclusion: The digital media post fundamental new challenges to our conception of the good—to the ways in which we think about other people, how they behave toward us, and how we behave toward them. In particular, the media are in the process of blurring or even erasing the difference between neighborhood morality and the ethics of roles—a situation unprecedented in human affairs.

Under the banner of the Good Play Project, our research team has been exploring a set of five ethical issues that need to be rethought—and perhaps reformulated entirely—in light of the ubiquitous new media. To begin with an issue of particular importance for young people, there is the individual's *sense of identity*. Youth have long engaged in various moves to determine who they are, how to present themselves, what kinds of personal and professional commitments to make. This state of affairs, quite normal, can lead to reasonable and wise decisions.

The new digital media, however, provide innumerable opportunities to generate multiple selves online, through the aforementioned games and networks. Ethical issues arise when youth misrepresent themselves in ways that could do harm to others, to family or friends—providing information that is misleading or hurtful, without taking responsibility for the effects of these self- or family portrayals.

For societies to function smoothly, individuals must be able to *trust* one another. A sense of warranted trust requires that individuals present information that is credible and that they can in turn make reasoned judgments about personal or factual information that they encounter in the media. But when so many identities can be spun, when there is a plethora of information available, much of it unreliable, it becomes a challenge to make trustworthy judgments and to earn and maintain the trust of others.

While the limits and extent of *privacy* have differed across time and across societies, it is generally expected that human beings may choose to keep certain forms of information private, or restricted to a few chosen friends and relatives; and that these individuals, in turn, will respect the privacy of others. But privacy risks becoming an illusion in an era where any and all bits of information—even those that one prefers to keep to oneself—may circulate anywhere and endure indefinitely.

Nearly all societies recognize the effort entailed in producing a work of art or science or invention; and in modern societies, these forms of creativity are typically protected by patents, trademarks, or copyright. Nowadays, however, just about anything—be it linguistic or graphic or musical—can be instantly transferred, transformed, borrowed, or passed off as one's own. The sphere of *ownership and authorship* of intellectual property requires rethinking.

A final issue on our research agenda is *participation in a community*— the sphere of good citizenship. As argued earlier, our species evolved under conditions of face-to-face communities, where all knew everyone else, and one could not easily run away or change one's identity. Now, of course, the size, scope, and longevity (or brevity) of online communities is unknown and probably unknowable. Under such circumstances, we need to probe the meaning of membership, of citizenship, as well as the paths for becoming an ethical citizen.

As a result of our studies of Good Play, I've become convinced that each of these five ethical flashpoints will have to be reformulated in the new digital era—not necessarily for the worse, but differently. We live at a time when identities can be endlessly spun and re-spun, sometimes in a healthy manner, but sometimes to the detriment of oneself or of others; when venerable clues to trustworthiness are typically absent; when information once deemed private can instantly be "outed"; when ownership of intellectual property (indeed, of any string of symbols) is easy to violate or ignore and difficult to protect; and when formerly circumscribed notions of a neighborhood cannot begin to address the essentially limitless communities in cyberspace—size, shape, and duration unknown and unknowable. The Internet places us in the midst of a world of personas whose identity and roles we cannot verify, a world where the customary regulators of human intercourse can no longer be relied upon.

At times this new dispensation has led to tragedy. Lori Drew, mother of thirteen-year-old Sarah Drew, believed that Megan Meier, another thirteen-year-old girl, was spreading nasty stories about her daughter on the Internet. With the aid of an accomplice and digital sleight of hand, Lori contrived Josh Evans, a fake sixteen-year-old male, and engaged Megan in seductive cyber-conversation. Lori hoped to entrap or embarrass Megan. Shortly after the contrived Josh abruptly cut off the relationship, young Megan committed suicide. While Lori was only convicted of three misdemeanors and the conviction was eventually overturned, the case underscores the potential for serious harm—even death—as a result of highly charged communications on an apparently innocent social network. Comparably tragic stories are reported on a regular basis. For example, as this book went to press, a gay teenage college student committed suicide after a webcast that captured a sexual encounter was posted. It is easy to see that old-fashioned notions of identity, trust, privacy, and community cannot simply be transferred to the new digital media.

Initially I had thought that each of these five foci could be considered in relative independence. But I now believe that they are inextricably interconnected. The primary reason for this conclusion: Once you enter cyberspace, however modest or parochial your intentions, you are in effect entering one or more communities, ones whose dimensions and reach are literally impossible to conceive, let alone to control. And because you are now part of one or more inherently limitless communities, issues of identity, privacy, ownership, and, above all, trustworthiness inevitably arise. To put it succinctly, all traditional bets are off.

Sometimes, fiction presents issues with succinct vividness. In his dystopian novel *Super Sad True Love Story* novelist Gary Shteyngart describes the "apparat," a digital device that allows its users to discern the full gamut of information about a person whom the user happens to encounter. In the presence of the protagonist, Lenny Abramov, a user can ascertain Lenny's exact age and ailments; the birthplace, identity, and diseases of his parents; and his income, savings, liabilities, most recent purchase, degree of athleticism, and religious and political leanings. It gets more intimate. In a description of his "fuckability," we learn of the kind of woman he likes, her ethnicity, self-esteem, income, and even which of three orifices he favors.

The vignette featuring the apparat touches on all five ethical issues. The apparat reveals a great deal about Lenny's identity, including material he'd rather not share; it invades his privacy; it raises the question of who owns this information, whether it can be trusted, and whether it should be shared. And since analogous information can be gleaned about anyone, all persons in the possession of an apparat can "undress" anyone in a community with whom they come in contact.

While implicating individuals of any age, the digital media pose particular challenges to young persons. Children cannot be expected to understand this concept of membership in remote and limitless communities—any more than they can be expected to understand the nature of professions or of citizenships. In my terms, they are "prepared" for neighborly morality (and for the role of good person) but not for the ethics implied in the role of citizenship in a cyber-community. And so they need firm guidance if they are not, inadvertently, to injure others or themselves. (More on this in the next chapter.)

By the time of adolescence, young people are not unaware of the pitfalls of involvement in the new digital media. Most youth know that they can get in trouble for downloading music illegally; that they can hurt another person by spreading information (or misinformation) that they gleaned on a restricted site; that they or others can perpetrate cyber-bullying. However, among American youth we have so far encountered lamentably little ethical sense with respect to these minefields. For the most part, American youth either ignore the ethical implications, worry only about negative consequences to themselves ("If I download illegally, I could get into trouble"), or belittle the importance of cyberspace altogether ("I spent way too much time online but it's just not that important"). Of course, there is no point in berating youth for these blind spots. It is up to elders (or more responsible peers) to model and promote ethical behaviors, and such modeling is possible only if elders or peers attain mastery over the digital media and become role models worthy of emulation.

And so: Having evolved as a species to practice neighborly morality, we are thrust as young people—ones who are often *very* young—into the ethics of roles, into the territory of citizenship. And yet, lamentably, neither the young nor their responsible elders may possess the cognitive and emotional equipment to handle these complex abstract spheres. I think of cyberspace as a new frontier. It is a wild west where we *may* be able to transplant some of the mores of the old country, but where, ultimately, new norms and practices will have to be fashioned for a terrain that no one yet quite understands. Such a hammering out is most likely to be carried out effectively if young and old can meld their respective zones of expertise. Specifically, young persons, who understand the new media intuitively, need to make common cause with older persons, particularly ones who are wise. Such elders are more apt to have achieved understanding of key ethical stances and can help determine where these stances are applicable and where they need to be rethought and perhaps transformed.

It's time to take stock of the status of "the good" at present and to consider its course, going forward. Throughout I have insisted on the difference between the neighborly moral—a local, long-evolving, and relatively stable set of principles and behaviors that may well have a biological basis; and the ethical—a nonlocal, more rapidly emerging and evolving set of principles and behaviors that clearly arises from, and must continue to adapt to, historical and cultural factors. In view of its longer history, indeed its prehistory, our sense of neighborly morality is far more firmly established than our sense of professional and civic ethics—in the sphere of things, a far more recent development. Put concretely, stealing goods from neighbors is unlikely ever to be endorsed; but whether the notion of stealing even makes sense in a digital world is a more vexing issue.

So while the traditional sense of "the good" endures, our overall concept of this virtue needs to be renegotiated at present: negotiated anew because of the powerful relativistic stream of thought throughout the land, especially the American land; and negotiated anew because of the surge in importance and ubiquity of the new digital media. I cannot predict whether we will end up with ethical codes that are necessarily better or worse than those that were passed down by our ancestors. Events involving humans have historical and cultural dimensions that are contingent, not rule governed, let alone a consequence of natural law. But I can predict that the sphere of "the good" will continue to pose challenges and I can assert with equal confidence that the ethical sense of the word *good* will continue to evolve, courtesy of these trends.

Considerations of the good (and what is not good) remain as important as ever. In the local sphere, delineations of the good evolve very slowly. In complex societies, and in the global sphere, the good is constantly being negotiated and renegotiated. At present, the postmodern critique and the new digital media pose formidable challenges to any simple-minded view of the good. Human biology will neither condemn us nor save us. As a species we have proclivities both for good and for evil, for altruism and for selfishness. In the face of claims that we are "born to be good," Thomas Hobbes acidly remarked: "Whatsoever is the object of any man's appetite or desires, that is it which he for his part calleth good." Our own sense of agency—individual and corporate—and our own understanding of current conditions will determine what is good, in which ways the good grows out of the past, and in which ways good must be forged and negotiated anew in largely uncharted territory.

The trend toward truth is powerful and upward; the fate of beauty is fragmented and likely to become ever more dispersed, more personalized, continually subject to revision in the light of new aesthetic experiences; the status of the good in its various senses lies squarely and permanently in the hands of our species. Though it may serve as an initial rough-and-ready guide, we cannot rely on neighborly morality as we attempt to navigate the shoals of work and citizenship in a highly complex and interconnected world.

As a start to this navigation, we need to appreciate the senses of work and of citizenship that have emerged in diverse cultures during past centuries and that remain vivid today. The ethics of law or journalism are not identical around the world, and notions of citizenship differ dramatically across countries and continents. Except when they are directly harmful to others, we should welcome, accept, or tolerate work or civic models that differ from our own—herewith the positive lesson of modern and postmodern thought.

Over the long haul, however, I doubt that the planet can survive if each nation—there are now close to two hundred, and still counting—has its own professional guidelines and its own mores of citizenship. Too much of the planet is interconnected and over time it will become ever more so. We need to evolve models of work that transcend national boundaries: Science, medicine, and air travel provide helpful current exemplars. By the same token, we need to evolve models of citizenship that can be embraced by the diverse populations of the world: Institutions like the International Court of Justice and documents like the Universal Declaration of Human Rights represent early efforts in this regard. Only in the light of converging notions of good work and good citizenship can we look ahead toward a good life on our fragile planet.

| # A Promising Start

reeks in the Socratic-Platonic tradition believed that all human knowledge is built in from the start, and René Descartes, the influential French mathematician and philosopher, thought that humans were endowed with "innate ideas." In sharp contrast to these "nativist" sentiments, British and American philosophers have inclined to the opposite view. On their "empiricist" account, initially the human infant is essentially a blank slate. Accordingly, the ambient culture—encompassing families, media, cultural institutions, the accidents of daily life—has virtually complete control over the kinds of human beings that emerge and what knowledge they ultimately display.

The intellectual tension between nativist and empiricist accounts proved surprisingly robust. Since the beginnings of scientific psychology, toward the end of the nineteenth century, major thinkers have sought evidence on how much knowledge, and of what sort, we can attribute to the newborn child and what happens in the ensuing years. As linguistically playful as his brother Henry, psychologist William James described the world of the infant as a "blooming, buzzing confusion." Sigmund Freud perceived in the infant soul a cauldron of strong, warring sexual and aggressive impulses. The influential Swiss developmental psychologist Jean Piaget conceded the existence of only programmed reflexes, gradually refined and refashioned by a set of complementary processes. On the Piagetian account, the process of *assimilation* entails the absorption of the world into the child's current repertoire of action; the process of *accommodation* entails the child's adaptation of his repertoire of action to the objects and conditions of the world. In our era, a time when far more native equipment and early knowledge are attributed to the child, Alison Gopnik, one of the world's leading authorities on early childhood, has penned two books: *The Scientist in the Crib* and *The Philosophical Baby*. (Readers of the present volume might wonder, "Is *The Artistic Infant* next?")

Nowadays, with a century of scientific research under our belts, developmental psychologists have achieved a rough consensus. Infants arrive on the planet with a definite set of life plans—"hardwired" physical and physiological developmental plans and "softer," more flexible social and emotional trajectories, as well as predictable milestones of cognitive development. Barring extremely destructive circumstances—and, fortunately, these have become increasingly rare—we can expect that in the opening years of life, children will learn to walk, jump, skip, and run; develop neural, muscular, and circulatory systems on a predictable time scale; and undergo changes associated with puberty shortly after the first decade of life. Children start to talk before the age of two; by that time they can also mentally represent and ferret out a well-hidden object. We now know that these toddlers also have some demonstrable knowledge of numbers, causal relations, human intentionality, and their own selves. Moreover, the world over, children are ready for formal schooling at five or six and can exhibit quite abstract forms of thought after the first decade of life.

But what can we say about the growing child's engagement with the true, the beautiful, the good? Expressed in personal terms, as children, what do we believe the world is like, how would we like it to appear, how would we like others to behave toward us, and how should we behave toward them? Here the story is surprisingly elusive; it has *not* been much told in the texts, the videos, and the research papers of developmental psychology. And so it's left to me to piece together an account of the developmental course of the three virtues. I do so in what seems the most appropriate sequence with reference to stages of development and to the contemporary forces of postmodern thought and digital media.

As I see it, there are broad proclivities, propensities, or dispositions with respect to each of the virtues. Even young children have no problem dealing with truth and falseness, beauty and ugliness, what's good and what's evil. And as far as we know, they deal with these virtues quite similarly across the planet. But—of equal, indeed greater importance—these dispositions can and will be refashioned in the light of developmental steps and in terms of the prevailing norms of the culture and of the era in which the child happens to grow up. Of special importance, particularly with reference to the understanding of truth, are the experiences at school. When it comes to the good, the models of influential older persons are potent. And, for their part, judgments of beauty are strongly influenced by peers and the media.

For much of childhood, the developmental course of the three virtues is relatively straightforward and unproblematic. But in a complex modern society, the onset of adolescence triggers new strains—and also new opportunities—with respect to the status and fate of the virtues. So, too, postmodern ideas (whether recognized as such or not) and digital media impact adolescents with considerable force. In the end, depending on this collection of influences, youth may end up as distressingly rigid in their views, completely laissez-faire or indifferent, thoroughly confused or reassuringly sophisticated and subtle. But even near the beginning of life, one can identify powerful messages that impact the child.

The first and the most important thing to say is that our three virtues, and the concepts to which they refer, are not part of the human genome, or the human species, in any simple or straightforward way. Indeed, the idea of the "natural" child, the wild child, the "raw" child is no longer cogent. The intrauterine environment already shapes the future human being: Is the environment healthy or diseased? Is the fetus alone or competing with one or more other fetuses? What sounds are on the outside, and are they soothing or jarring, in one language or several, produced by human-fashioned musical instruments or picked up from the natural environment? Equally, and at least as importantly, what are the expectations of the parents or of the extended family? Do they want a girl or a boy? Do they know the sex of the fetus, and does it matter to them? Have they expectations about the health of the child, either because of family lore or because of genetic testing, ultrasound, or other exploratory investigations? And how, if at all, does this information affect what the prospective parents do, say, and think about the impending infant?

The long-term effects of such prebirth factors are in most cases relatively modest; but no such claim can be made about the impact of the environment following birth. Once in the open air, the infant proves supremely sensitive to the objects and signals in the environment. It matters enormously whether there is sufficient and appropriate food; whether there is regular, soothing warmth from the caretaker; in what manner the infant is dressed, undressed, addressed, and, on occasion, redressed. Such signals, of course, go well beyond the ambience of the crib and the home. Is the wider community at peace or at war? Does the family feel secure and comfortable, or tense and embattled? More generally, what are the attitudes toward a new child? Is he or she seen as a blessing from God, an additional hand in the home or on the farm, an unexpected burden in an already crowded village, or a welcome future member of a thriving society?

Few would question the impact on the child of parents, other adults, older siblings (or a twin) in the immediate environment. Additionally, powerful institutions insert themselves between the home, on the one hand, and the broader society, on the other. From early on, children are exposed to the dominant media. When I was growing up in the middle of the last century, *media* meant radio at first, and then television. Now of course, in a "developed" society, children are surrounded from a young age by a mélange of television sets, CD and DVD players, personal computers, and handheld assistants—and all but the least developed societies now feature cell (if not "smart") phones and, perhaps even "one laptop per child." In the Internet era, children are not mere consumers: Many participate, early on and sometimes quite actively, in assembling, editing, or even creating messages. With respect to our concerns here, all of these forms of media present views of the world (truth), in various forms and formats (beauty), and with different models of human relations (goodness)— and these representations are sometimes consistent with one another, but often not.

Less tangible institutions are potent as well. Across the globe, most communities feature one or more religious traditions. Young people grow up attending temple, church, or mosque, with daily prayers and nightly rituals, and these religious traditions leave a powerful stamp. Despite their enormous differences in philosophy, both the Jesuits and the founding Communist, Lenin, claimed: "Give me a child until age seven, and I have that child for life." The absence of religion in the child's life is also significant, though it matters tremendously whether other families in the area are similarly secular, or whether one's home harbors the only atheists or agnostics in the village. Many communities now offer museums, playing fields, and playgrounds for all toddlers—and often a lot of education, and perhaps also miseducation, occurs in these public spaces.

Of course, after the opening years of life, educational institutions exert the most direct, powerful, and long-lasting impressions on the child. At one time, most children did not receive a formal education; as recently as a century ago, formal education began around the age of six or seven and ended just a few years later. Nowadays, in any developed society, infant-toddler centers, preschools, and kindergarten begin exerting their influence in the opening years of life; half or more of young people receive postsecondary education; and some of us—including, no doubt, some readers of this book—continue to collect degrees and to retain at least one foot in educational institutions.

At the risk of rehearsing what you (and perhaps your grandparents) already know, I trust I've made the case that there is lot of information, an unprecedented amount of "data" available on the supply side. Many human beings and many human institutions stimulate the child, and only a fool (or a full-blown genetic determinist) would suggest that the child is impervious to these entities. Some of these entities (e.g., churches) have very clear educational goals for children, while others (e.g., the Cartoon Network) have only incidental goals.

When we consider the "demand side," it is clear that young persons seek sufficient food, drink, physical comfort. When these "creature comforts" are lacking, the young child will flail, scream, and go to considerable lengths to attain them. With respect to satisfaction of these wants, the child is wired, so to speak. But other needs soon come to the fore. Like other primates, young children seek warmth, comfort, hugs—indeed, signs of love. And, in addition, once these demands have been met, young children come to desire information, data, knowledge of all sorts.

On to the task at hand. Under reasonably benign circumstances, the child begins to seek information and to raise questions with respect to our trio of truth, beauty, and goodness. From infancy, she observes the regularities in her world (where and when the parent appears, how food is prepared) and the irregularities (an absent parent, an unexpected form of nourishment, a surprise visit from a stranger). A certain amount of regularity is appreciated. But too much predictability—of sounds, sight, taste, smell—soon becomes boring: As psychologists put it, the child "habituates" to the milieu and ceases to attend. And so, in an effort to remain engaged, the child becomes intrigued by events and experiences that deviate from the predictable. (So, too, the adults who wish to hold the child's attention offer a literal or figurative "peek-a-boo.") Not too many, perhaps, not too often, but enough to spice up her daily informational diet.

With respect to truth, the infant or young child is initially alert to what we might call the practical truths, or the truths of practice. If the infant smiles, the caretaker will smile back; if she screams, the caretaker will come to her side; if she attempts to crawl out of her crib, she'll be firmly repositioned to the center of the crib or the sides of the crib will be raised and clicked into place. (Note that truths of this sort apply to other mammals as well.) Violations of these practical truths are noted: Depending on the nature of the violation and the emotional state of the child, such violations can be intriguing (Mommy's hat looks funny), or upsetting (Why does my Daddy look so strange?).

Sometime in the second or third year of life, the young child goes beyond recognition of the practical truths of her surround. Now that the child has begun to speak and understand language, words that convey truth and falsity enter her vocabulary. Of course, by this point, the young child is already qualitatively different from any other creature. Especially in a pedagogically precocious environment, where parents read books to children, messages of what is right/correct/true and what is "off the mark" are ubiquitous. And yet, at the same time, the scope of judgments of "truth" is not clearly demarcated.

Words of approval ("Right," "That's it," "Good for you") can acknowledge that the child has spoken; that the child has said something relevant; that the response is audible, felicitously expressed, or grammatically correct; or that it exhibits a certain truth value. Disentangling various connotations of truth (what's absolutely correct, what's acceptable under the circumstances, what is strictly taboo) is a challenge that never ends.

Well before psychologists adopted the term *egocentrism*, it was known that young children are focused on themselves. While such a focus likely includes a narcissistic or selfish component, egocentrism is fundamentally a limitation of perspective: Children see the world exclusively or primarily from their own often (and perhaps necessarily) idiosyncratic point of view. Egocentrism can be demonstrated quite literally when a child asserts, falsely, that a scene shown to a person seated opposite of herself appears identical to the way that she herself sees it. Put in the terms of our analysis, the young child assumes "What's true for me must be true for you."

But in the last few decades, psychologists have also documented some surprising results that challenge a strong version of childhood egocentrism. As early as the second or third year of life, young children begin to develop a "theory of mind." This theory acknowledges that unseen mental states (beliefs, desires, intentions, emotions) can cause external behaviors, and that other people may well possess beliefs that differ from and perhaps even conflict with mine. (To continue the above example: "What's true for me may *not* be true for you.")

The crowning achievement in the child's developing theory of mind occurs around the age of four. At this time the child becomes able to represent a false belief—that is, she now understands that another person may misperceive the external world. The ability to conceptualize a false belief shows that the child recognizes that beliefs are mere representations of the world; as a representation, a belief is not necessarily an accurate mirror of the world but can be partial, biased, or completely erroneous. Going beyond her own perspective, the child is able to judge propositions as "right" or "wrong," "true" or "false."

An example: Susie and Beth see a toy placed in basket A. Susie leaves the room, and thereafter Beth moves the toy into basket B. When Susie returns to the room, will she look for the toy in basket A (where she initially saw it) or in basket B (where it was moved, without her knowledge)? Until about the age of four, Beth believes, erroneously, that Susie is aware of the manipulation that occurred outside of her view; accordingly, Beth expects Susie to retrieve the toy from basket B. Once the theory of mind has coalesced, however, Beth is aware that Susie holds a false belief—namely, that Susie, not being privy to the manipulation, continues to believe that the toy is in basket A.

This insight, apparently not available to other primates, is fundamental. For the first time, the child clearly understands that individuals (including the child herself) hold beliefs, and that those beliefs can be right or wrong—in our terms, true or false. She can capture this knowledge in propositional form and assess propositions asserted by others. Of course, these beliefs are still far from those established by history, science, or mathematics; and yet they lay the groundwork for propositional knowledge in the culture that eventually competes for the status of truthfulness.

Initially, as we've noted, the child's sense of what is true, and what is not, retains an egocentric component; it is formed primarily on the basis of her own perceptions of the world. But even before formal schooling commences, children become willing to accept a truth uttered by someone else. This acceptance of testimony occurs chiefly with respect to persons who are older, well known to the child, and deemed to be trustworthy. Clearly the capacity to accept testimony forms the basis of much of education—the child is expected to treat as truthful the content conveyed by a trusted teacher or textbook or program (broadcast or downloaded). The child also picks up the rules of conversation in her society; in the case of modern society, these rules would include the following sentiments: Say what you mean, be brief, be salient, be relevant, be truthful unless you have a compelling reason not to.

And so, in just a few years, the young child has made a number of crucial steps forward: from simple perception to the appreciation of practical truths; from truths observed in practice to truths that can be encoded in propositions; from an assumption that other's truths are identical to one's own to an awareness that others may have a different representation of the conditions in the world; from a reliance on one's own perceptions to a willingness to accept the testimony of more knowledgeable adults.

Turning to a second virtue, we find that a rough-and-ready sense of good and bad already emerges early in life. Even in the first year, infants gravitate toward adults who are helpful to others and avoid those who behave in a neutral or hindering way toward others. By the second or third year of life, children also have a keen sense of what others desire from the child. When the child does what adults desire, she is rewarded with approval—smiles, and perhaps the phrase "Good, Sally." When the child goes against the desires of powerful adults—running into the street without looking in both directions, throwing food on the just-ironed tablecloth, hitting a younger sibling—then the vocabulary of admonishment intervenes: "No," "Don't do that," "You're a bad boy, Johnny." Anyone who has been around children knows that phrases of approval and disapproval are soon internalized—so much so that one can hear the child muttering "Good Johnny" or "Bad Johnny" after the feedback has been given or even later, in recollection, while playing with blocks or dozing off in the crib.

Many scholars have spoken of the birth of morality in the second or third year of life. Much like the early stages of knowledge more generally, the sense of good and bad is often quite egocentric: As the philosopher Thomas Hobbes observed, we tend to collapse "the good" with what we desire, "the bad" with what does not meet our own needs. But by the age of four or so, as noted with respect to truth, such egocentrism is already on the wane. The growing child is becoming aware that what he himself desires may not be what the world wants of him; and that sometimes the world requires a behavior or action that goes against his self-interest. Freud called this milestone the establishment of the Superego: the emergence of a little voice inside the head that approves or—mostly—disapproves of what we say and do. And indeed, by this still tender age, most children in most cultures exhibit the signs of shame or guilt—a private and/or public awareness that one has not adhered to the standards of the community and is therefore worthy of, and may receive, condemnation.

Soon another important milestone occurs. By the age of five the child can distinguish the moral from the merely conventional. Put concretely, the child acknowledges the difference between a classroom violation that is merely one of convention (e.g., we will put on our blue smocks before painting and not our red smocks) from a violation that smacks of morality (we will chastise kids who bully their classmates). The child already realizes that the decision to wear blue rather than red, or vice versa, is not of great moment and could be changed without due fuss. But the child is likely to become upset if the teacher suddenly ignores or sanctions bullying—because such behavior, the child now understands, constitutes a moral transgression.

From a child-rearing perspective, consistency of judgments is crucial. When individuals and institutions concur about what is good, and what is not, moral development can occur with relative smoothness. Trouble ensues when an individual adult gives mixed messages—approving of swearing on Monday, punishing the swearer on the Sabbath—or when different adults give different messages (Mommy swears often, while Dad expresses his disapproval with vehemence) or when what is considered a mere violation of convention by one authority is considered a moral breach by another. In a complex world, inconsistencies in moral judgments are frequent. Not surprisingly, many (indeed, too many) young people grow up uncertain about what is good and what is bad.

Note that I have avoided making specific judgments about what is to be considered "good" or "bad." Attribution of moral judgments may be universal—the realm of human proclivities; but the items to which they are applied can vary enormously—the realm of societal norms. Consistent with the idea of neighborly morality, certain precepts— don't harm your neighbor, don't steal from him, don't lie to him—are widely accepted across diverse cultures. But the exceptions or reservations are notable as well. In a warrior society, males are trained to hit other persons—or at least *certain* other persons—and the capacity to injure or kill "the enemy" is seen as a virtue. In the Dickensian world of Oliver Twist, the epithet *good* is applied, indeed restricted, to the successful pilferer. As Lionel Bart's Fagin intones to his ragamuffin gang of lads, "You gotta pick a pocket or two, boys."

As was the case with truth, the first years of life also witness significant milestones in the realm of the good. What is first seen as practically positive or negative, good or bad, becomes captured in words. Various connotations of *good* become disentangled—the realm of convention is not equivalent to the sphere of morality. With the wane of egocentrism, the child becomes aware that what he wants to do may not be seen as good by others, or vice versa. He may well internalize these judgments, feeling shame or guilt when he does not live up to widely held standards. And he may also note—and perhaps become upset—when one valued person's judgment of good and bad is at variance with that held by another equally treasured person.

Perhaps reflecting their own scholarly priorities, perhaps reflecting the priorities of society in general, perhaps reflecting the greater differences across societies, psychologists have less to say about judgments of beauty in early life. To be sure, terms of approval or opprobrium apply to scenes, objects, and experiences, as well as to behaviors and to assertions about the world. Without necessarily aspiring to moral judgments, individuals regularly signal to one another what they crave, what they enjoy, what they find awesome, and what they prefer to ignore or to shun. The signaling can be done by facial expression, bodily position, the inclination to return to an activity or not, and, of course, by linguistic description. All kinds of descriptors (and their opposites) may be used: *wonderful/terrible, amazing/disgusting, awesome/awful, cool/yucky.* My thesaurus lists dozens of additional evaluative contrasts; I'd be surprised if any language lacks a comparable vocabulary of evaluation. And of course, children take note of these characterizations and will often echo them in their own chatter.

Across many societies, adults employ terms like *beautiful* to signal the objects whose appearances they cherish and the experiences that they seek to re-create, while applying terms like *ugly* or *repellent* to objects and experiences that they shun or disapprove of or find disgusting. These instances may come from the world of nature (a stately mountain top, a roaring brook); man-made objects (a painting, monument, or piece of jewelry); or an amalgam (a house set at the edge of a forest, with recently picked flowers on display in a treasured vase). Choices on what to wear, how to wear it, how to groom oneself, how to furnish one's home, how to garden, what to eat and how to eat it, all have aesthetic dimensions, whether choices are made deliberately or casually, remarked upon or simply enacted. These choices are certainly noticed by children, and may be the subject of commentary when the favored configurations are featured ("A super house"), transformed ("They painted the shutters"), or destroyed ("What a shame, the new house is ugly").

We take for granted the language spoken around us. Awareness of the phenomenon of language arises when we can use (or find ourselves frustrated that we cannot use) more than one language. In the same way, we take for granted the aesthetic values attached to the area in which we spend our formative years and become aware of this chiefly when we are exposed to a significantly different palette of artistic or natural values. Whether it is urban or sylvan, crowded or sparse, mountainous or flat, near seawater, alongside fresh water, or in the parched desert—any of these can constitute an initial aesthetic for young persons. Both the setting itself and the choices and commentary made within this setting constitute a necessary baseline.

As it happens, I grew up in a leafy urban setting and vacationed in areas with mountains, lakes, and rivers; these became, and to some extent remain, even after several decades, my foundational notions of natural beauty. How different these are from notions absorbed by contemporaries who grew up in the countryside, on farms, and who vacationed near the ocean. Of course, the initial milieu can also serve as a negative example. If (for whatever reason) one has come to loathe the scenic milieu of one's childhood, once one has a choice, one strives to embrace its opposite or at least a radically different surround.

Evolutionary psychologists may be on to something when they note the preferences across the globe for certain natural scenes— recall the worldwide favorites identified by Alexander Melamid and Vitaly Kolmar. Perhaps in our subconscious we have retained intimations of the plains of East Africa, where our predecessors wandered for hundreds of thousands of years. But evolutionary scholars miss the widely divergent ways in which the aesthetic taste for man-made objects "evolves" (note the quotation marks) across cultures and historical eras. Does one paint the face, and if so, with what substance and what forms? Are the valued bodies fat or thin, self-consciously muscular or modestly contoured? Does graphic art favor human representation or spurn it, or even outlaw it; and, if representation is foregrounded, is it realistic (warts and all), does it idealize, or is it closer to geometric simplification or even caricature? When we become aware of the decorations and objects favored by another group, do we copy them, depict them in deliberately contrasting fashion, work out something new, or fashion an amalgam of the two styles? The very fact that we can so easily come up with a rationale for each of these contrasting results demonstrates the inadequacy of accounts founded primarily on biology or, for that matter, accounts based primarily on economic considerations (the cost of materials, the market value of the object).

As this discussion of the virtues in early childhood comes to a close, it's important to note that societies place differing importance on the respective realms. Everywhere, judgments of what is good and bad are very important: They count heavily both because the society wants to preserve its moral code and because adults do not want young people to hurt themselves ("Bad boy, don't go near the tool shed") or others ("Be careful with your fork"). By and large, these judgments are made verbally. Societies also have a vested interest in the truthfulness of their descriptions of the state of the world—its physical properties, its biological properties, and, most important, what human beings are like. Accordingly, explanatory accounts ("That's a dog, not a wolf," "Look, the moon is fuller than yesterday," "Uncle John is just pretending to be angry") are part and parcel of daily conversation.

When it comes to the sphere of beauty, however, the variation is far greater. Some cultures and subcultures direct a great deal of attention to the appearance of objects and to the choices about how they are made, displayed, and altered, and among those cultures, some have an extensive vocabulary for describing gardens or wall paintings or music that is performed live or on recordings. Bali and Japan are often cited as oases of artistry. Other societies, for whatever reason, direct less energy and attention to aesthetic features; still others rarely put their judgments into words. These variations necessarily are reflected in the extent to which the young are oriented toward aesthetic choices, in the kinds of choices that they make, and in the likelihood that they will be aware of them consciously and put their judgments into verbal descriptions or exclamations.

That said, we do know a lot about what produces pleasure in young children, and from these preferences we can make reasonable guesses that prove relevant to judgments and experiences of beauty. In societies where social scientists have made observations, they find that young children love stories, particularly those with clear heroes and villains; infants prefer lullabies but by the time they are able to run around and dance, young children prefer music that is loud, regular, with a strong beat; toddlers like displays that are large, colorful, featuring big and attractive animals and other creatures; they gravitate toward video games that are colorful, fast-moving, dramatic, and punctuated by loud noises. Young children are fascinated by magic; they become especially excited when an intriguing object or creature disappears or appears suddenly, or is transformed from one state to another. Indeed, being enterprising, many psychologists have made use of these preferences in designing experiments that involve young children.

Studies reveal that preschool children are essentialists. That is, they believe that the phenomena of the world each have a fundamental essence—an essence that is crucial and transcends superficial appearances. A dog may be painted a different color or have its hair shaved off or even undergo a surgical transplant but it still remains a dog. Only if its "innards" were somehow magically replaced might its "doggedness" somehow be undermined. Essentialism applies to humans—girls are girls, boys are boys, and that cannot be changed. And it applies as well to subcategories of people: Certain humans are seen as inexorably "liars" or "heroes" or "friends." For the young child, this essence proves extremely difficult to challenge.

Why is this relevant to the study of beauty? It turns out that the inclination to search for essences extends early on to man-made objects: A painting is different from a rock, because the painting is made by a person and therefore possesses part of that person's essence. A child can recognize a work done by one friend as being different from a work done by another, or a daub made by accident as different from a daub made as part of an effort to depict something. Moreover, a young child—call him (A)—will interpret a squiggle made by another child (B) differently, depending on the model that was on display when B made her squiggle. And of course, once a stick has been anointed a hobby horse, woe be to the person who tries to treat the horse as a stick or even as a dog! Viewed as a whole, these findings indicate awareness, early on, of the special status of certain objects, such as those that are central to artistic experiences.

Admittedly, with respect to the study of beauty in early childhood, we do not have the same amount of research, or the same degree of confidence, as we encountered with respect to the cases of truth and goodness. Perhaps we should not be surprised, nor should we be disappointed. After all, in the end, as I've argued in these pages, the sense of beauty turns out to be far less convergent, far more individualized than is the case with other virtues. Still, we can at least draw some tentative conclusions. From an early age, children find certain sights and experiences interesting, memorable, and worthy of revisiting; such children respect the status, and—indeed—the essence, of these entities; and they can clearly distinguish those whose causes are natural from those that are created by human beings, and, indeed, by specific human beings for specific purposes, including expressive ones.

So far, in this description of the first years of life, I've given a picture of human development that occurs whether or not formal schooling is in play. This approach reflects my belief that truth, goodness, and beauty are perennial human concerns: ones that date back thousands of years, to a prehistorical era, ones that would be found across all contemporary cultures, irrespective of the importance placed upon formal schooling. Half a century ago, at the height of

Piagetian influences, I might have characterized these developmental courses as being "natural" or universal. Nowadays we are keenly aware of the roles played—deliberately or inadvertently—by adult models and by institutions that are present from the crib.

No doubt, facets of truth determination, moral behavior, and matters of taste continue to develop in the ensuing decades of life, even in the absence of formal schooling; and how they develop, or fail to develop in the latter case, would make a fascinating account. After all, preliterate cultures have complex taxonomies of the world—full-blown "folk theories" about the stars, the crops, kinship relations; intricate rules about what is prescribed and proscribed with reference to marriage, property, worship, birth and death; and a concern with craft and decoration that we can appreciate—and even hold in awe. But in an account of the virtues in a postmodern, digital era, I necessarily focus on what happens as a consequence of schools and schooling.

Educators pursue four principal pedagogical goals. First, produce a population that is literate and numerate. (This goal is universal, uncontroversial, and will not concern us further.) Second, provide the tools whereby future citizens can learn the truths of the society. (This goal is achieved through the transmission of key disciplinary lenses and practical procedures of work.) Third, ensure that the important moral laws (typically drawn from the ambient religious and legal codes) are known and enforced. Finally, transmit those human creations—narratives, crafted objects, decorations, dances, songs—whose forms and messages are most valued by the culture.

Let's now consider the ways in which educators in our time can achieve these ambitious goals. Within the school context, truths exist in three major disciplinary families. The first is mathematics—certain statements or laws are true by virtue of definition ($5 = 1 + 3 + 1$) or proof (the angles of a triangle sum to $180°$). The second is history—the recording and transmission of names, dates, and events, with as much accuracy as possible. Literary and other records are essential for history, even if they are not necessarily sufficient. The third is science—the effort, through observation and experimentation, to describe, model, and explain the physical, natural, and human worlds.

Note that disciplinary understanding is not the same as the mere accrual of facts (sometimes termed subject-matter knowledge). Facts are fine but they do not in themselves involve any disciplinary understanding. Moreover, in this day of handheld devices, there is little point in memorizing facts that are instantly available at one's fingertips. Rather, educators should help students to understand the ways in which disciplinary specialists establish and confirm knowledge. This acquisition necessarily involves immersion in the kinds of activities in which specialists are regularly engaged—carrying out proofs in mathematics, making systematic observations and conducting experiments in science, or poring over documents and graphic materials in history.

Establishing these various truths is hardly an easy or straightforward matter. Even mathematical truths can be contested, especially when new branches of mathematics are established. History is a matter of construction and reconstruction, crafting accounts that are revised both in terms of discoveries of new documents and by virtue of the fresh vantage point provided by the present era. As philosopher Karl Popper insisted, science is a matter of subjecting existing claims to the most rigorous tests. The possibility of falsification is *the* earmark of scientific work—and, not incidentally, the reason why creationism (or its successor stealth position "intelligent design") is not science. New paradigms cause old ones to be rejected as limited, misleading, or even false. And new paradigms are not necessarily true for all time but are themselves subject to partial or complete replacement. Still, the succession of paradigms is by no means arbitrary: By and large, newly accepted paradigms are steps on the road to better established and more broadly based truths.

So far, I've been reviewing the "truths of school" without particular attention to age. When working with young people, there is an additional challenge to the establishment and transmission of truth—particularly the truths of science. Put directly, science is not common sense—often, as Nelson Goodman liked to quip, science refutes common *non-sense*. Cognitive psychology has documented this assertion amply. Nearly all young people harbor much nonsense—numerous misconceptions about the world—and children arrive at these in the absence of formal tutelage. If any of us are to appreciate the truths of science, schooling must address directly this state of affairs.

A short list of such misconceptions can introduce the challenge: If we rely on our common sense, we believe that the sun revolves around the earth and not vice versa, that objects fall to the ground as they lose or dissipate energy, that all animal species were created at the same time and have not changed since that founding instant, and so on. These statements would be instantly endorsed by most schoolchildren (I'll not speculate about those of us who are no longer in school!). It does not suffice simply to tell eight- or twelve-year-olds that these views are wrong, and that they (or the erroneous views) should "shape up." Rather, to become a genuinely disciplined thinker, one needs to adopt entirely different worldviews—that is, to substitute a Copernican view of the solar system, with the sun at the center, for a Ptolemaic view, where all celestial bodies revolved around earth; or to substitute a Darwinian view of evolution as occurring over millions of years for a biblical story of creation in less than a week.

In considering how best to educate young people with reference to science (and other subjects), our own decades-long work on "teaching and learning for understanding" becomes germane. Scientific thinking is not primarily a mastery of facts—though knowledge of some facts is certainly necessary. Rather, scientific thinking involves two challenging tasks: (1) to think in terms of claims, and the kinds of evidence that would either support or refute those claims;

and (2) to master the current prevailing models of paradigms of scientific thought. Though they change slowly, paradigms of scientific thought do change. The Aristotelian physics of Greek times slowly gave rise to the Newtonian physics of the Enlightenment; and Newton in turn yielded pride of place to the views of Einstein in the first part of the twentieth century, and to even more complex and even less intuitive quantum-mechanical or superstring theoretical accounts of the physical world in our own time.

Of course, one does not need to master the paradigms—continually shifting—in all of the natural, physical, and social sciences. No one can! But if one wants to be involved at all meaningfully in understanding the truths as they have come to be established in our time, one at least has to "get with" the program. And that is why, around the world, there are so many calls now for an early focus on education in STEM subjects—science, technology, engineering, and mathematics.

In the late 1950s the British scientist-turned-novelist C. P. Snow highlighted the importance of mastering STEM culture, and nothing since has proved him wrong. But all too often, Snow has been invoked to suggest that the *only* truths, or the *most important* truths, are the ones of science. The entire burden of the present book is to argue that there are several truths and orders of truths, and that none merits absolute hegemony over any other. Those individuals equipped with only scientific truths are as hapless as those who know only mathematics, or only history, or only the arts, or only the practical truths of the workplace and the marketplace.

So we must ask: How can we combat the misconceptions and half-truths that young persons come up with on their own, or that they absorb from others?

The blunt answer: There is no easy or royal or foolproof road to the determination of truths. As educators, we must help young people to discern the inadequacies of their earlier folk beliefs, and to construct better, more veridical accounts. Our studies suggest two complementary approaches.

The first approach entails *constructive engagement*. Young people need to confront the inadequacies of their intuitive beliefs. If the earth is flat, then how come we can circumnavigate the globe? If all species were conceived at the same time, then how do we account for the fossil record? If human values have not changed in thousands of years, how do we explain the widespread acceptance of slavery until recent times? We must raise these issues explicitly, or help students identify them on their own, and then prod them to reflect on the paradoxes and puzzles.

But the dis-establishment of erroneous or inadequate under-standings is not enough. As a complement to constructive engage-ment, we need to introduce and model the kinds of explanations employed by experts. And this means equipping young people with the *ways of thinking* associated with major disciplines, such as the sci-ences and history. Only if one dons the lenses of the biologist, and looks at the sources of evidence at the expert's disposal, can one be-gin to understand the processes of evolution. Only if one immerses oneself in the history of ancient Greece, or the culture of antebellum Southern society, can one appreciate why most persons thought it was acceptable to enslave another human being. Over time, and with judicious scaffolding by sympathetic mentors, young students will shed their misconceptions and begin to embrace the truths of knowl-edgeable experts.

Constructive engagement and the modeling of expertise can begin in the early years of schooling and should continue indefinitely. But we must take note of an important change that occurs toward the end of the middle years of school—say, about the age of twelve. At that time, lessons shift from a focus on mere statement of facts, of unadorned propositions, to a presentation of "propositional attitudes." During the initial years of school, the student is simply told that "matter (colloqui-ally, 'stuff') is neither created or destroyed"; or "Napoleon regained power briefly after he left Elba"; or "the earth is not flat, it is spherical (colloquially 'round')." As they become more sophisticated cognitively, students encounter a new way of presenting information—one that goes beyond bald statements of truth and falsity. Relevant now is the attitude of the speaker or author toward the stated proposition. "Scientist Isaac Newton *claimed* that matter is neither created nor destroyed" or "Historian R. R. Palmer *contends* that Napoleon regained power after he left Elba." Note here that the information is no longer presented as a straight assertion. Rather, the student learns that the fact was claimed (or asserted or argued or doubted or denied) by a particular authority; henceforth, we need to take into account the reliability of the source.

If student understanding is to continue to grow, awareness of this shift is crucial. If students remain ignorant of how "propositional attitudes" work, they are likely to misunderstand the nature of scholarly inquiry and the way that it progresses, or fails to progress. Conversely, once students come to appreciate that scholarship is a continuing conversation among experts—through words, through experiments, through the proposal of models—they are well positioned to pursue truths about the world, both those that are long established and those that are being negotiated at the present moment.

And so, the educational trajectory toward the establishment of well-founded truths is reasonably clear. The job of the educator is to help the student understand the limits of his early intuitions; to expose him to the tools whereby the establishment (and, on occasion, the dis-establishment) of truth occurs in various disciplines; to sensitize the student to the role, over time, of assertions and counterassertions by experts; and, importantly, to provide enough background knowledge so that the student is able to appreciate those consequential changes in understanding that are the hallmark of scholarship.

In our time, formal schooling focuses primarily on the truths as established by disciplinary specialists. Perhaps that is appropriate—at any rate, it is unlikely to change. But we should take note of two exceptions. First of all, in many countries, a significant proportion of students are assigned to a vocational track—and that placement can occur as early as the years of middle childhood. In that track, of course, much of the learning focuses on practical truths, and these are best conveyed by being "on site" and "on the case." The second exception is professional training, which begins much later, typically after secondary school or even after college. In professional training, internships and mentorships are key. Professional schools often require field experiences (e.g., teaching hospitals or laboratory schools) and include practitioners as faculty members.

Without doubt, a focus on the establishment of truths occupies the lion's share of formal schooling; accordingly I've treated "education for truth" at some length and with an eye toward schooling across the age range. But this is not to say that the other virtues are unimportant—only that they tend to be treated incidentally, rather than focally, in modern secular schools. I'll consider each in turn, indicating the little that is routinely addressed in school and suggesting what more might be done.

First, the sphere of morality—the conveying of what is acceptable ("good") or unacceptable ("bad") behavior in the community. As children begin to attend school, new considerations arise. What is honored or disparaged at home becomes complemented and perhaps complexified by new kinds of moral concerns: those of the teachers, the rest of the staff, and the other students.

In the past, much of schooling involved the study of sacred texts—and of course, those texts were studded with examples of virtuous and pernicious behaviors, along with awe-inspiring accounts of the rewards and punishments attendant thereto. That's why these texts were featured—at that time, in the agenda of school, knowledge of good (and evil) trumped mastery of truths and mastery of disciplines. Frequently, the most evocative passages dominated class recitations and were committed to memory. In most schools, an acceptance of the received wisdom with respect to the moral course was assumed, though sometimes discussion of alternative behaviors or responses was tolerated, if not encouraged.

Nowadays, in modern secular societies, there is far less explicit concern with sacred texts—and sometimes, indeed, explicitly religious teachings are forbidden. And yet, it would be erroneous to assume that morality is accordingly absent from the curriculum. Indeed, it is salient in what has sometimes been termed "the hidden curriculum." To begin with, every school has its rules of acceptable and unacceptable behaviors, along with the punishments that accompany deplorable actions like bullying or cheating. Second, adults in the school (including those who are not designated teachers) model the kinds of behaviors that they value, and—either explicitly or implicitly—demarcate those that they will not tolerate. And of course, schools are embedded in broader societies with their own roster of preferences, tolerances, and explicit proscriptions.

Pure didactic pedagogy—simply listing what is allowed and what not, along with attendant rewards and prescriptions—rarely succeeds in engendering morality in children. Unless young people have some sense of *why* certain actions are to be avoided, unless they have a chance to put forth their own views and offer their own justifications, these strictures are unlikely to be internalized and followed voluntarily. (Obviously, if the punishment is severe enough, students will obey; but as soon as the punishment is lifted, or ways of avoiding it are discovered, obedience dissolves.) "Constructive engagement" is preferable to a charter of "do's and don'ts." When students have a chance to discuss, debate, hear alternative perspectives, and undergo changes of mind without being penalized for doing so, a genuine, lasting moral compass may be installed.

Since the early years of life, the child has known how she should treat others and how she would like to be treated by them. Morality—

in its pristine neighborhood form—is clear in that sense. But as I've argued, the "ethics of roles" entails the ability to think of oneself as a worker and/or as a citizen, and to act in accordance with the responsibilities attendant to that status. Probably the child gets the first inkling of work and citizenship in school—and in that sense, she is able to think about how adequately to fulfill the role of student, and the role of member of her homeroom or class. But the ability to think systematically and systemically about the demands of roles, qua roles, is not within the ken of the child during the first decade of life.

In recent years, given the rise of antisocial behaviors even among young children, many teachers have asked me about what they could do, early on, with respect to moral and ethical behavior. In my view, the emphasis in the first years of school should fall on those words and behaviors that are most likely to register on the young mind: impressive and convincing "live" role models of desirable behaviors and reasons; exposure to literature and other media that highlight moral and immoral examplars, while dramatizing the consequences for those who honor the codes and those who transgress; thoughtful reflection on morally tinged events that happen in the course of daily activities; consequences that seem appropriate, given the circumstances of specific acts and particular actors. These recommendations, along with modeling by an effective community, are the most important steps that can be taken, prior to the opportunities and challenges posed by adolescence. Happily, they don't take much time and money—what is needed is the *will* to do these things and the *vigilance* to keep them always in mind.

I turn, finally, to a consideration of beauty in the firmament of formal schooling. As a matter of fact, the inclusion of art—whether painting, dance, or music—as important in its own right has rarely been a feature of formal education—neither yesterday, nor today. (Literature is a somewhat different affair, because it is often part of classes dedicated to the mastery of one's native language.) When music has been included, it typically functions as a way of preparing students to perform in the school band, orchestra, or chorus. Visual arts have traditionally provided skills in drafting or depicting scenes when photographic equipment did not exist or was not available.

As one who has been involved in arts education for more than four decades, I regret this limited tableau. I wish that there were more focus on the arts and on beauty—both in the traditional sense of beauty and in the more expanded and individualized sense introduced here. Alas, unless national and international priorities change radically, much of arts education is likely to occur at home, after school, or on weekends—if it is to occur at all.

There is, however, one respect in which a concern with the arts, with beauty, does fall within the purview of education, as currently construed. Schools are seen as the primary mode of introducing those artifacts and experiences that are particularly cherished in the community or the nation. And so, for example, in European societies, students study the paintings and works of music of their own culture or of Western civilization, European style. The educated European needs to be familiar with the works of Shakespeare, Rembrandt, and Beethoven. And within specific cultures, there are more specific foci: Thus the compositions of Purcell and Elgar are heard in English schools, while the paintings of Giotto and Titian are familiar to children in Italian schools. The patriotic reasons for such curricula are clear enough; it's less evident whether students are expected to reach specific conclusions with respect to the nature, locus, and scope of beauty.

Thanks to developmental research, we can discern clear patterns in the perception of art—at least in modern Western societies. (Alas, we lack comparable data from other cultural traditions.) When confronting pictorial art, for example, children pass through a predictable set of stages. In the early years of life, their preferences are based on their apprehension of the object being depicted, and whether they like the depicted object (a doll or a devil), the colors (dark brown or a rainbow), or the associated story (fairy tale, Bible story, space adventure). Youngsters deal with the painting, drawing, or piece of sculpture as a straightforward presentation of the world. To be sure, even preschoolers recognize that a work of art is produced by a human being. However, the existence of the "mind behind the art work" is not salient until well into the school years.

As they near adolescence, young people pay increased attention to the fact that the painting is not simply another object—the creator had various goals in mind and wanted the work to be perceived in certain ways. Accordingly, formal features, such as style, expression, and composition, become more prominent. The young person begins to adopt a "pictorial attitude." For the most part, school-age children spurn works of art that are abstract, eccentric, or caricatured, in favor of those that are realistic—closer to photography. Quite possibly, this palette of preferences reflects a broader tendency to favor the kinds of works that are displayed by the majority society—that capture some kind of a popular consensus for beauty.

But not entirely. Among Western preadolescents with a continuing involvement in the arts as creators, a desire may arise to push the envelope, to do something that is more exotic, more outlandish, less conventional. Such a preteen is able to put his own personal mark on a work, to reveal something of his own person, his own values, his own history, his own perhaps idiosyncratic aesthetics; an artistic turn has been effected. Access on the Internet to peers who share the same, perhaps eccentric, tastes also broadens the ensemble of possibilities. And indeed, while adult models and sanctions loom large in the apprehension of morality, peer preferences typically dominate the artistic sensibilities of younger persons.

When it comes to issues of truth and goodness, societies are rather firm on what should be transmitted to children, either formally, through school, or informally, through parents, media, and other people and institutions. But in matters of beauty and, more broadly, of tastes in the arts and in nature, there is far more latitude—both in terms of whether to educate formally and, if so, in what ways.

Here's my view and my prescription. All young people will acquire and exhibit aesthetic preferences. But only those who are exposed to a range of works of art, who observe how these works are produced, who understand something about the artist behind the works, and who encounter thoughtful discussion of issues of craft and taste are likely to develop an aesthetic sense that goes beyond schlock or transcends what happens to be most popular among peers at the moment.

We now inhabit a world in which one has access to countless works of art, reflecting many styles, topics, formats, and aesthetic values. Certainly, young people can and should be exposed to those works that are cherished by the people who are closest to them. But I think it an injustice to limit exposure to only the "local favorites" so to speak.

So, instead, from an early age and throughout the school years, I recommend introducing young people to a wide range of works of art, in several artistic domains. Young Americans, for example, ought to see paintings and sculpture not only from Western civilization but also from prehistoric cultures, and from other major cultural traditions, such as pre-Colombian, Islamic, or Buddhist. By the same token, youth should have the opportunity to savor stories, music, drama, dance, and poetry from several, though obviously not all, cultural traditions.

How to handle judgments of beauty? Given limits of time, I certainly believe that we should favor those works of art—and those aspects of nature—that have gained wide acceptance over time. Mozart rather than Salieri or Ditters von Dittersdorf; acclaimed Japanese painter and printmaker Katsushika Hokusai rather than his contemporaries during the Edo period. Necessarily, such choices will reflect aesthetic standards, including judgments of beauty. But these canonical favorites should be tempered in two ways.

First of all, we should recognize that works of art have come to be cherished not only for the embodiment of beauty in its own right but also for their interestingness, memorability of form, and capacity to inspire revisits. And so, as fellow inhabitants of "the museum without walls," we should give young people the chance to behold works that have been valued, whether or not the epithet *beauty* is readily applied. For example, we might create a slide show of the works featured in the 2008 exhibit *Design and the Elastic Mind*—or for that matter, those that garnered prizes in a nearby arts competition.

Second, and of great importance, we should help young people to notice distinctions that matter. Given two portraits, or two sonnets, or two mazurkas, we should avoid assertions about which is better, which is more valuable, which is more beautiful. Rather, we should encourage young people to notice, and to articulate, the differences that they can discern between various "tokens" of the "type"—for it is the *capacity to distinguish* that truly matters. (And not infrequently, we'll find that our young students notice differences that have escaped our allegedly more developed tastes.) Once consequential distinctions have been identified, then and only then can we talk about whether one is better, and, indeed, whether one is more beautiful than others, and if so, why.

Students will likely, and perhaps inevitably, disagree about which work of art they prefer, which they think is better, which they consider more beautiful and why. And that is precisely where the genuine education occurs—whether in school, at home, at the movies, or on the playing field. And, if my earlier argument is correct, such learning will not necessarily involve adoption of the cultural or classroom canon of beauty. Rather, it will materialize as the young person comes to know his own standards, identify the reasons for them, and remain open to changes of mind, on the basis of his continuing experiences, and his exposure to new items, new tastes, new arguments, and new refutations.

Animating our enterprise here is the fate of the trio of virtues in an age characterized by postmodern critiques and suffused by digital media. Many of the educational recommendations already mentioned remain apt in the current era and for students of different ages, and there is no need to rehearse them further. And so in what follows, I'll focus on the education of adolescents. At this pivotal time of life, the powerful biological drives of adolescence meet the potent cultural forces of postmodern ideas and digital media.

As background, it is fair to say that the threats posed by postmodern ways of thinking are not much of an issue for the developing young person. Even if such children hear (or overhear) challenges to the verities, even if they can repeat these challenges verbatim, I doubt that they have much meaning. In a sense, the postmodern critique makes sense only in the context of possessing a premodern or modern point of view, and, at least explicitly, young children lack these (or any other systematic) views. Indeed, as quintessential essentialists, young children are bent on discovering The Truths, The Ultimate Moral Code, The Decisive Canon of Beauty. They simply assume that there is a conventional wisdom, if not an "essence," and that it is their job to ferret it out. Even if the ambient society itself has doubts—increasing doubts—about the status of these verities, these doubts cannot have much meaning or consequence for the still-developing mind.

We see this phenomenon clearly at work in studies of moral development. As detailed by Lawrence Kolhberg and confirmed by many other researchers, young children seek actively to discover the moral code, the right thing to do. Scattered research confirms an analogous picture with respect to truth and beauty. That is, in the case of the arts, young individuals believe that there is a right way to depict (realistically) or to versify (with rhymes), and that school texts represent a concatenation of firmly established, eternal truths.

But with the arrival of adolescence, things change dramatically. In the moral sphere, adolescents begin to challenge the culture's code, often adopting a complete, almost a perverse relativism. The same child who, a few years earlier, would not countenance lying, stealing, or cheating may now marshal reasons why such hitherto immoral behaviors are justified, respectively: "because the government lies all the time" or "because the boutique makes too much money" or "because it does not hurt anyone and it will get my parents off my back."

A parallel case occurs with reference to the assertion of truth or truths. The adolescent must come to grips with two new conditions. First, there is the recognition that the truths encountered in texts and lectures have not been enunciated from "on high" and for all time. They are merely assertions, the propositional attitudes of specific persons or groups of persons, and are accordingly subject to the limitations of human frailty. Second, students are now studying separate disciplines, typically taught by different teachers in different classrooms that foreground different sources of information. Adolescents encounter one body of truths in history, a second in math, a third in science, not to mention the assertions made in other disciplines encountered in school or via the media. Just how to evaluate these truths against one another, and how to synthesize truths into a broader picture of reality, is a daunting task, one that is rarely part of the explicit agenda of schools. No wonder many adolescents despair of evaluating and sorting out the truths that they once took for granted.

Indeed, one of the defining features of adolescence is consistent and spirited attacks on the orthodoxy of the society. The flowering of a critical spirit proves particularly problematic in fundamentalist households. (*Fundamentalist* here signifies a rigid view of the world, whether religious or not.) Throughout childhood, offspring in these households adhere readily to the canon embraced by their community. When they become adolescents, particularly if they live in pluralistic societies, these young people encounter contrasting points of view and become able, themselves, to contemplate other possible worlds—historical, scientific, aesthetic, religious. The seeds of skepticism have been planted. The principal challenge to elders in such societies is to make sure that the young person's worldview remains sheltered during adolescence. For should the young person prove able to resist the Circean temptations that present themselves during adolescence, she will in all likelihood remain in the fundamentalist fold for life.

Even setting aside fundamentalist homes or communities, challenges to the regnant orthodoxy may not last if the signals in the ambient culture are powerful and univocal. We thus have the surprising phenomenon of young adults, capable of more complex or nuanced thinking, "regressing" to a simpler formulation that has been embraced by their society. Under such conditions, seemingly modernist or postmodernist sentiments yield to a premodern sensibility.

But given the pervasive irreverent and iconoclastic adolescent mentality, we need to ask: Is there a relationship between adolescent worldviews, on the one hand, and postmodern ideas, on the other? To be sure, the embrace of heterodox sentiments occurs whether or not the young people have ever heard of postmodernism, and whether or not they understand or agree with any of its "anti-virtue" assertions. Yet, as I've suggested before, the postmodern critique gives strength and sustenance to tendencies that have long been observed among youth, particularly those who live in Western societies or in societies influenced by Western ideas. In recent decades, both in school and via the media, nearly all young persons have been encouraged to acknowledge diversity within and across cultures; to honor the perspectives of those who come from different backgrounds; and to avoid any rush to judgment about the thoughts and behaviors of others with respect to what is true, and what is good, if indeed those descriptors retain any transcendent validity. Taken together, these ideas, which are part and parcel of postmodernism, extend and exacerbate the signal features of modern adolescence.

Whether or not young persons have heard of the postmodern perspective, and whether or not they take it to heart, nearly all young persons are deeply engaged with the digital world. They take for granted the barrage of information and the overlaying of voices that define our oversaturated world. For them, it is the norm—indeed, it is as difficult for a fifteen-year-old to conceive of a wholly analog world as for a seventy-five-year-old to imagine a world without dial telephones, telegrams, or mass rail and air transportation. Still, the fact that young people can use these new technologies deftly does not make it easier to solidify their sense of the true, the beautiful, and the good—indeed, at the height of adolescence they may despair of doing so.

With respect to the digital media, young people exhibit a paradox. As I noted earlier, they tend to belittle the importance of life online; when asked, they say that their blogs and social network sites are not that important, that what *really* counts are *real-life* encounters with *real-life* phenomena. I take them at their word. At the same time, most young people in developed societies spend the bulk of their daily waking hours engaged with the media—both in and outside of school. Necessarily the media are, or become, their primary source of data, knowledge, experiences—on nearly all matters including those that pertain to truth, beauty, and goodness. Whether they know it or not, whether they like it or not, their beliefs, views, and conclusions are in significant measure a sum, a distillation, or—more probably—a morass of the contents, the forms, and the formats of the new media.

We seem to be at the epicenter of one of the rare moments in cultural history: a time when dramatic changes in the life cycle intersect with unprecedentedly seismic changes in the technological environment. Moreover, the changes in the technological environment continue unabated, if not occurring even more rapidly than before. To be sure, the biological clock of adolescence has not changed much: A genealogical generation still spans a quarter-century. In contrast, the length of a technological generation seems to shrink with every digital breakthrough. As a result of these interacting factors, it is challenging to describe what *is* happening, to anticipate what *will* happen, to offer recommendations about what *should* happen with respect to our virtues during a digitally suffused adolescence. Yet it's time to take stock and to tender a few recommendations.

Let's first consider the realm of beauty. When it comes to the arts, many youths will hit upon a favored genre, and a favored style within that genre. Whether or not they employ the term *beauty*, or a surrogate (*cool, wicked*), they will wax enthusiastically about works of that ilk. Often, perhaps even typically, youths believe that they are rebelling against parental and teacher preferences—and that may be the case. But these preferences are far from being unique. Indeed, most adolescents follow *their* crowd almost slavishly, whether its preferences are best described as premodern, modern, or postmodern. In this regard, the challenge posed by beauty with respect to the adolescent sensibility proves quite different from the challenges with respect to truth and goodness. In my view, we should strive to expand adolescents' notion of artistic possibilities and to stretch their sense of what might be considered beautiful.

On their own, or owing to stimulation of peers, some adolescents will explore the arts quite widely, perhaps canvassing different art forms as well as diverse cultural traditions. Certainly, the digital media enable this process. These adventurous souls should be praised for their endeavors, introduced to traditions with which they may not have been familiar, and encouraged to share their discoveries with less adventurous peers.

But, barring these exceptions, adolescent curiosity rarely extends beyond the conventional preferences of one's peer groups. Nor, given the priorities of all but the best-funded public schools, can most students look to formal arts education as a means of broadening their horizons of beauty. (Independent schools are more likely to present a menu of artistic options.) It thus falls upon family members, friends, and neighbors, and—if one is lucky—nearby museums or community centers to offer, offline, a broader palette of aesthetic options.

Whatever the venue, the sequence I'd recommend is straightforward. One begins with sheer exposure to a wider range of art works—a wider opportunity to see, hear, even feel. Next, one raises provocative questions: What do you see or hear? What differences do you notice within the work and in comparison to other works? Why are these important? What else caught your attention? What is the creator trying to achieve? How does this relate to other parts of your life, of the lives of others? These questions should stimulate careful attention and, assuming that peers are actively engaged, reveal the many facets of a work of art that can be noticeable.

Noticing, discussing, arguing, reflection are the entry points of choice—for people across the age span. But, when it comes to adolescents, the subsequent steps can and should vary. Some participants will want to explore historical or cultural dimensions; others will focus on aesthetic aspects, such as style or expression; still others will focus on value judgments—and these value judgments can range from financial value to a personal value system.

Note that the goals here are quite different from those pursued with respect to the other virtues. There is no desire to lead the youth to specific conclusions. Or, put differently, the conclusions reached should be those of importance to the particular young person, and these conclusions can and should continue to change and deepen over time. Our goal in the arts should be the development, in each person, of a portfolio of personal preferences, and the reasons for them, and, as appropriate, a record of what seems beautiful, and why.

Enter the media. More than ever before, youth are now exposed to the potpourri of fads, fashions, and styles of living that have been adopted all over the world. A century ago, most young people saw with their own eyes the clothing, the houses, the media of their neighborhood, or possibly their nation—and nothing more. Their aesthetic sensibility was necessarily circumscribed and typically parochial. Nowadays, thanks to television, movies, and the web, billions of young people see for themselves and on their own the aesthetics of many other cultures. Watching MTV or surfing YouTube, they become aware of the numerous ways in which individuals can decorate themselves or one another, express themselves in line, color, story, or song; they are exposed, sometimes on an hourly basis, to the diverse aesthetics of a "Silk Road" world. Indeed, the digital media present more options, more quickly, and in more ways than ever before. Canons of beauty, and of the arts more broadly, are destined to keep changing, and young persons can participate in bringing about these changes; no one—not biologist, not economist, not psychologist—can predict with any precision the ways in which they will change. Nor should we: When it comes to beauty, or to the arts more generally, let innumerable flowers bloom, let ten thousand tastes emerge.

At this historical moment, the reluctance to pass judgment, characteristic of postmodernism, joins forces with the instant digital accessibility of the global artistic landscape. And so there is a welcome opportunity to broaden the artistic horizons of young persons and to help them develop their own increasingly individualized senses of beauty.

Let me introduce an idea that I find promising. Youth should be encouraged to keep a portfolio of artistic preferences. While such a portfolio could be kept in one's mind, it is far preferable for the portfolio to exist in tangible form: either through the collection of physical artifacts or, as a sign of the times, by means of digital files. Young people should be encouraged to place in that portfolio any artistic objects or experiences—made by famous artists, unknown artists, friends, or themselves—that they feel is worth preserving. In addition, they should be encouraged to record their own thoughts: what they like, what they value, and why. And they should pay special attention to changes of heart over time—what they no longer value as much, what they have come to value anew, and why.

Ideally, the artistic portfolio should be shared with others—family, friends, and, when possible, adults knowledgeable in the arts. Teachers of the arts not only provide a useful sounding board; they may also be able to call attention to features that are less obvious to the youth. In this way, young persons will begin to solidify their own artistic identities, their own individualized senses of beauty. And consistent with the notion of identity as formulated by psychologists, this identity is defined in part by the way that the adolescent is (or is not) received within the broader community.

Keeping in mind the contrast between childhood and adolescence, we turn next to goodness. As we've seen, young children naturally learn to deal with moral issues in relation to those around them. This "neighborly morality"—with all its cultural wrinkles—seems to be part of the human condition; in any case, changes in the morality of the neighborhood occur rarely and very slowly. Yet, in a way that could not have been anticipated twenty-five years ago, even very young people, via the Internet, find themselves members of large communities, communities whose size, scale, and duration are not only unknown but inherently unknowable. To one's evident obligations toward one's neighbor, or toward one's cousin, we must now add the ethics of roles—the behaviors and beliefs that the responsible worker and the responsible citizen need to adopt, if our world is to be viable. And that is because any participant in the digital media is necessarily connected to an indeterminate number of others in an indeterminate number of places.

In preparing young people for these roles of digital worker or digital citizen, we have little precedent on which to draw. These roles are newer, not anticipated in prehistory or traditional history, and changing rapidly. Both roles clash with the concrete here-and-now ways of thinking characteristic of the child or the preadolescent. Ten-year-olds are not adults, and no act of will can magically double their age or sophistication or maturity.

Here, far more than in other spheres of their lives, I see as essential the intervention of parents and other knowledgeable elders. Such adults need to be part of the digital world of their children, guiding wherever possible, playing the same games, participating in the same social networks, and, should all else fail, limiting or even proscribing the unchaperoned uses of these media. Of course, unless the adult restricts his own behavior in analogous ways, he can scarcely expect the child to undertake restraint on her own. Yet, by far the preferable way to guide the child is through constructive engagement ("Let's play SimCity together," "Do you want to chat today on Club Penguin?") rather than through dictated nonengagement ("You can't use the iPad") or through confusing modeling of the proscribed behaviors ("... but I can").

When it comes to young children's use of digital media, then, the foregrounding of good behavior, and the minimization of destructive behavior, takes precedent. Healthy habits established at that time are crucial. For once the years of adolescence approach, any effort to control the use of digital media is likely to founder and may well produce counterproductive reactions.

Our own studies with adolescents tease apart two ethical dimensions of the digital world. For starters, there is the ethics involved in dealing with other persons, often ones remote and unknown. Most young adolescents have a *consequentialist* attitude toward these remote actors: Since the digital world is not that important anyway, one should do what one likes with respect to these others, unless negative consequences ensue. Then, in addition, there is the regular, if not constant, exposure to groups or cultures that have a quite different set of ethical concerns and practices. Youths behold a dizzying range of behavioral models and can potentially interact with individuals from the full swath of societies. Here one encounters a range of reactions. Adolescents of an idealistic cast of mind can be very disturbed by practices in other cultures that they find repugnant (for example, treatment of women or of gays); they are moved to attempt to bring about changes that they consider desirable. Others, of a more relativist or postmodern persuasion, are inclined to be quite permissive, accepting, or indifferent with respect to alternative mores.

In an ideal world, youth might be able to sort out these ethical fault lines and entanglements on their own. And given the resistance to adult interference, this approach might be preferable. Yet several strands of research confirm that this state of affairs is unlikely to occur spontaneously. In particular—and here they resemble other age groups—young people tend to interact digitally primarily with those peers with whom they are in agreement. Moreover, there are few sanctions for engaging in ethically dubious ways; regulation is spotty and, more often than not, behind the times.

As I mentioned in the last chapter, our Good Work Project included a broad exploration of the ethical senses of young Americans—aged, roughly, from fifteen to thirty. In many cases these young people could distinguish between behaviors and actions that were ethical and those that were not. Yet to our surprise and disappointment, we discovered that these young people often exhibited an ethical sense that was unjustifiably thin. They told us that someday, when they were rich and famous, they would behave ethically at the workplace and would insist on hiring individuals who were themselves ethical. But for now, they did not want to be held to account for ethical lapses—their peers performed compromised work and so it was permissible for them to stray as well.

These findings stimulated a program of action. As part of our Good Work reflection sessions with adolescents and young adults, we present true stories from our own research, each setting forth a dilemma encountered at school or place of work. There is the reporter on the school newspaper who is determined to write about a rape on campus but is threatened with reprisal by the head of the school if she acts on her stated intention. After all, recruiting of next year's class is about to occur, and publication of the story is likely to scare off prospective students. There is the excellent college teacher, long revered by his students, whose rigorous grading practices are now keeping some students from gaining admission to competitive graduate programs. There is the aspiring, idealistic Asian-American actor who is offered a plum part; however, that role requires her to perform in a stereotypical way that undermines her fundamental beliefs and values.

Such dilemmas powerfully document the differences between neighborly morality and role-related ethics, as I have defined these concepts. Our cases do not encompass territory where the Ten Commandments or the Golden Rule will tell you what to do. They are suffused with shades of gray and layers of complexity. Indeed, the dilemma involving the school newspaper is even more vexing than might appear to be the case. On the one hand, the reporter's grandfather was a famous journalist with a reputation for integrity; on the other hand, the reporter's younger brother wants to gain admission to the reporter's school next year. Rarely are these dilemmas a simple case of "right vs. wrong"; frequently, those confronted by a dilemma must pit right vs. right or wrong vs. wrong, or choose the lesser of two evils, if not the greater of two goods.

While students often resist passing judgment on public figures, the same students find these dilemmas fascinating and show little hesitation in making recommendations. The challenge to advise others faced with a dilemma seems to unleash their critical faculties. But it is premature to declare our sessions with students a success. Indeed, in a few cases, exposure to these dilemmas, and intense discussion thereof, seems to cause students to dig in their heels. Far from becoming convinced of the need for responsible actions, students may defiantly embody, embrace, or at least defend selfish or compromised work. Nor can we be certain that this apparent regression is to be avoided at all costs. Sometimes, in order to embrace the good, one must invest time and energy in donning the garb of compromise, if not the cloak of the unambiguously wicked. As observers have contended, ever since Adam and Eve left the Garden of Eden, one cannot know and live the good unless one has confronted evil. *Paradise lost* before *paradise regained*. No wonder Dante's fabled Comedy begins with the Inferno and reaches celestial regions only in its final pages.

And yet, I can report that most students who enroll in these sessions find them worthwhile. Often they report that they had never thought about such issues, or had previously seen only one side of the dilemma. Now they have a fuller appreciation of the operating forces and feel that they themselves might well behave differently in the future. Reflection and constructive engagement may not suffice to produce ethical human beings; but in my view, they constitute essential first steps. Accordingly, we are eager to identify venues where we (and others) can initiate such sessions as well as means for linking participants directly and digitally.

As noted, whether consciously invoking postmodern sentiments, students sometimes refuse to pass judgment on the protagonists in a case. But from the educational standpoint, it is not acceptable simply to declare that anyone's position is as valid as anyone else's. The arguments adduced, the reasoning employed, the examples analyzed, and the transparency surrounding one's own and others' positions are all relevant factors. With respect to a particular moral or ethical issue, there may not be a decisive right or wrong. But we should help young people value those individuals who recognize moral and ethical dilemmas, wrestle with them publicly, strive to arrive at the proper course of action, reflect on what did and did not happen, and attempt to apply those lessons to future encounters.

The Good Work sessions have not focused particularly on digital life. And yet, they can clearly be adapted to this area of concern. Educators can feature websites, YouTube offerings, or articles from Wikipedia that raise ethical issues, and they can engage their students in discussions, debates, and role play that foreground the ethical issues. Leaders can call attention to or dramatize online situations where adolescents commit or become victims of unethical behaviors. Youths may relinquish their indifference toward ownership of intellectual property when they themselves have worked hard on a creation, only to see it usurped without credit on YouTube. Or youths may refrain from cyber-bullying when their own young siblings become victims.

Moreover, in a digital era, Good Work sessions can transcend geographical and cultural boundaries. The digital media provide an unprecedented opportunity to de-parochialize Good Work discussions—indeed, to make these reflections global. In the process, students not only learn about the perspectives of citizens from other societies; they also learn how to evaluate, in a civil manner, the most appropriate course of actions. Students should take the lead in these interchanges; sensitive facilitators can make timely interventions, providing context or ensuring that alternative points of view are heard. The most informed judgments of good and evil are likely to come about when one has surveyed a range of views on this topic, reflected on the strengths of each, and arrived at a philosophy, or at least a rule of thumb, with which one can live comfortably. At the very least, one has a firmer understanding of one's own moral and ethical compass. And, at best, for themselves and for the planet, individuals from diverse moral and ethical traditions can work together to forge a code that encompasses the most praiseworthy and beneficent features of these diverse traditions.

We turn, finally, to the realm of truth. With adolescents, the challenge is to recognize that there are indeed several truths, not just one truth; that each truth is subject to alteration, in the light of new knowledge or new understandings; and yet that the search for truth is important, worth pursuing over time, and ultimately leading to more authoritative accounts of the world. In the terminology I've introduced here, adolescence should mark the transition from a single established truth to multiple emerging truths. Hammering out this insight, and its implications, has essentially been the task of liberal education. Thanks to the work of William Perry and other authorities, we now appreciate that a challenge to any received notion of truth is ordinary and to be expected during the college years. The challenge has been exacerbated by the postmodern critique, which calls into question *any* confident assertion of truth.

A focus on truths should be a special hallmark of the adolescent years: in the modern world, the years of secondary school, college or university, and vocational or professional specialization. To begin with, this is the period of life in which youngsters can have distance from their learning. For the first time, they can be comfortably metacognitive with reference to various disciplines and methods, as well as to the possible interrelations (and tensions) among them. And so educators can and should help to nurture that part of cognition which stimulates reflection about its own modes of operation.

Adolescence is also the time when lifelong habits of learning need to be consolidated. To be sure, the acquisition of discipline, of working regularly and hard, should be well launched far earlier. But it is during adolescence that one's stance toward truths, and how one will continue to establish them, once formal schooling has ended, becomes a lifelong habit of mind.

When it comes to beauty, young people should work out their canons largely by themselves. When it comes to goodness, elders can provide some wisdom, but young people need to hash out the reasons for their own moral code and then decide whether to stretch to accommodate or merge with others. When it comes to truth, the role of formal education is clearest, the need for regular, careful interventions most urgent.

In an important sense, the means for approaching truth operate across the age terrain. When working with children, one certainly wants to make one's approach to knowledge and one's uses of source as salient as possible. By the same token, as I'll detail in the next chapter, the need to keep methods, sources, and modes of verification in mind remains constant throughout life.

Still, with adolescents, two interventions prove particularly fruitful. First of all, one can undertake careful detailed study of individual cases, using original documents or carrying out actual experiments. In history, for example, one can look at what actually happened at the Wannsee Conference, after which the Holocaust was launched; or at conflicting accounts of the discovery of Troy or the founding of Rome. In science, one can examine the various accounts over time about the function of the brain or the reasons for the current configuration of continents or the causes of combustion. Or one can replicate well-known laboratory experiments, altering the conditions in systematic, controlled ways. Then, too, as exemplified by the "Theory of Knowledge" course developed by the International Baccalaureate schools, one can look directly at the methods used by different disciplines and discern how they complement or supplement one another. Such an examination can occur only in later adolescence, at a time when young people have already shown some mastery of a number of fields of knowledge and have sufficient distance to be able to make judicious comparisons across those fields.

How is the study of truth affected by the digital era? Never before in human history have so many accounts been available of the past and the present, of science and magic, of persons famous, slightly known, completely obscure, until they have their proverbial "fifteen minutes" on the world stage. And, thanks to wikis, blogs, and tweets, the propositions and demonstrations in various sectors can be changed from one day to another, or even from one moment to another. No wonder even those who have never heard of the postmodern critiques penned by Jean-François Lyotard or Richard Rorty can despair of the possibility of establishing what is true and what is not.

During this period of life, the youth is likely to establish an enduring stance toward the digital media. Earlier, the child may well have sampled widely, but probably did so largely in an accepting manner (if it says that, well, it must be so). Now the youth needs to consolidate the means by which he will make determinations of what is valid, what needs more evidence, and what does not merit further attention. By the same token, while younger children may well have created some content on the web, adolescents becomes major contributors to websites, photosites, videosites, and sites connected to particular hobbies and interests, not to mention the ubiquitous social networks. Whether the youth approaches these web 2.0 opportunities with a focus on truthfulness, with complete indifference to truth value, or somewhere in the "truthiness" between, will have significant consequences for himself and for all with whom he comes into contact.

How, then, to guide adolescents toward truth in a digital era? In brief, it is up to disciplinary specialists and other experts to make explicit the ways in which evidence is gathered and conclusions drawn. They (and, as appropriate, we) must be as explicit and transparent as possible. They must show how they evaluate new claims and on what basis they dismiss them, consider them briefly, ponder them seriously, or even change their own understanding of what is true. Importantly, they need to share the strategies that they adopt when confronted with a plethora of information, some of which is contradictory. For example, in considering which book to read on a topic of interest, an expert will consider the reputation of the publisher, the track record of the author, the credibility of the reviewers and the blurbers, and, perhaps, a sample page from the beginning, middle, and end of the book. Analogous canons will arise from scientists evaluating journal articles, lawyers evaluating witnesses, journalists evaluating informants. Truth, it must be made clear, is not a question of bias or gut instinct; it consists of carefully-arrived-at conclusions on the basis of cool and consistent review of the evidence.

The advent of the digital media has not fundamentally altered the establishment of truth. The insights, findings, and methods of disciplinary specialists and of practitioners are enduring. But any expert who wants to remain current, or even relevant, must rethink his or her processes in light of the digital media—what they emphasize, what they afford, and what they may render obscure or even invisible. And even more so, any educator working with adolescents must think constantly about how best to use the digital media, and how, as it were, to reinvent the methods of establishing truth, so that they will be clear to "digital natives."

Of course, establishment of truth is not the exclusive province of the expert. Sometimes experts have been wrong—briefly or even over long periods of time. Sometimes the rank amateur has discerned a state of affairs that was missed by those with much more knowledge and experience. And, as any quick-witted youth will remind us, there is a wisdom in crowds. The digital media underscore this point dramatically. A survey of sixty reviewers on amazon.com may prove more informative and more useful than a front-page review in the *New York Times Book Review*, and Wikipedia has sometimes "outsmarted" the *Encyclopedia Britannica*.

The crucial point: Assembling all these forms of expertise, with other relevant sources of support, puts us into the best possible position to discern the actual state of affairs. And so, important Converging Truths, if not the Ultimate Truths, are more likely than ever to emerge in a digital era.

In comparison with earlier cohorts, young people today emerge as a Fragmented Generation—a generation that has lived through so much in a few years and has been exposed to so many experiences, alive and virtually. At least in the eyes of their elders, today's youth harbor—indeed, they constitute—a mountain of unassimilated and unorganized information, whether or not they are aware of it, and whether or not they would be bothered, were it pointed out to them. A virtual barrage of truths, beauties, and moral precepts besieges the psyche of any "connected" child. Natural proclivities, if any, are overwhelmed by competing norms. Here may lie a clue about why youths have been attracted to the person of President Barack Obama: A young person of textbook fragmentation in parentage, residence, and belief systems—like them, wedded to his smartphone—against the odds proved able to put these fragments together in a coherent way. But needless to say, we are not—and young people are not—all Barack Obamas!

In the end, despite their looming presence, neither postmodernism nor the digital media need distance or block adolescents from embracing a legitimate version of the three virtues. Indeed, as I've suggested, one can discern hopeful signs. A lovely, individualized sense of beautiful experiences and objects can emerge; a robust sense of how to treat others—globally as well as locally—is possible; and those with patience and tenacity can march steadily and even confidently toward a sturdy sense of truth.

Thanks to a world that is physically healthier if not mentally saner, most of the young people born in the twenty-first century will survive to their majority. Had they been born 250 years ago and lived into their twenties or thirties, changes post-puberty would have had to be modest. The truths of science and history did not change that quickly—Newton reigned supreme; the sense of beauty in their cultures were less contested; and, as Kant put the finishing touch on his writings, the ethical strains that are part and parcel of any complex society had not yet fully erupted.

Now, however, no such assumptions can or should be made. Thanks to the French Revolution, the Marxist revolution, the computer revolution (take your pick!), the pace of change has quickened, and the places and periods of stability are few and far between. Parents, institutions, societies that seek to impose their versions of the virtues on the young have their work cut out for them. Even if, unlikely as it may seem, one has—in one's youth—worked out one's schema of truth, beauty, and goodness pretty well, these are certain to be challenged in the decades ahead. Just how the trio fares during the adult years concerns us next.

Chapter 6 | Learning
Throughout Life

Once upon a time, the category of childhood scarcely existed. Portraits in the Middle Ages depicted young children as either helpless infants or miniature adults. After 1500, along with the rediscovery of classical knowledge, multiple openings to the New World, and increasingly enlightened (if not Enlightenment) notions of education, the principal contours of childhood became evident. Educators like Comenius and Pestalozzi, philosophers like Rousseau and Vico, writers like Wordsworth and Dickens, explored the unique sensibilities of childhood. But stasis was now posited at the other end of childhood. Having passed through the ages/stages of childhood, the young adult peaked just before beginning a long (or not so long), inexorable decline. As Shakespeare put it:

The sixth stage shifts
Into the lean and slippered pantaloon,
With spectacles on nose and pouch on side;
His youthful hose, well saved, a world too wide
For his shrunk shank, and his big manly voice,
Turning again toward childish treble, pipes
And whistles in his sound. Last scene of all,
That ends this strange eventful history,
Is second childishness and mere oblivion,
Sans teeth, sans eyes, sans taste, sans everything.

This view of a differentiated life cycle is seen clearly in the scheme proposed by Jean Piaget. The seminal psychological thinker construed cognitive development as a set of stages that culminated in the "formal operational thinking" of the adolescent. The formal operator is able to envision all possible permutations and combinations of a situation. (How many ways can the chess player put the king into check on the next move?) She is also able to think abstractly. (As a newly sworn-in citizen, what are my rights and what are my obligations?) The formal thinker can describe the world in terms of propositions; evaluate whether those propositions are individually true; and fit the propositions together into a coherent overall framework— witness the competent scientist, historian, psychologist, economist, or chess player. Or, equally powerfully, the formal thinker can show why such systemization is not possible, in principle or at least at present. Turning to the realm of ethics, we find that the formal thinker can transcend the habits of neighborly morality and consider the responsibilities attendant to formal roles—that of worker, of professional, of citizen.

But in the decades since the Piagetian cognitive scheme was first vetted, scholars have challenged the idea that people reach their cognitive peak at age fifteen or eighteen. In what has come to be called "post-formal thought," psychologists now recognize the importance of subsequent stages of cognitive development. I'll argue that these later stages can usher in new stances and understandings of truth, beauty, and goodness: that truths can be more firmly established; that experiences of beauty can be more effectively individualized; and that individuals can fulfill roles in ways that are more ethically sound. Moreover, given the longer lives that most of us will lead (even longer than in the Piagetian era, let alone in Shakespearean times), and the multitude of changes occurring in the world each passing year, it is crucial that we continue to engage the three virtues in optimal ways over the decades.

In fact, this lengthened life span ushers in opportunities. On the purely cognitive plane, we now believe that adolescents are just beginning to be able to think in terms of coherent systems of thought—let's say, in the political sphere, reasonably comprehensive understandings of socialism, fascism, and representative democracy. To be sure, the adolescent should be able to master the precepts of one or more of these systems. But in contrast, the capacity to think about systems (metasystemic thinking), or to compare systems (e.g., national socialism vs. democratic socialism), awaits further cognitive development— ordinarily such a facility does not come into its own until the twenties, if indeed it is ever achieved. Just think of the difference between the high school senior armed with SAT achievement-test facts and the graduate student preparing to take her general examinations. It is not an "information gap"—it is a gap in systemic thinking. Only in maturity can individuals appreciate and compare and, as appropriate, synthesize the kinds of propositional and practical truths embodied across the several disciplines and crafts.

Similar progress occurs after adolescence in the realms of personality and interpersonal relations. Even the precocious adolescent still entertains an egocentrically tainted view of the world: egocentric in the sense that the world seems to be focused—sometimes even exclusively—on his or her current concerns. (Is everyone going to the dance except me? Am I competing with everyone for that internship?

Is the whole school—or the whole world—watching me?) At later stages of development, an individual has a far greater capacity to de-center: to assume a distance from her own agenda, to understand and help others achieve their goals, to create situations in which others realize their potentials, and to lead effectively by stepping into the background and allowing—indeed encouraging—others to assume greater independence and to receive most of the credit. In the best-case scenario, such development continues until the later years of life, culminating in mature judgment, effective mentoring, responsible trusteeship in various fields, and, indeed, wisdom.

"Stage views" of adult development now reflect these trends. At one time, as scholars and laypersons, we posited—and were content with—only three postchildhood life stages: adolescence, adulthood, and old age/senility. Now a stage of emergent adulthood (or pro-longed adolescence) is widely recognized. (Are your grown children still living at home? Do they still call several times a week to ask for advice and seek help?) A stage of early old age is acknowledged (active retirement). And many are also recognizing a "third stage" of adulthood—the period between ages fifty and seventy-five—when life's initial ambitions have been achieved, limitations have been accepted, and the now mature adult seeks to relate actively to the world in a new, often determinedly prosocial way. At this time, perhaps more so than at any other point in the life cycle, the person has the potential and the time to appreciate the various truths across several realms; to refine his or her distinctive sense of beauty; and to tackle sensitively and sensibly the often vexed ethical issues that arise at the workplace, the ballot box, or the town square.

The trends I've mentioned point to continuing development, at least through the middle years of life, and in the happiest circumstances until the ages of sixty, seventy, or even older. These trends reflect not only human psychology; evidence mounts that our bodies and brains can grow and adapt for decades after adolescence. Yet, as should be evident, these developments are only *possibilities*, by no means necessities or imperatives. If there are millions of individuals who continue to develop, for decades, there are certainly untold millions who have reached the high point of development by the middle of the second decade of life. Such individuals stagnate, are content to maintain their current (often fragile) understandings and outlook, actively resist growth, or even regress to more primitive modes of thought and action.

It would be disingenuous to pretend that such a continuing or even expanding sense of agency during the adult years—as I'll call the latter periods—is entirely within the control of the individual. Bad luck can throw off one's hoped-for life course. If one has to work twelve hours a day at the same boring job (or at two or three equally joyless workplaces) to keep the family fed and clothed, there is less time for any kind of personal growth. If one inhabits a religious or social environment that strongly dictates conformity, pressures mount to remain as one was, or as one's neighbors are, or as they appear to be. If one inherits a constitution—mental or physical—that is frail, efforts to continue to grow, to change, to develop, are more difficult to mount and sustain. Still, one can take heart from inspiring examples like those of Theodore Roosevelt, who overcame physical infirmities, or Winston Churchill, who overcame learning difficulties, and led long and ever more active lives, or, even more dramatically, Helen Keller, who, despite lack of sight and hearing, achieved and shared deep insights about the human condition. More recently, we encounter impressive examples of women reared in strict Islamic settings who risked life and limb to escape an abusive arranged marriage and to initiate a new life, alone, in a new world.

Some factors that limit growth are beyond one's own control. The anthropologist Claude Lévi-Strauss distinguished between "cool societies," which change at glacial speed, and "hot societies," which are in frequent, indeed constant, turmoil. Compare "cool" ancient Egypt, where significant political changes occurred over the centuries, with "hot" China in the twentieth century, which transmogrified in very short order from empire to republic to totalitarian communist regime, to a distinctive blend of socialism and capitalism. Clearly, an individual has the greater opportunity to change, develop, and grow in a setting that itself is being constantly transformed.

Of course, change is not always easy, nor is it necessarily desirable. With respect to relations among human beings, alternative scenarios exist. Traditional "cool" societies are marked by the dominance of a few strong ties. Individuals come to know intimately a small set of relatives, neighbors, and friends, and to depend on this deeply entrenched social network over long periods of time. In sharp contrast, modern "hot" societies spurn or devalue such deep ties in favor of numerous, far weaker, far more flexible ties. Denizens of such societies know a great many persons, but inevitably much more superficially; they can contact these individuals in numerous ways, but may do so only sporadically. Traditional society is distinguished by the same set of family pictures or other mementos or heirlooms that remain on one's front table or desk for decades; modern society is marked by a large and rapidly evolving rolodex, a rich database in one's personal digital assistant, and dozens if not many hundreds of entries on a favorite social network site.

Without question, in a rapidly changing world the ability to make use of many weak ties proves advantageous. Such ties not only expose one to far more information and experiences but also afford one the opportunity to compare different versions of truth, to develop one's own distinctive sense of beauty, and to think clearly and to act responsibly with respect to complex ethical and moral dilemmas. Too much flexibility may prove a hindrance in a society that remains at a relatively low temperature; but, clearly, greater flexibility becomes a mark of survival in any "hot" society.

From the opening years of life, those of us who happen to have been born and raised in "hot" societies are more accustomed to

change and more likely to have become able to deal with, to anticipate, and even to grow fond of continuing major alterations in the
landscape. At the same time, it must be recognized that the attenua-
tion or loss of deep, intimate, long-lived ties can be personally painful.
Moreover, indices of happiness and trust tend to be higher in societies that have maintained such strong links among human beings.
Still, given the trends in today's world, it is evident that people will
need to be able to survive—and to arrive at viable versions of the
virtues—in fast-changing, relatively "hot" milieus.

Painting with a very broad brush, we could say that in most societies, throughout most of history, notions of truth, beauty, and goodness were relatively consensual. In our terms, truths were established
rather than emerging; beauty was traditional rather than individualized; vexed interpersonal issues were adjudicated by neighborly
morality or not at all. Conceptions changed slowly, sometimes even
imperceptibly. For centuries in Europe, portrayals of Christ and the
Virgin Mother were the primary preoccupation of visual artists.
Moreover, often there was a tendency to collapse the three virtues—
what was seen as true was also beautiful and good, and the reverse
implicatory sequence obtained as well.

Not that we should remain content with brush strokes that are
too broad. Even in the distant past, views of the three virtues did
change. Sometimes, change was due to powerful leaders—say, Moses
for the Hebrews, or Shi Huangdi of the Han Dynasty. Sometimes,
changes came about as the result of cataclysmic events—say, the
Black Plague, the Lisbon earthquake, or the melting of the icecaps.
More often, changes—both beneficent and malevolent—occurred as
the result of the meeting and clash of cultures, the guns of war, the
spoils of the victor, the adaptations of the vanquished. Of course, not
all changes are permanent—civilizations roll back as well as march
forth. The Middle Ages (once called the Dark Ages)—beloved by
Henry Adams—were far less dynamic than the centuries that pre-
ceded or follow them.

Few periods of history compare with our own in terms of the speed and decisiveness of changes. Just about everyone over the age of thirty-five can remember vividly the fall of the Berlin Wall, the surprisingly brief hegemony of Western democracy coupled with market capitalism, the shock of the attacks of 9/11, natural disasters like Hurricane Katrina or the tsunami of South Asia, the worldwide financial meltdown in the autumn of 2008, the Gulf oil spill two years later. Circumstances once considered permanent and resolved—the Cold War, the inviolacy of the borders of the United States, the natural corrective force inherent in financial markets—did not withstand brutal facts and factors. From one decade to the next, inhabitants of countries like Afghanistan, Iran, Iraq, Israel, Poland, Romania, Venezuela—even the relatively calm United Kingdom and the United States—were exposed to dramatically different notions of good and evil. And with each cohort of artists challenging the core values and practices of its predecessors, any effort to maintain a constant or consistent aesthetic seemed doomed. Not only did these changes occur at warp speed; but in contradistinction to earlier eras, individuals became aware of them almost instantly. It has been claimed that within two days of its occurrence on August 31, 1997, 98 percent of adults around the world had become aware of the death of Princess Diana.

How, then, does a rapidly altering terrain, including a kaleidoscope of virtues and vices, affect individuals who are well past their initial development and their initial stages of learning? At one time, we might have thought that we could not teach new tricks to an old dog, let alone to a middle-aged human. But today, a newly reigning cliché—lifelong learning—must become more than a cliché. Learning ceases to be the targeted burden of childhood and adolescence; it becomes the privilege—but also the obligation—of an entire lifetime. We now know that, contrary to long-held beliefs in the scientific community, the adult nervous system remains plastic, flexible, and capable of effecting new neural connections. Indeed, we have little reason to believe in biological constraints on the acquisition of new knowledge, tastes, and values.

And yet lifelong learning can be difficult, elusive, even in the best of situations. For those of us who remain in school, literally or in effect, continuous learning *appears* to be easier. After all, we are surrounded by the paraphernalia of education—teachers, students, curricula, courses, books, computers, libraries, the worldwide web. Learning is literally within the reach of one's own or one's neighbors' hands. And yet, we all know individuals within academe who remain stagnant, set in their views, oblivious to the changing winds, waters, and words. And even if one grows within one's own field of expertise, it is perfectly possible to remain paralyzed in other spheres. Sometimes, individuals do not even try to grow or deepen in unfamiliar domains. At other times, despite valiant efforts, growth in new spheres proves very difficult. Though we can admire and respect their daring, Nobel laureates and other winners of prestigious prizes rarely distinguish themselves in new sciences, arts, or crafts.

There is another imposing obstacle along the path to lifelong learning, even for those of us blessed to live the life of the mind. Lifelong learning would be easier if one could just extend the path of college or graduate school—one more course, one more exam, one more degree. But all too often, the seemingly well-trodden path contains tortuous zigs and zags. Many of us who mastered the truths of a particular discipline or craft would find it straightforward to continue digging deeper into that same groove of knowledge. But disciplines can change fundamentally—splintering, coalescing, reconfiguring. Moreover and crucially, nowadays much work is no longer discipline based—it is problem centered (and appropriately so); it involves interdisciplinary content knowledge as well as the capacity to work fluently and flexibly with individuals from different disciplines as well as different cultures. These stretches may prove to be formidable; there are many more claims about the importance of interdisciplinary work than there are clear-cut demonstrations of *successful* interdisciplinary work. And when multidisciplinary work succeeds, it is often far from clear why it succeeded and how that success might be replicated and modeled for others.

That said, in the broadest possible terms, it has become much easier for adults, both within and outside of educational institutions, to remain in tune and in touch if they so wish. The ubiquitous media—old, new, mechanical, electronic, digital—enable that contact. Anyone regularly engaged with the Internet and the web—anyone who blogs or who reads blogs—will be exposed as often as he or she likes to what is new, noteworthy, changing.

Of course, the flow of information is hardly an unabashed good. Many of us feel overwhelmed, in over our heads, much of the time. The new imperative has become synthesis—the capacity to gather, prune, organize information of all sizes and shapes and forms, and to repeat the cycle indefinitely. "The synthesizing mind" is able to take in copious information; apply reliable criteria in determining what to attend to and what to ignore; exhibit the capacity to put things together so that one can hold on to them (a synthesis "just in time"); and then, unless one happens to be a hermit or a troglodyte, communicate the gist of the synthesis to others in an effective and memorable manner. In truth, we have just begun to understand the challenge of effective synthesis, let alone develop the pedagogical and digital tools that can make it a reality for most persons. Advantages will flow to those of any age with a head start on this process. Ideally, one should blend the youthful ability to take in and store new information with the well-honed judging and evaluating capacities of older persons.

Inevitably, some individuals have readier access than others to information, knowledge, and quality syntheses. Yet in the end it is up to the individual to decide whether he or she wishes to keep up with what is happening in the world. One's continuing development depends principally on the kind of environment—day in and day out—in which one chooses to spend one's time. One can remain with the same group of friends or search for new ones; one can play games with the same people or seek new partners and opponents; one can visit and revisit the same works of art, or seek out new ones; one can have the same conversations repeatedly or deliberately bypass these linguistic and interpersonal ruts. Especially in a digital age, one can choose to visit the same sites, chiefly those that agree with one's views and tastes and moral code, or one can choose to visit new sites, particularly those that reflect new framings and raise new questions. In any reasonably democratic society, no one else dictates these regimens; the responsible person is the individual in question.

Many factors determine the choices one makes about how to spend one's days and nights: the need to hold on to one's job (or advance to a more attractive one); the desire to maintain one's health or improve one's finances; the goal of becoming a responsible citizen; the quest to maintain friendships or seek new ones, to convey one's values to intimates, to quench one's own curiosity or to hold one's own in conversations with valued others—those older or younger, wiser or in need of wisdom. Few people will explicitly state as their objective the pursuit of truth, beauty and goodness. And yet, lifelong learning cannot afford to skirt these vital dimensions.

First truth. Within one's own work and life spheres, there will doubtless be more practical truths. In my own case, what it takes to write and then publish an article or book has changed numerous times over the decades; and if I continued to proceed just as I did in the early 1970s, I would have little success. I used to "be published and wait for reviews"; now, unless I am determinedly proactive, I'd wait forever without anyone taking notice of the publication. The changes are even manifest in the slower-changing realm of teaching. I used to deliver hour-long lectures with, at most, an occasional slide and an occasional aside. Now nearly all of my teaching is seminar style, lectures are available online, and discussions are punctuated with ample PowerPoint presentations and timely access to the web for both the students and me. The politics of the workplace, as well as the processes of work production, are ever changing: Widely shared beliefs are not what they once were nor will they remain frozen in the decades to come. Which is not to say that all previous knowledge is evanescent. Certain practical and propositional truths obtain across the ages in writing and publishing: in teaching the young, caring for the sick, making a sale, and keeping a client. It is as important to cherish those perpetual truths as to remain open to new ones.

But one's work life is by no means the only, nor even the most salient, area of changing truths. Anyone interested in what is happening in the world needs to track our growing collective understanding (as well as, of course, our continuing confusions). New findings pour in from the several sciences; historical revisions are the order of the day. (Nor do economics and psychology and literary criticism remain unchanged, nor should they!) We do not understand the Civil War or World War I (then called the Great War) or the Cold War in the same way as our grandparents did. The gulf in understanding between earlier eras and our own is even greater when it comes to the sciences—from our burgeoning knowledge of the birth, age, and extent of the universe, to the nature and flexibility of genetic material, to the course of early hominid evolution. Even the ways in which science is conducted have changed enormously—projects now involve dozens or even hundreds of researchers, experiments probing temperatures close to absolute zero, speeds far exceeding sound, technology at the nano-level, vast simulations inconceivable before the computer age. (If items on standardized tests of science have changed little, they reflect more about the test-makers than about the stability of science per se.) It is not easy to keep up with the cavalcade of new truths; but if one makes the attempt, one is likely to attain better understanding of the world in its numerous facets.

It goes without saying—at least in this book!—that one should continue the effort to converge toward truths. What factors determine whether, as an adult, one will be successful in this goal? To begin with, a commitment to pursuing truths, wherever they may rise, and even when they go against a cherished held belief, is necessary. In light of this commitment, it is also vital to keep informed, to follow the latest findings, to evaluate them critically but not cynically. In some fields, this "checking in" can be intermittent; but as one who has sought to follow the biological sciences over the decades, I can testify that one must remain constantly vigilant if one has any hope of "keeping up."

When it comes to practical truths, one must be equally vigilant. While they are less likely to be written about, changes in the lab, the workshop, or the atelier can be quite rapid and, particularly in a highly technological age, quite dramatic. Not infrequently, the apprentice may in some respects be more "current" than the master.

Here lies an important dimension of adult development in our times. Perhaps in earlier eras, the elders held nearly all of the intellectual as well as the political cards. No longer! Today, in many ways, young persons have both the intellectual vigor and the technical skills that are at a premium across the virtues. Older and supposedly wiser persons do well to listen to, watch, and learn from their youthful contacts (be they children, grandchildren, students, apprentices). And yet, the relationship is and should be reciprocal and complementary. When it comes to the commitment to pursue truth, and the ability to discern the trivial from the vital, older persons have much to give to their younger counterparts—and it becomes their responsibility to do so.

In the sphere of beauty, too, change is the order of the day. But change here is far less linear. After periods when artistic trends move inexorably toward greater complexity and abstruseness, there is a virtually inevitable reaction in the favor of the simple, the straightforward, the determinedly demotic. And yet the *form* of that reaction cannot be predicted. In the visual arts, minimalism, pop art, old-fashioned realism were all (possible and actual) reactions to the arcana of abstract expressionism. Within music, minimalism, extreme regularity, fusion, third stream, unabashed romanticism were all (possible and actual) reactions to the intricacies of serial music.

Adult development allows us to recognize our individuality—the ways in which we resemble all individuals or some individuals, but equally and more importantly, how we differ from all other persons. This increased insight accompanies our experiences with a wide range of individuals and our continuing and thoughtful reflection on the nature of these experiences—most especially, those that encompass the realm of the beautiful. With reference to the arts, we can acknowledge those works—musical, literary, cinematic, graphic—that prove popular, even beloved, by other persons. At the same time we can come to understand—and to cherish—our own particular and perhaps even peculiar tastes, our individualized sense of beauty. I like to think of this growth as the continuing accumulation of a personal, richly annotated portfolio of all our significant experiences with works of art (and, for that matter, our encounters with nature).

It's been claimed, intriguingly, that after one enters one's forties, the human mind finds it extremely difficult to absorb truly new aesthetic norms. Proclivities become sclerotic. Put concretely, so the claim goes, if you are a Westerner in his fifth decade whose mind has not been exposed to the arts of Asia, you can never truly appreciate Indian reggae or Chinese ink-and-brush scrolls or Balinese dance.

In a literal sense, this claim cannot possibly be true. Despite the jokes of Jack Benny, a beloved comedian of the radio era, there is nothing sacred about the age of thirty-nine. Moreover, so much depends on one's own earlier experience—its breadth, its continuity— and one's own openness to change, that individual differences here must dwarf developmental (life-stage) or cohort differences (the place and date of one's birth).

Still, just as older scientists have increasing difficulty in accepting new paradigms—even the redoubtable Albert Einstein could never embrace the seemingly quirky though powerful truths of quantum mechanics—older eyes and ears do not readily absorb strikingly new artistic genres. I would go further. The sophisticated eye and ear may well be able to assimilate a new form—and indeed may even be able to put into words why that new form has merit, why it has mesmerized younger critics and youthful audiences. And yet, at a gut level, at the feeling level, at the depth of the experienced "tingle," it may indeed be difficult for a forty-, fifty-, or seventy-year-old person to accept easily, and to gain pleasure from, a work of music, film, literature, dance, painting, or sculpture that deviates significantly from the hitherto known and valued presentations. An entirely new area of art—say, computer-generated graphics or electronic music—may prove particularly elusive. The central tendency of our sense of beauty may have become fixed by then, and alterations are accomplished with increasing difficulty. That is why "golden oldies" radio stations and classic films exercise an almost hypnotic power over those who were once there, once young.

Note that these limitations in the altering of taste have virtually nothing to do with initial predispositions. The genres that one comes to like (or to loathe) are due almost entirely to one's own experiences of living in one or more cultures during a specific historical era. The norms are emergent, not given. Once they have become entrenched, however, due largely to age and repetition, these norms prove increasingly difficult to alter—constituting a challenge to our emotional as well as to our cognitive systems.

That's the sobering news, but it's not the last word. A growing aversion to "the new" need not be fatal. As I've argued here, the important challenge in the world of arts is the capacity to notice differences. If I am unable to make discriminations within a new art form, medium, or genre, then clearly I cannot relate to it in a meaningful way. But if I can learn to make the consequential distinctions—and any kind of help from any source, human or electronic, is welcome—I've crossed an important line. At least, I understand what the fuss is about. And perhaps—just perhaps—I'll be able to transition from noting the critical difference to being able to enjoy it, even to crave it. Earlier I traced some of my own "changes of tingles" with references to the works of painter Anselm Kiefer and composer Elliott Carter.

Changes in artistic sensibility affect artists as well as members of an audience. For decades, composer Igor Stravinsky could not hide his contempt for the twelve-tone serial music pioneered by his contemporary Arnold Schoenberg. Yet Stravinsky's much younger contemporary, conductor Robert Craft, kept exposing Stravinsky to new serial music. And to everyone's surprise, almost as soon as Schoenberg had died, Stravinsky began to compose in this demanding genre—and, in the view of many, gained a new lease on his composing life. Here's a case, in the realm of beauty, where young and old joined forces in a powerful way. As I write, Elliott Carter has passed the age of one hundred and is still writing compositions that are powerful and beautiful. Having opened up so many musical pathways in earlier decades, he is able to build upon them, synthesize them, and even change them significantly in his second century. (The great evolutionary biologist Ernst Mayr published five books while in his nineties.) The novelist Philip Roth, the poet W. B. Yeats, the painter Gerhard Richter, and the choreographer Merce Cunningham are other artists whose later works spoke to audiences of the time. If one continues to be open to the world and to keep one's instruments of creating in good order, there are no insurmountable barriers to continued aesthetic growth.

In considerations of adult development, the realm of morality and ethics has been marked by controversy. Lawrence Kohlberg—the principal scholar of moral development of recent times—saw moral judgment reaching its high point by the third decade of life. At the "post-conventional" stage, the young adult thinks through moral issues on her own; she is able and willing to oppose the regnant rules and regulations, if these are deemed unjust; for her part, she is also willing to accept the consequences, to engage in civil disobedience in the manner demonstrated by such moral exemplars as Mahatma Gandhi, Martin Luther King Jr., Aung San Suu Kyi, Liu Xiaobo, or Nelson Mandela.

Our own studies suggest, however, that in the "realm of the good," stances develop far more gradually, and may continue to grow and deepen throughout one's active life. Here again, clarity about this realm is enhanced if one honors the distinction between neighborly morality and the ethics of roles.

With respect to neighborly morality, we do not find, nor should we expect to find, important new injunctions. Prescribed and proscribed actions with respect to our neighbors have evolved over tens of thousands of years and are unlikely to change in fundamental respects. Cheating, lying, stealing, maiming, killing—all remain taboo. And yet, it is apparent that the means and the range of neighborly morality are constantly under negotiation. In my lifetime, I have seen my loyalties expand beyond members of my own ethnic group (during childhood, German-Jewish families living in northeastern Pennsylvania) to a much broader sphere, and that shift continues to change and broaden to this day and, I trust, for as long as I live. Many who once distanced themselves from those of different racial or ethnic backgrounds or alternative sexual orientation no longer do so. In many parts of the world, the inclination toward pseudospeciation—the belief that some groups are not truly part of the human family and so do not merit being treated as conspecifics—is on the sharp decline. Yet, it would be naïve to consider these inclusionary trends to be inexorable: Stereotyping and stigmatizing remain powerful human inclinations that can be activated by events or demagogues.

When it comes to "the ethics of roles," the picture is quite different. Changes are the order of the day, and these can continue to jolt many of us. Professions come and go—and once-secure professions, such as print journalism, change in a manner of years, or even months. (In 1993, the *New York Times* paid more than $1 billion for the *Boston Globe*; in 2011, the paper is worth only a small fraction of that amount.) New professions emerge; teams composed of different professions or disciplines have nearly become the norm. Just how to behave, and what to believe, in these altered professional environments has to be a source of continuing change and, no doubt in many cases, continuing confusion. For example, how—in the throes of the 24/7 news cycle—can the journalist take the time to confirm sources? Should the doctor reject a treatment that he has customarily recommended once a prestigious website has declared it ineffective? How do lawyers and agents deal with intellectual property at a time when it is so easy to transmit any and all contents on the Internet? Even professionals who want ardently to do the right thing can be at a loss; if our research group wanted to help them, we'd ideally need a constantly changing "Toolkit" for each profession.

Consider the rapid changes in my own field of psychology. When I announced to my teachers, four decades ago, that I felt it was vital to study the effects of brain damage on cognition, these teachers (whom I still venerate) assured me that I was wasting my time—that little of import about the human mind had been or would be ascertained by the studies of the brain or of damage to the nervous system. Thirty years ago, when I proposed to a funding agency that it support a newly emerging field called cognitive neuroscience, I was dismissed out of hand. Today, no one would dare to take such foolish stances. They are obviously false. Indeed, psychology has given way to cognitive science, and cognitive science is fast giving way to cognitive neuroscience, not to mention cognitive social neuroscience and other splinter sub-disciplines.

Virtually no one can anticipate the ethical issues that arise in newly emerging disciplines like these. What does one do after inadvertently uncovering information about a developing nervous system that suggests a person—perhaps even a fetus or a newborn—is at risk for a learning disability? Particularly a disability for which there is no known effective intervention? How is one to think about the development and marketing of an expensive drug that could significantly improve the attention or memory of a well-heeled student preparing for her college entrance examination? Is it proper to recommend genetic engineering that could enhance the athletic competitiveness of a child? Anyone involved in the helping, measuring, or teaching professions can be—or soon will be—confronted with dilemmas like these. And yet, so far as I know, there is little guidance—no courses in graduate school, no license in neuro- or bioethics—that prepares one to confront these challenges.

In the ideal, the ethics of roles expands over the course of the life cycle. At the workplace, the young adult thinks primarily of responsibility to his boss and to his family; the middle-aged adult thinks more broadly about the responsibility to the organization and to the core values of the profession that she has joined; and the mature adult, whom we dub a "trustee," assumes partial responsibility for the overall health of the profession and its relation to the wider community. A parallel expansion may occur with respect to citizenship. While the young adult thinks primarily in terms of his street or his city, older persons may see themselves as citizens of ever larger collectivities—climaxing, in the most dramatic cases, to the entire planet. It may be useful to think of, and perhaps assemble, an ever expanding and deepening annotated portfolio of experiences in the moral and ethical realms.

With respect to "the good," we again encounter a terrain where young and old can join forces productively. Almost always, new fields of work are populated by younger scholars and practitioners. They know the technical ins-and-outs of the new terrain. Yet neither their own experiences nor their earlier role models necessarily prove of much help in dealing with the "dilemmas of the good" that arise. Older individuals may not have the technical knowledge of the new profession or discipline. Yet, at least in the happiest cases, these mature persons are alert to ethical quagmires and can draw on relevant examples from other, longer-existing realms (as well as designating apparently similar examples that are no longer comparable or no longer relevant). And so, for example, methods and prototypes from medical ethics dating back to the Hippocratic era may provide help-ful clues about how to deal with issues that arise in such newly emerging fields as genetics counseling or neuroeducation. By the same token, modes of speech and action once forged in the Athenian agora can continue to inspire those involved in civil action today.

Though we now realize that development—cognitive, social, emo-tional—can continue throughout one's active life, we must concede that such development is neither certain nor easy. Keeping up with what happens in spheres of interest and concern, reflecting on the meaning of these occurrences, attempting constantly to update one's own understanding are crucial steps. Whether in the realm of truth, beauty, or the good, one must be leery of retaining old habits of thought and action, even if they are comfortable, and remain open to new lines of thought and action, even if they are initially uncomfort-able and threatening. Perhaps in distinctive ways, the attitudes and expertises of young and old can complement one another.

Even if the phrase *postmodernism* had never been uttered, even if we were chugging along without the new digital media, continued productive learning throughout one's life would constitute a formida-ble challenge—or, for those belonging to the "glass half full" cohort, an inviting opportunity. Not all strive for this learning—many are content to remain buried in their foxholes or resting upon their easy chairs. And not all those who so strive will succeed—we smile at the autodidact or the bootstrapping expert who thinks that he has scaled new heights, but who has actually fallen flat on his face! And since (perhaps beneficently) the nervous system does not know what is wrong with it, we are spared the knowledge that we ourselves have failed in efforts to remain informed, current, ahead of the pack.

For those who are not digital natives, and for those who do not keep up with the changes in the speed, style, and delivery of information via new media, continued learning poses ever greater challenges. We risk falling further and further behind those who have mastered the media, who know the latest tricks and have access to the most current "apps," who can combine and synthesize knowledge at an ever more rapid rate. This is one of those areas where the Matthew Effect—"the rich get richer"—reigns supreme. To those with digital intelligence, much is given, and the more that has been given, the greater the cumulative advantage. Immanuel Kant reflected brilliantly on some of the world's greatest enigmas while wending his way around Koenigsberg 250 years ago; but it is anyone's guess whether, in the assimilation and organization of information, he could compete today with a precocious youngster armed with a versatile handheld device.

Older persons can choose to avoid the digital media—at the risk of missing much, if not most, of what is happening in the world, both technologically and substantively. Those of us, no longer young, who venture into the new digital media find much of our worldview challenged. We encounter a plethora of alleged truths on the Internet, the full gamut of moral and ethical codes and mores, and a constant barrage of ever-changing aesthetic presentations that may or may not lead to experiences of beauty. The search for firm truths, universal ethics, a consensus on beauty seems doomed, or at least continually receding.

Yet, as they survey or surf the media, adults are also advantaged. Having knowledge and standards, they can bring these to bear on the copious information that is available. Understanding the nature of claims and counterclaims, of rival forms of expertise, and of the changing nature of understanding, older persons can be in a privileged position to make judgments of truthfulness—not in the sense of absolute or final truths but, rather, in the sense of data or information converging toward truth. And here, those capacities that emerge after adolescence—for systemic thinking, for putting one's own agenda aside—place one in good stead.

Much the same line of reasoning applies to experiences of beauty and choices in the ethical realm. The new digital media present an unending diet of objects and events to apprehend and evaluate. Initially, these can overwhelm. But preparation in one's earlier years can prove an enormous boon. That preparation ought to include some kind of portfolio—tangible, virtual, mnemonic—well stocked with references to earlier experiences. In the case of beauty, that portfolio consists of experiences felt to be beautiful (or instructively not so). In the case of the good, that portfolio consists of one's experiences with ethical dilemmas (successfully navigated or less so). Well-considered judgment can lead to a heightened sense of individual beauty and to better-conceived and substantiated actions at the workplace and in relevant civic spheres.

As I write these words, I recall the apt words of John Gardner (no relation), a treasured mentor. Gardner spoke admiringly of a colleague who had an "uncluttered mind." The abilities to assimilate and absorb quickly may be helped today by access to the latest media and technology; but they do not substitute for clarity of vision, purpose, and method. Take in all the information that you can; organize it as well as you can; but do not lose sight of what is truly important, truly valuable, and how you can use that knowledge in the service of "the good." Here again, older persons, particularly those who have maintained and reflected periodically upon their portfolio of prior experiences, may offer a perspective that is valuable to those who succeed them.

While the rise of the digital media may seem sudden and dramatic—particularly for so-called digital immigrants—the postmodern perspective has been in the air for decades. Accordingly, it proves less surprising and less insidious for most adults. I've argued that the postmodern perspective does not loom menacingly during childhood. Even if the child is regularly exposed to skepticism about the verities (say, she lives in a postmodern household!), that skepticism is unlikely to have much force. After all, what does it mean to reject truth or beauty or goodness if one lacks a full-blown sense of these terms and concepts? And indeed, *the* cognitive assignment of middle childhood, as researchers have come to understand it, is precisely to learn the society's views, the conventional wisdom as it were, with respect to truth, beauty, goodness—their details, their embodiments, their enemies.

Any consensus with respect to the trio is likely to be challenged during adolescence—unless such defiance is forbidden by a totalitarian or fundamentalist community. Teenagers are able to think of the world in ways other than it is, and this cognitive advance means that received wisdoms do not automatically receive a "pass." That is why protest marches are common for fifteen-year-olds, much less so for five-year-olds or fifty-year-olds. As the years mount, the realities of earning a living, raising a family, fighting the ravages of aging and disease come to the fore; the luxury of challenging the status quo becomes the province of a minority elect—if indeed that minority is allowed to express itself. For every aging *enfant terrible*, there are legions who march steadily into the ranks of old farts. As Winston Churchill famously quipped, "If a young man is not a socialist by the time he is 20, he has no heart. . . . [I]f he is not a conservative by the time he is 40, he has no brain."

(Note the difficulty of determining the truth these days. When I looked up this quotation on the web, I found versions of it attributed to Georges Clemenceau, Benjamin Disraeli, David Lloyd-George, George Bernard Shaw, and Woodrow Wilson. Clearly it is a saying that is all too readily attributed to a certain kind of politically aware middle-aged Western male living in a democratic society [particularly if he happens to be named George!]. But if I am right, one should ultimately be able to discover the author of these words, if not the sentiment.)

Old hat or new wine, the "postmodern perspective" is here to stay. It exerts an effect on individuals of all ages, whether they've read the relevant works or never heard the relevant words. Like a bobo doll that keeps bouncing back to rubbery equilibrium each time it has been knocked to the floor, the reservations and reversals embodied in post-modern thought cannot be permanently stifled. Indeed, thanks to the digital media, these doubts are more insistent than ever. One advantage accruing to adults is that they are probably familiar with the critique and so can put it into perspective. While a challenge to the very possibility of truth may seduce a teenager for a time, it is more likely to be taken in stride by those who have "been there before."

What happens during the adult years when the postmodern critique intersects with the virtues of the beautiful and the good? With reference to beauty, it becomes all too easy to proclaim "de gustibus non est disputandum." But then one is left with the unpalatable conclusion that anyone can like anything, for any reason; and that there is not even the possibility—let alone the legitimacy—of agreement among individuals. With respect to art and entertainment, people can always vote with their feet—deciding which events to attend, which objects to buy, when to toss fragrant bouquets or to hurl rotten tomatoes onto the stage. But the risk exists, particularly as we age, of ignoring new objects and experiences that might be meritorious—and simply becoming creatures of habit, continuing to favor the same artists, the same works, the same theaters, even the same seats and the same refreshments.

In this regard, the new digital media can provide help. Nowadays, one can easily access hundreds, thousands, even tens of thousands of critiques of what is beautiful (and you can substitute whatever evaluative adjective you favor). Indeed, it is easy to be exposed to any and—it sometimes seems—all individuals' senses of what they value and why. Moreover, other persons on one's aesthetic wavelengths, or neural networks programmed with respect to one's preferences, can offer a steady diet of objects and experiences that one should be predisposed to like. One's current satisfaction quotient may go up. But perhaps one ought deliberately to instruct these human or computational "nudgers" to stretch a bit—offering not just those items that one has a 90 percent chance of liking but also those where the batting average may be lower, yet with concomitant rewards that may enlarge your consciousness, increase the secretion of serotonin, and heighten your chances of flow. On such an account, each individual has the option of determining how open or closed he wishes to be with respect to new aesthetic offerings.

A continuing development of a sense of beauty rests on a broadening notion of artistic merit. As I argued earlier, beauty in the classical sense, indeed beauty in any sense, need not be *the* arbiter of works of art. Features such as interest, memorability of form, the potential to induce awe are equally valid considerations; one's own pleasure zone can pleasurably extend as one adopts a more latitudinarian stance. The risk, of course, is abject resignation with respect to *any* standards—the conclusion that "anything goes," the refusal to render any judgment of beauty or merit. Happily, however powerful as a rhetorical stance, such a position proves to be impossible in practice. As human beings, we will make choices, establish preferences, sometimes change them; we may as well proceed in as informed and open a way as possible.

So long as they remain open to new aesthetic experiences, adults can look forward to happy outcomes with respect to the realm of beauty. If adults have the motivation to take advantage of new media, exploring unfamiliar works of art, surveying a range of praise and criticism, and then stepping back and forming their own judgments, the prospect of a genuine individualized sense of beauty is enhanced. No new cognitive capacities are needed here—voluntary exposure to new experiences starts early in life and has no statute of limitations. But the capacities to see one's whole self clearly—not as one would like to be seen *but* as one actually is—and to discern both similarities *and* differences from others—lay the groundwork for a personal sense of beauty. And so long as one keeps an open mind, that sense of beauty can continually be altered and enhanced.

Which leaves us to ponder the headline "Morals and Ethics Meet the Postmodern Challenge." For most observers, the postmodern challenge has been most salient with respect to the moral sphere, broadly conceived. All but the most benighted are aware that people, groups, cultures, differ deeply in their views about how to live; what boundaries to honor; what is appropriate with respect to worship, sex before or outside of marriage, sexual preference, polygamy, contraception, the death penalty, euthanasia, collective guilt, and a host of other "hot button" issues. And even when there appears to be a consensus or near consensus within a particular community or nation (say, for the sake of argument, in Dubai or Poland or Costa Rica), one simply has to cross a border or traverse a body of water to encounter—head on—cultures or subcultures with radically different views of what is proper, what is acceptable, what is taboo.

How these contrasts are dealt with differs dramatically across individuals and societies. The gamut runs from the defiant intolerance displayed by a fundamentalist group like the Taliban to the perhaps too-forgiving stance of Scandinavians—at least before an influx of immigrants from a multitude of cultures put the fabled Scandinavian tolerance to an unprecedented test. The head of a Muslim family kills his unmarried daughter because, willingly or not, she has had sexual relations with a Swedish male. As justification, the father explains that this putative murderous act draws on, in fact is dictated by, his deepest religious belief systems, thereby challenging the mores of northern Europe. Practices of neighborly morality clash head on with universalist views of citizenship. And of course, within the host society, individual reactions differ, even within families.

In the area of ethics and morals, as in other areas, individuals can and do change their minds in the later decades of life. To take a personal example, I used to believe that freedom of the press was paramount and that the press could and should publish as it wishes. In 2005 a Danish newspaper published a set of cartoons that ridiculed Islam. The reaction was swift. There were riots in several Islamic cities, people lost their lives, serious threats were lodged against the offending cartoonist and the editor who permitted their publication. These severe consequences caused me to change my mind. I now believe that the press should not publish needlessly inflammatory materials—in this case, cartoons that ridicule religious leaders and icons. The press should be able to express its opinions freely and honestly but should do so in clear and unambiguous language, not through inflammatory graphic imagery and caricature. As I put it, freedom of the press remains an important value—indeed, a core value of the profession of journalism. But pursuing a utilitarian or consequentialist line of argument, I also believe that on some occasions the press should engage in self-censorship. Here a universal ethical principle gives way to more traditional or parochial forms of morality.

(Of course, in these days of the Internet, any and all images will be circulated—no way to stop it. And so it is necessary to introduce a distinction between the responsible press and the other—call it "irresponsible"—press. On my revised ethics, the responsible press can continue to publish all views, but should take special efforts to do so in ways that are not needlessly incendiary.)

The potential to change one's mind with respect to the virtues remains important throughout the life cycle. Perhaps, as a thoughtful adult, one should not easily change one's mind, particularly on issues where a wide consensus has obtained among informed individuals and where one has long held a certain point of view. Yet, one should equally avoid the stance of the fundamentalist. (As noted earlier, when I use the term *fundamentalist* I do not refer to a person of rigid religious beliefs. Rather, I use the term to designate *any* individual who makes a commitment *not* to change his mind on any topic—or indeed on all topics.) It is rarely worth spending time trying to change the mind of a fundamentalist, because he has committed himself irrevocably to a totally different set of assumptions.

An individual is least open to changing his or her mind when three conditions obtain: (1) One has had a long-term adherence to a particular view; (2) that view contains a strong emotional or affective component; and (3) one has taken a public position on that view. Conversely, when a viewpoint is relatively new, is not accompanied by deep-seated emotions, and has been kept private, changes of mind are less difficult to effect.

Individuals, groups, and cultures will differ on which spheres afford easy mind changes, and which prove more refractory to change. Judgments of truth depend largely on the sphere in question. They are probably easiest to change with respect to areas of knowledge about which one knows little (e.g., how many strings in superstring theory, how to secure a certain sound on a Chinese string instrument), and correlatively more difficult as one becomes more knowledgeable and as the issues impact one's own life. As a general rule, judgments and experiences of beauty are the easiest to change, because one's relations to others are less likely to be at stake—unless one happens to be a widely known artist or critic.

In contrast, the areas of morality and ethics may prove most difficult to invade and alter—views tend to persist, to carry strong emotional overtones, and, especially as one becomes responsible to or for others, to offer occasions for public pronouncements. Often, the moral values are part and parcel of a religious position to which the individual has a long and strong emotional bond. It takes a truly dramatic event—say, the discovery by a homophobe that one or more of his *own* offspring are gay—to trigger or facilitate a change of mind in the moral arena.

At times, however, mind change with respect to ethical issues is possible through less dramatic interventions. Occasionally one meets and likes someone from a determinedly different walk of life. In the course of spending time together, one gradually discovers that this person has views quite different from one's own. At such times, it is possible to have conversations that change one or even both minds. Robert Wright speaks of such encounters as the exercise of "moral imagination"—the capacity to put oneself in someone else's shoes. Commissions on Peace and Reconciliation in war-torn societies build on this potential of human intercourse. The capacity for such empathy need not decline over the life span—and perhaps in the best instance, it can even flourish, particularly if one remains alert to the experiences of others. That is what appears to have happened in the case of former presidents John Adams and Thomas Jefferson. Long bitter foes, they reconciled and even found themselves more often in agreement as the decades passed.

One other reason to remain open to mind changes: Sometimes, nearly everyone happens to be wrong. Despite the seemingly entrenched consensus that financial markets will inevitably correct themselves, more than one great financial upheaval has occurred in less than a century. Despite the belief that the end of the Cold War spelled the triumph of democratic capitalism, state capitalism is now in the ascendancy. I will not forget what the notable scholar of linguistics Noam Chomsky once told me: "I never accept anyone else's word about anything." Accumulating experiences that one has been wrong, or that others have been wrong, may make one more willing to consider alternative descriptions of reality. Modesty and flexibility do not particularly correlate with age: They reflect traits that one can either denigrate or cultivate.

Life lasts longer nowadays for most of us than it did in earlier eras. And exposure to a range of propositions, experiences, and values has never been greater. Those with flexible minds, with open minds, are at a distinct advantage overall, as contrasted to those who want to adhere to every word uttered by their mother and father, if not to every word of the Holy Mother and the Holy Father. So are those who know how their own mind works and can marshal that metacognitive knowledge in cases where the course to pursue is not clear. Finally those who have greater distance from themselves may, paradoxically, come to understand better the ways in which they are truly distinctive. They may also be in a better position to determine what they can learn from the young, and what they might transmit to the young.

As I've argued here, our era has ushered in a playing field that puts younger and older persons in an admirably complementary position. Adolescents and young adults generally have a mastery of the new media; they also have grown up in a world where postmodern ideas of diversity, relativism, and skepticism are part of the intellectual atmosphere. For their part, adults have had far more experience in making judgments in their areas of expertise, the realm of beauty, the spheres of work and civic action. Moreover, particularly if they have accumulated and kept track of their learnings, they can bring a soundness of judgment to the trio of virtues that complements the greater vigor and learning capacity of young persons. Working together, young and old can master the media and the varieties of modernist thought, rather than being overwhelmed by them.

Such complementarity and synergy represent an inspiring aspiration. Yet, sooner or later, we all must come to grips with our own mortality. Writer Albert Camus may have exaggerated when he declared that "there is but one truly serious philosophical problem and that is suicide." But it takes a truly benighted individual to ignore the reality that he or she may die at any moment, and, barring a bizarre circumstance, is likely to die before his or her descendants. Initial proclivities are long past; societal norms have long since been absorbed; the inexorable forces of biological decomposition, gradual or aggressive, with or without concomitant cognitive decline, come to the fore. One's own growth is at or near an end; the focus shifts toward what younger persons can learn from the words and the examples of elders.

As conceived by my teacher Erik Erikson, the final years of life are characterized by a struggle between feelings of integrity and feelings of despair. The individual ponders the ways in which his life has made sense to himself and to others, the contributions he has made, as well the hurts, physical or psychological, short term or more long lasting, intentional or not, that he may have inflicted on others. He ponders as well his own aspirations and missions, where he has succeeded and where he has fallen short of his own or another's (or of still others') wishes. And assuming that he lives in a community that is supportive or at least attentive, others will be curious to learn just what he has valued, and why, and which lessons he would pass on to future generations. Of course, this "demand" is greater in societies that move slowly, and where elders are honored for their wisdom, than it is in societies, like most today, that move rapidly, have little memory for the past, and are attracted to the young, the swift, the facile, and the novel, be it exemplary or egregious. Nevertheless, particularly at trying times, the lessons of experience prove valuable, if not invaluable.

And so, if we are to look to those who are long-lived or deeply lived, which configuration of virtues is most vital to cherish and to pass on? I would single out two: the practical truths of a life that was lived well, and the morals and ethics of a life that served others. To some extent, these truths and good-nesses can be verbalized, and that is why we sometimes hang on to the words of those who are about to depart. But far more powerfully, it is the lives rather than the words of these elders that attract our attention and, as appropriate, activate our moral imaginations.

It is a source of regret to me that so many young people today find no one to admire, or restrict their admiration to individuals known only to them and their immediate circle. I am gratified that I can look to twentieth-century public figures like John Gardner or Eleanor Roosevelt or Mahatma Gandhi or, in the contemporary world, to Burmese dissident Aung San Suu Kyi, cellist Yo-Yo Ma, social entrepreneur

William Drayton, scientist and naturalist Jane Goodall, philanthropist George Soros, pioneering microfinancier Muhammad Yunus—and admire the truths that they discovered or affirmed, the beauties that they admired or created, and the values that they embodied and passed on to the young. The generations of our world would be diminished in the absence of the models that they have provided. And it is worth underscoring, as well, that these admirable figures have continued to seek out, and to learn from, the lively young in their midst. In this way, they epitomize that complementarity between younger and elder persons that may well be at a particular premium in our postmodern, digital era.

Conclusion | # Looking Ahead

At the outset of this book, I contrasted the austere splendor and unity of the Middle Ages, as portrayed by historian Henry Adams, with the pastiche of direct quotations, paraphrases, and putatively original materials collated by the contemporary author David Shields. The worldviews presented in these works could not be more different. Adams assumed that, at least in the ideal, there can exist a world that is true, beautiful, and good—and at a single historical moment. The passages selected by Shields present a contrasting perspective: extreme skepticism that these virtues make sense today.

I've wondered whether, if Adams and Shields could somehow be brought together, they would have anything to say to one another. Adams could hardly bear the America of a century ago. In contrast, Shields seems fully to embrace the artistic possibilities of the contemporary world—the incredible capacity of the digital media to combine and recombine all matter of literary and graphic creations. He appears as well to accept the major tenets of postmodernism. I was therefore somewhat surprised to discover, while surfing the Internet, that Henry Adams's autobiography *The Education of Henry Adams* is one of the books most admired by David Shields. Whether or not Adams would have any use for Shields's ideas, we can assume that Shields would at least pay his respects to a literary master of an earlier era.

My undertaking here has been to navigate between the nostalgic utopianism of Adams, on the one hand, and the postmodern skepticism and literary latitudinarianism of Shields, on the other. Perhaps both would be offended by my efforts. Adams would likely see me as far too accepting of recent challenges to truth, beauty, and goodness. He would have no use, I suspect, for the epistemological chaos concerned with the new digital media. (It's hard to picture him with a cell phone or a personal computer.) For his part, Shields would likely see me as retrograde for having put forth and defended my own versions of truth, beauty, and goodness, and as lamentably unappreciative of the literary achievement of an "assembled work" like *Reality Hunger*.

Whatever the verdicts issued by Adams or Shields, I do believe that my enterprise is justified. The virtues need to be reframed in the current era, using the analytic and disciplinary tools most appropriate for the task at hand. I've focused on the two factors—one epistemological, one technological—that seem especially challenging to traditional perspectives. But I must emphasize that the trends observed today are not products exclusively of postmodern thought or the digital media. Uncertainties about the nature of truth, beauty, or goodness have been raised since classical times (indeed, formed the basis of much of Socrates' dialogues and Plato's writings). Throughout history, one can find thoughtful teachers, philosophers, and artists who have wrestled with many of the issues raised in these pages. A history of human thought could be formulated in terms of the constant and the changing facets of truth, beauty, and goodness: to borrow a phrase from the humanities—three great chains of being.

Yet, I would not have written this book just to pour new wine into old bottles. Arguments and perspectives that may once have been clear to some philosophers and to some artists are now part of common discourse, at least throughout the developed world. One could quibble about whether the differences are better characterized as quantitative (increased skepticism about truth, greater reluctance to talk about beauty, more awareness of different senses of the good) or qualitative or, indeed, quantum leaps. I'm content to characterize them as significant, worthy of extended treatment, containing ample promise but also considerable peril.

Over time, I have changed my mind more than once about the productive and the destructive aspects of both postmodernism and the digital media. I believe that all reflective individuals need to be exposed to the postmodern critique and to engage with its tenets and implications. In that sense the critique can be salutary. Yet, to the extent that skepticism about these concepts closes off considerations of what might be valuable in time-tested views of truth, beauty, and goodness, it can be destructive. Perhaps, I've suggested, there can be a productive synergy between the abundant if irreverent energies of young persons, on the one hand, and the accumulated experiences of their elders, on the other.

All things considered, I am upbeat about the potentials of the new digital media. Initially, they can overwhelm and appear to place the virtues in constant if not permanent jeopardy. But in the end, all three of the virtues can be strengthened by dint of their positions in the digital media sphere. Chances are enhanced for more firmly grounded truth; possibilities abound for a meaningful personal sense of beauty; and our burgeoning contacts with the full swathe of humanity could lead, ultimately, to a shared sense of goodness.

Yet, I scarcely take these outcomes for granted. To put it baldly, we have plenty of potential to screw things up. One motive for writing this book, at this time, and in this way, is to lay out some of the more positive potentials of the new media and to suggest how they might be realized with our students, our youth, ourselves.

The postmodern and digital challenges weigh differently on each of the three virtues—the dangers and opportunities they pose vary from realm to realm, and our responses to these challenges should vary accordingly. To many people, the search for truth or truths seems clear enough. We can argue about whether there is one truth or more than one truth, and how firmly truths can be established. But unless you do not believe in reality, in the way(s) that things are (or are not) and the way(s) that they can be described, the search for truth(s) seems reasonable. As disciplines, the sciences have certainly established truths; by the same token, practitioners in any domain that has been around for a while can chronicle the practical truths that have stood the test of time. These processes should and will continue.

Similarly, every society, and, indeed, every individual, has some sense of what it means to be good, and some thoughts about how to achieve the good. As we learn more about different religions, belief systems, and cultural practices, we come to appreciate that our sense of good may not be the same as that held by other persons or other cohorts, in other places and at other times. And as societies become more complex, we need delineations of the good with respect to specific professions and varieties of citizenship. And so we may or may not succeed in arriving at a consensual view of the good. But the search for the good, the drive to struggle over different ideas of the good, and the hope that some kind of workable consensus might arise remain essential. These impulses date back almost as far as the written record. They will almost certainly remain with us as long as there are thinking and feeling human beings attempting to inhabit—rather than to destroy—a single, small planet.

Beauty poses a host of issues that seem less salient with reference to the other virtues. First of all, there is the question—discussed at some length in these pages—as to whether our sense of beauty has a biological basis or whether it is largely or even wholly determined by our cultural environment. Perhaps the truth of the matter lies somewhere in between—which only raises more questions. Even if there is a biological basis for initial judgments about the beauty of specific objects and experiences, to what extent can these judgments be altered?

Then there is the question of the *realm* of beauty. In this work, I focus almost entirely on works of art, but certainly natural elements (like mountains or lakes or forests) appear beautiful to people, and other human inventions (scientific theories, mathematical proofs) are often considered beautiful as well. We must ask whether these realms would require separate treatments of beauty.

Given my focus on the arts, the issue arises of whether fashioning of beauty is—or ought to be—the purpose of art. In the past, and across cultures, there was widespread consensus that the arts (or their equivalent, if the word did not exist) were dedicated to the creation of beautiful experiences—and considerable consensus on what constituted beauty. Irrespective of whether the production of beauty was preeminent for the artist, the experience of beauty was clearly a cardinal motivator for most audience members. Nowadays, however, owing in significant measure to technologies both new (computers) and not-so-new (cameras, records), beauty per se is far less salient in the arts. Features such as the interest of the ideas and concepts, and the memorability of the form in which these are presented, have become correspondingly more important.

The experience of beauty in the realm of the arts therefore does not completely parallel the accumulation of propositions in the realm of truth, nor the status of human relations in the realm of the good. The course of beauty is far less predictable, and the opportunity for an individualized experience of beauty is far greater, than is the case with the other pair of virtues. Perhaps, indeed, the definition of beauty is a moving target. Also, to put it crisply, beauty is less a matter of life and death than are the other virtues. Agreeing on the good, and protecting against evil, are important for survival. It is equally vital to be able to distinguish truth from falsehood.

Yet, experiences of beauty remain among the principal reasons for being alive, for wanting to remain alive, for sharing the joys of living with others. To be sure, from the point of view of evolutionary theory, our job on earth is simply to reproduce abundantly and then get out of the way. But once we go beyond sheer survival—and most of us are fortunate to be in that position—the quality of one's life proves of the essence. And a life bereft of beauty—or, if you prefer, without the potential for beautiful experiences—is empty.

And so by no means is there an identical "story" for the three virtues. The story of truth is convergent and confirmatory. The story of beauty is divergent, reflecting endless unpredictable variation, with the possibility of diverse meaningful personal experiences. The story of goodness proceeds on two different planes, the first (neighborhood morality) far more entrenched than the second (the ethics of roles). To put the matter in the vocabulary of this book, while we can remain divergent with respect to cultural conventions and local customs, it is imperative that we retain neighborly morality and converge with respect to ethical concerns and judgments.

What, then, might the future hold for our three virtues? With respect to truth, I anticipate continuing debate: Are we converging on a single or small set of truths, or will there be an ever greater plurality of truths, drawn from different disciplines and perhaps in some sense incommensurate with one another? In the postmodern spirit there will continue to be voices that insist on the predominance of hegemony and struggle. According to this account: Rather than disinterested pursuit of truth, even at the cost of one's own personal stake, we are best off simply allowing alternative political, economic, social, and cultural positions to contend—and may the most rhetorically convincing contender prevail!

The peril that I discern is well epitomized by Wikipedia. No one has an explicit mandate to evaluate the truth of entries in this web-based resource. The measure of acceptability is whether a statement has appeared in some other publication. Wikipedia simply represents the current consensual view of a subject—neither expertise nor truth per se enters into the equation. And so, even if inadvertently, this remarkable creation represents the triumph of digital media in a post-modern garb.

Indeed, for many young people (and some who are no longer young), the actual truth value of statements is no longer privileged. These persons are interested principally in authenticity (Does the speaker *seem* real, committed, engaged?) and in transparency (Does the speaker reveal where he or she is coming from, or does she dissemble or hide?). Should these trends continue, then sheer truthfulness may become less important. Still, the idea of transparency rests on the assumption that there *is* an underlying truth, which one either foregrounds or shields. Transparency depends on—indeed presupposes—tests of truthfulness. In the end, a position that brackets truth harbors its own destruction, if not its own self-contradiction.

Moving on to our second virtue, we have survived the period in which "beauty" was effectively banished from the lexicon of "art talk." (To be sure, it was never banished as a personal experience, as can be testified by anyone who has ever eavesdropped on visitors at a museum of fine arts, a national park, or a venerable tourist attraction.) For nearly all individuals, emanating from nearly all groups, certain objects and experiences—family portraits, evening entertainment, athletic contests, high art—will continue to hold a special place, a place in which interestingness, memorability of form, and pleasurable feeling somehow come together and invite further exploration. However, the *kinds* of experiences that are judged to be beautiful, by individuals and by groups, will vary, often unpredictably, because the history, culture, technologies, and vagaries of art cannot be predicted—and I am personally grateful to the Fates that this is the case.

Before the fact, who could have predicted the revolutionary effects of Pablo Picasso's paintings, T. S. Eliot's poems, Igor Stravinsky's compositions, Martha Graham's dances—and the speed with which they were absorbed into the canon? In other words, I would put my money on the Survival of Beauty long before I put my money on the Science of Beauty. At the same time, beauty per se has probably relinquished, for all time, its preeminent position in determining membership in the pantheon of Great Art.

Our notions of goodness, in the individual moral sense, are far more entrenched than our conceptions of beauty. What we expect of friends and neighbors, and what they expect of us, has not fundamentally altered over the centuries—though we are perhaps more tolerant in some ways and less tolerant in others. In an era of many weak ties, and virtually unrestrained mobility, we may well be less accountable than we once were; but the basics of the Golden Rule and the Ten Commandments need not be recalibrated.

Yet in the recent past, ethical life has become much more complicated, due to the diverse and frequently altering professional and civic roles that individuals occupy in complex, highly differentiated societies. Insights from biology, anthropology, or history cannot provide reliable guidance about how to assume these roles in a responsible manner. These professional and civic spheres, and the problems and puzzles that they spawn, are novel and complex; their solutions cannot be readily deduced from what has been done before and how it has been articulated. Over the decades, rough-and-ready norms can develop—as has happened, for example, in professions like journalism or architecture, and with respect to membership in democratic states or in supranational entities like the European Union. But rarely are these instances ones of black and white; all too often one is weighing one "right" against another, or choosing the lesser of two evils.

The centrifugal forces at work here are great, and at times parties may conclude that they have to "agree to disagree." Yet if ever there were a case where pressures to reach consensus will mount, it is in the fulfillment of the ethics of roles. We cannot have a viable global society in which professions or businesses in each nation, let alone in each community, go their own way. Nor can we deal with issues like the spread of disease, the threats of terrorism, the realities of climate change, and the need for fiscal responsibility and transparency on a nation-by-nation or even region-by-region basis. As Benjamin Franklin quipped at the signing of the Declaration of Independence, "We must indeed all hang together, or, most assuredly, we shall all hang separately."

The realm of "the good" is threatened by antipodal forces: a mindless absolutism, on the one hand, and a feckless cultural relativism, on the other. We cannot legislate goodness from on high, but we also should not throw up our hands in resignation and simply declare "Whatever." Postmodernist critiques are appropriately cautionary and occasionally devastating, but they cannot be allowed to become decisive. The digital media can play a positive role in exposing us to a range of alternatives, in presenting for debate the diverse views of "the good," and in modeling practices that have proved effective beyond our borders and outside our consciousness. An abundant supply of "best practices" on the part of the media may be necessary, but it cannot suffice.

Ultimately, we require a deep and continuing dialogue between citizens, on the one hand, and media practitioners (who aspire to be professionals), on the other. To the extent that citizens call for broad and well-rounded presentations of alternatives, this message pressures or frees media to be even-handed and comprehensive. But to the extent that citizens do not fill their roles responsibly—are indifferent or fixated on celebrities or interested only in dredging up support for their opinions and prejudices—the media will simply expand the fog of ignorance and prejudice.

My own belief—more properly, my own hope—is that the inexorable facts of globalization will ultimately prod individuals, groups, and institutions to search for a "good" that transcends individual borders or any single, received sense of moral absolutes. This emerging "good" need not be purchased at the cost of distinctive and diverse local practices, so long as the pursuit of the local does not undercut the imperative to seek transcultural consensus on the most pressing issues of the time. In other words, maximum latitude or divergence with respect to matters of convenience and convention, gradual convergence with respect to ethical standards.

The concurrence of postmodernism and the digital media may, ironically, hold out the potential for a second age of Enlightenment. Toward the end of the eighteenth century, thinkers in Europe and in the emerging American nations were inspired by the operation of reason tempered by skepticism, the decline of prejudice and the rise of tolerance, the pursuit of scientific understanding, the realities of technological progress, and the emergence of well-designed, robust institutions. These and other factors led to a view of the human condition that was hopeful and that could be realized on a universal scale—where all had the right to life, liberty, and the pursuit of happiness. Despite the wrenching transformations of the nineteenth and twentieth centuries, this conception has remained alive. It undergirds institutions like the United Nations and highly regarded documents like the Universal Declaration of Human Rights.

Without question: two cheers for the Enlightenment, but not yet three. For all its brilliance, the Enlightenment remains far too Western in its conceptualization. The ideas of the Enlightenment are not literally universal; they were forged largely in Western Europe, by a small group of articulate and influential philosophers and philosophes, all males, of course, nearly all practicing Christians. If we are to have an ethical framework that is truly universal, it needs to take into account, to build upon, to incorporate powerful ideas and concepts from other

significant philosophical and religious traditions, ranging from Confu-
cianism to Islam, from Buddhism to secular humanism, and not ex-
cluding key precepts and practices emanating from the indigenous
populations of the several continents. Profound wisdom characterizes
many cultural traditions. In various guises and places, this task has
begun—but if it is to solidify and to gain widespread approval, its
achievement will require sustained dialogue, mutual learning, and
generous amounts of humility.

No one acquainted with history could predict with confidence the
fate of our three virtues. With respect to truth, who could have anticipated the indeterminacy of quantum mechanics or the laws of non-
Euclidean geometry? With respect to beauty, what does one make of
a century that began with Marcel Duchamps's urinal and ended with
Damien Hirst's shark? And with respect to goodness, what sense do
we make of a time (our own) when a father carries out an "honor
killing" of his daughter while a team of scientists attempts to clone a
human being? Writer Virginia Woolf once declared that "[o]n or
about December 1910, human character changed." Granting poetic
license, this statement captures well the unexpected forms and formats that our species has assumed in the past century.

Yet, if futurology is a risky profession, history is a necessary one.
Those ignorant of history are condemned to repeat it. Equally imperative is philosophy. We all have underlying philosophies of life and
knowledge—the only difference is whether or not we are aware of
them. Without the insights of science and the fruits of technology, we
would still be living in the Dark Ages—literally and metaphorically. In
this book, I have applied some contemporary lenses to a set of ancient concepts. I cannot claim to know the future fate of these concepts, individually or corporately. But I can state with confidence that
they will continue to be important, that they will have to assimilate
newly emerging entities like postmodernism and digital media, and
that the analytic tools on which I've drawn here will continue to be

relevant. Just how they will be brought to bear, and what conclusions will be drawn, I cannot say.

In the opening pages of this book, I described this inquiry as inherently multidisciplinary. And I have kept my word! At various points and in various places, I have drawn on history and prehistory (for example, with respect to the origins of writing and of philosophy); biology and evolutionary psychology (to explain why certain scenes are attractive to human beings around the globe, but also why this truth does not begin to account for the power of individual works of art); sociology and anthropology (the tastes and predilections of different groups, for example, with reference to canons of beauty); humanistic scholarship (descriptions and evaluations of specific events and works); and three strands of philosophy—epistemology (the nature of statements reflecting our knowledge), aesthetics (judgments of beauty and other valued qualities), and ethics (the beliefs and actions that humans ought to pursue). This disciplinary quiver may be more abundantly stocked than one would like, but I don't see how one can do justice to the ensemble of issues without taking into account key scholarly perspectives, individually and corporately.

Yet, I have been critical of two perspectives that have in recent years dominated much of scholarly discourse. From the realms of biology and psychology, many scholars have sought to explain human thought and behavior through the lens of evolutionary psychology (some decades ago, called sociobiology). Doubtless, our evolutionary past and our biological present place certain limits on what we can conceive and what we can do. Darwinian concepts have been vital in helping to define and account for those limits. And yet, I have insisted throughout that the issues most important to the present task gain relatively little purchase from the evolutionary lens.

Our search for truth, and our capacity to evaluate truths, relies on our sensory organs initially. But ultimately, the quest for truth is far more dependent on statements and sets of statements that are verified through informal practice and systematic scientific or scholarly investigations. Provisional and more firmly established truths emerge from human beings working together to make sense of their world. Likewise, our experiences of beauty may initially foreground features of environments friendly to our hominid ancestors; but those canons are soon overwhelmed by the history, customs, practices, and accidents of the particular collectivities in which we and our forebears lived. And while our moral stances toward neighbors draw on evolutionary constraints, our ethical stances have emerged far more recently, primarily through the interactions among reflective workers in the several professions, and through comparable interactions among responsible leaders and citizens in various political jurisdictions.

Lurking in the background of much contemporary discourse has been another powerful discipline—mainstream economics. Over the decades economic consensus has rested on two widespread assumptions: the wisdom, or even the perfection, of the market; and the rationality of "*Homo economicus*." But empirical studies by psychologists, sometimes collaborating with economists, have almost completely undermined the view of human beings as fundamentally rational creatures. We operate via heuristics, and not by statistical computations; not infrequently we are quite irrational. And of course, frequent though unpredictable meltdowns—most recently in September 2008—give the lie to any coherent notion of the inherent wisdom of the market. "Chaos" or "wild swings" or "irrational exuberance" seem more accurate descriptors.

Asked to characterize human beings, I assume neither rationality nor irrationality. I believe that rationality is a hard-worn victory but that humans have the capacity to enhance their reasoning powers and deploy them judiciously, particularly if they are aware of, and vigilant with respect to, the traps of irrationality and self-delusion. I have long admired Freud's statement that "[t]he voice of the intellect is quiet but it does not rest until it is heard." Humans are not inherently rational but can develop their rational muscle. With respect to goodness, markets are not inherently wise but human beings can attempt to regulate them wisely. After all, those countries that had regulations firmly in place—for example, Australia, Canada, Chile, Singapore—have so far fared the best in the aftermath of the most recent financial meltdowns.

I see this "market perspective"—particularly when extended beyond the village marketplace—as inimical to the achievement of the virtues. Truth should not be a product of a formal vote or an informal consensus of what "feels" right: It should be the emergent product of propositions that have been tested and tested again. Beauty is not what most people admire or indeed pay for; rather, it is a description of the phenomenal experiences of individuals—be it a couple or a multitude—in the presence of objects and events.

Finally, the market is not the mechanism *par excellence* by which the "good" of excellence, engagement, and ethics should be determined. At most it should be factored in along with other considerations, ranging from reason to religion. For inspiration on these matters I look instead to three redoubtable thinkers. Echoing Thomas Hobbes, I believe that a world governed solely by market forces is likely to be "nasty, brutish, and short." What makes us human in the best sense is our potential to go *beyond* individual self-interest and to think instead about what makes sense in terms of the general welfare, the common weal. Those who cite Adam Smith in favor of unfettered markets forget that he presupposed a citizenry that embodied "moral sentiments." And it is inspiring to recall the words of anthropologist Margaret Mead: "Never doubt that a small group of committed people can change the world. Indeed, it is the only thing that ever has."

Whatever their vogue in today's academy (and its chattering classes), neither evolutionary psychology nor mainstream economics has much to say with respect to the two contemporary forces that we've been examining here. Postmodernism has no more patience for the assertions of evolutionary psychology or of economics than it does for the assertions of any other scholarly discipline—except perhaps the one called deconstructionism. And the speed, complexity, and intricacies of the new digital media would have perplexed Charles Darwin and Adam Smith as much as they have confounded commentators in our own time. We are all in uncharted territory: An amalgam of disciplines, judiciously titrated, is more likely to be illuminating than bets placed on any single scholarly lens.

Looking ahead, there is every reason to believe that we will continue to need an armamentarium of existing disciplines to understand our world and, no doubt, new iterations that emerge. These disciplines, I believe, can temper the current prominence of evolutionary and economic accounts. As more groups of human beings become visible and vocal, anthropological and sociological lenses will loom large. No longer are certain groups invisible; no longer are societies dominated by a single gender or a single racial or ethnic group; diversity reigns supreme, and a wide spectrum of voices will be heard (as they should be).

At one time, history was largely political and military—a narrative of victors and victories, punctuated by those men who commanded their ranks. Now, of course, we have all kinds of subfields, ranging from economic history to social history to the history of groups, like African-Americans or Hispanic-Americans or women. Such clusters of history will continue to be written and rewritten. Whether or not we continue to hold a printed paper in our hands, journalists will continue to fashion the first draft of history. As such, these historians of the contemporary scene will tell us what is happening and seek to explain its significance. To their ranks will be added bloggers and other instant chroniclers. It will be crucial to devise criteria by which to judge these new entrants to the realm of historical and journalistic documentation; otherwise "anything goes," a situation that may please full-blown postmodernists and uncritical digerati but is destined to frustrate the rest of us.

Working in tandem to the aforementioned disciplinarians are scholars in the humanities. Rather than focusing on the sequence of events (natural or historical) and their possible causal relations, humanists direct their attention and analytic skills to specific events and specific works—how they have been achieved, how they come to harbor often diverse meanings (and what those meanings might be), and how they fit into the landscape of their era. Sometimes, the humanists illuminate a specific work, like *Guernica* or *Moby Dick*; sometimes they clarify an epoch, like the classical or romantic era; and sometimes they challenge our received classificatory systems, as did the chroniclers of the exhibition *Design and the Elastic Mind*. So long as human artifacts matter, humanistic scholars will be essential handmaidens in their interpretation.

One of the most alarming aspects of reductionism—whether of the natural scientific (evolutionary theory) or social scientific (economic analyses) varieties—is the sometime implication that humanistic study is expendable. (This is no idle threat: Fewer than 5 percent of university students today major in a humanistic area of study.)

To be sure, scientists, particularly those dealing with the biological and the human spheres, will continue to loom large in our discussion of the virtues. Already, in the wake of influential books like E. O. Wilson's *Consilience*, scientists have laid claim to much of the terrain of this book. They do so in two ways: in presenting fundamental explanations of what humans do and why they do it; and in offering links that connect the disparate sciences, from the lowly atom or molecule all the way up to the social group or the level of the superorganism (a label applied equally to a swarm of ants and the members of any self-organizing human institution).

I've signaled my own skepticism that everything human can or should be consigned to the data, the models, and the theories presented by scientists. I'm equally skeptical that the huge arena called Life can be stitched together along a single "great chain of being." But one would have to be an intellectual Luddite to ignore the findings and explanatory models of scientists; and one would be a hermetic fool not to integrate relevant claims and findings whenever they seem germane. And with the emergence of more nuanced interdisciplinary models—for example, those emanating from studies of behavioral economics or cultural evolution—investigations like the present one may be enriched.

Last, but perhaps also first, are the tools and the preoccupations of philosophy. I do not have formal training in philosophy, but it is probably not an accident that I always read two clusters of book reviews first: those dealing with the biological sciences and those dealing with philosophy. If one is interested in the nature of knowledge and how to think about it, philosophers reliably offer the most profound ideas—dating back to the original Athenians and reaching forward to those interested in the mind today.

Accordingly, I find it necessary and appropriate to think of my inquiry as one rooted in philosophy. Only through philosophy can one begin to think about the nature of statements and claims that invoke the terms *true*, *beautiful*, and *good*, and the territories where these statements (often highhandedly) obtain. And once one goes beyond the delineation of statements, one invades the subfields of philosophy—epistemology for truth, aesthetics for beauty, ethics for goodness. I hope that I have redeemed my amateur's love of philosophy in the ways that I have explored these terrains.

But philosophy also gains from its contacts with other fields. As a psychologist I'm particularly interested in efforts to join the experimentation strengths of my field to the conceptual powers of philosophical analysis. My teacher Nelson Goodman quipped that a psychologist was a philosopher with a research grant; he also observed that cognitive psychology is the most interesting branch of philosophy. Anthony Appiah, a contemporary philosopher, has even coined a term—*experimental philosophy* (no longer an oxymoron)—to describe a partial merging of these fields.

All of which is to say: So long as human beings are interested in the issues of truth, beauty, and goodness, we will continue to draw on philosophy and other humanistically oriented fields. A famous debate that occurred in Davos, Switzerland, in the summer of 1929, between Enlightenment thinker Ernst Cassirer and Martin Heidegger, celebrant of irrationality, is no less relevant today. Perhaps certain fields, such as brain science or genetics, will become more vocal; perhaps others, such as psychology or sociology, will become less dominant; but I don't expect the nature and interchange among key disciplinary participants to become less vigorous in the foreseeable future.

A s this inquiry draws to a close, I'd like to offer two observations. Though they pull in different directions, they are equally crucial. First, the role of chance, fate, vagaries, will be important, perhaps decisive. In all matters involving humans, the shake of the dice matters, and often profoundly so. We can hardly conceive of our understandings of the physical and biological worlds if the twenty-five-year-old Albert Einstein had not worked at a patent office, or if the twenty-five-year-old Charles Darwin had not traveled on the *Beagle*. And yet, despite the power of Einstein's physics and Darwin's biology, neither of their disciplines has been as prominent for our inquiry as the forces of history, the influences of history and histories, which in turn are studded with chance occurrences. How can we possibly anticipate the effects—positive, negative, unanticipated, in all likelihood chaotic—of artificial intelligence, nanotechnology, genetic manipulation, global warming, and the possible convergence of human neural networks and computer "neural networks" into an unprecedented Singularity?

My other observation: Despite the role of contingency in human affairs, individuals *do* matter—leaders, those who work with them to help achieve their mutual aspirations, those who seek—courageously or destructively—to undermine the leaders' mission. The efforts and choices made by individual people can play a decisive role in the fate of mankind. Thanks to Galileo Galilei, we have an altered understanding of the truths governing our physical environment. Thanks to James Watson and Francis Crick, we've gained an enhanced understanding of the natural world. Thanks to painter and sculptor Michelangelo Buonarrati, we have a richer notion of beauty; thanks to dancer Martha Graham, we have an expanded notion of what counts as beautiful. Thanks to Mohandas (Mahatma) Gandhi and to the founding figures of major religious and philosophical traditions, we have a fuller sense of the good person, the good action, the good life.

We cannot all achieve these pinnacles but we need not go gently into the dark night. Our choices need not be dictated by our own genes or by the impersonal features of supply and demand. We can all assemble around a campfire, a conference table, or a website and participate in lively conversations about the virtues. We can go further. Drawing on centuries of scholarly and practical knowledge, we can sift through the morass of information and move steadily toward the establishment of truths. Starting early, contemplating the range of artistic and natural creations, we can assemble a portfolio of beautiful objects and experiences, perhaps fashion our own objects of beauty, and arrive at our individualized aesthetic sensibility. As for morality and ethics: We should honor neighborly morality and respect the conventions of diverse cultures. At the same time, we should strive to become good workers and good citizens, not just within our own society but across the global community. Our actions should transcend self-interest. In so doing, we can provide powerful models that inspire our fellow human beings to act in responsible—indeed, in ever more responsible—ways.

Acknowledgments

This book grew out of a series of three lectures delivered in the autumn of 2008 at New York's Museum of Modern Art. For their indispensable support, I thank Emma Enderby, Pablo Helguera, Glenn Lowry, Jennifer Russell, and Wendy Woon. As discussants of lectures, I was privileged to have Peter Galison on Truth, Paola Antonelli on Beauty, and Antonio Damasio on Goodness.

My wife Ellen Winner gave the manuscript a careful reading, offered many good ideas, and provided the book's title. In addition, for their helpful comments on various portions of the manuscript, I thank Eric Blumenson, Michael Connell, George Klein, Tanya Luhrmann, Sara Rimer, Zak Stein, Marcelo Suarez-Orozco, Sandy Thatcher, and Steven Weinberg. Because of the generous support of Judy and Jamie Dimon and the MacArthur Foundation, I've been able to explore the digital media—special appreciation to John Seely Brown, Jonathan Fanton, Bob Gallucci, Julia Stasch, and Connie Yowell. My assistant

Kirsten Adam has been a wonderful partner in preparing many aspects of the lectures as well as the book manuscript—without her help, I'd still be working on the manuscript! Jessica Creighton, our office partner, was always there, and cheerfully so, when we needed her help.

At a time when book editing is a vanishing art, Lara Heimert gave the manuscript several detailed and probing readings and made many valuable recommendations. I am in her considerable debt. At Basic Books, I also thank Christine Arden, Sandra Beris, and Adam Eaglin for their expert help with the production of the book. And for their incredible support over the years, I owe special thanks to Ike Williams and Hope Denekamp, valued literary agents and friends.

HOWARD GARDNER
Cambridge, Massachusetts

Notes

Preface

x   **"The whole Mount . . . ":** H. Adams, *Mont-St. Michel and Chartres* (Boston: Houghton Mifflin, 1933). This book was circulated privately in 1904 and initially published in 1913. I obtained the quotations from a 2009 edition issued by CreateSpace. The quotations are from page 104.

xi   **"The life span of a fact . . . ":** D. Shields, *Reality hunger: A manifesto* (New York: Knopf, 2010), pp. 21, 52, 136, 160.

Chapter 1: The Virtues and the Challenges

3   **Modernism and postmodernism:** A host of works are helpful on these subjects. See C. Belsey, *Poststructuralism: A very short introduction* (New York: Oxford University Press, 2002); C. Butler, *Postmodernism: A very short introduction* (New York: Oxford, 2003); P. Gay, *Modernism: The lure of heresy from Baudelaire to Beckett and beyond* (New York: Norton, 2007); F. Jameson and S. Fish, *Postmodernism* (Durham: Duke University Press, 1991); G. Josipovici, *Whatever happened to modernism?* (New Haven: Yale University Press, 2010); G. Kitching, *The trouble with theory: The educational costs of postmodernism* (State College: Pennsylvania State University Press, 2008); C. Lemert, *Postmodernism is not what you think* (Malden, MA: Blackwell Publishers, 1997); S. Lukes, *Moral relativism* (New York: Picador, 2008); and J.-F. Lyotard, *The postmodern condition* (Minneapolis: University of Minnesota Press, 1984).

3   **New digital media:** See N. Carr, *The shallows: What the Internet is doing to our brains* (New York: Norton, 2010); M. Ito et al., *Hanging out, messing around, geeking out* (Cambridge, MA: MIT Press, 2009); H. Jenkins, *Convergence culture: Where old and new media collide* (New York: NYU Press, 2008); J. Lanier, *You are not a gadget: A manifesto* (New York: Knopf, 2010); M. Levinson, *From fear to Facebook: One school's journey* (International Society for Technology in Education, 2010); N. Negroponte, *Being digital* (New York: Vintage, 1996); J. Palfrey and U. Gasser, *Born digital* (New York: Basic Books, 2010); C. Shirky, *Here comes everybody: The power of organizing without organizations* (New York: Penguin Press, 2008); and C. Shirky, *Cognitive surplus* (New York: Penguin Press, 2010).

5   **"The safest general characterization . . . ":** A. N. Whitehead, *Process and reality* (New York: Free Press, 1979), p. 37. Originally published in 1928.

5   **"War is peace . . . ":** G. Orwell, *1984* (New York: Signet Classic, 1981). Originally published in 1949.

6   **"Only one thing on earth . . . ":** Albert Camus quoted in R. Riemen, *Nobility of spirit* (New Haven: Yale University Press, 2008), p. 75.

6   **"[t]here are no hard distinctions . . . ":** Pinter wrote this passage in 1958. He quoted it in Anne-Marie Cusac, "Harold Pinter interview," *The Progressive*, March 2001.

6   **Books about beauty:** U. Eco, *On beauty: History of a Western idea* (London: Secker and Warburg, 2004); E. Scarry, *On beauty and being just* (Princeton: Princeton University Press, 2001); and R. Scruton, *Beauty* (New York: Oxford University Press, 2009).

7   **Truthiness:** The term *truthiness* is generally attributed to the American comedian Stephen Colbert. It refers to propositions that one wishes to be true rather than to those that have been demonstrated to be true; or, as Colbert has put it, to statements that one assents to through one's guts rather than through books.

8   **"In the form of photographic images . . . ":** S. Sontag, *On photography* (New York: Picador, 1973), p. 174.

10   **"Children hope against hope . . . ":** B. Schlink, *Homecoming* (New York: Pantheon, 2008), p. 127.

10   **"'Ma-at' meant truth, justice, balance . . . ":** M. Atwood, *Payback debt and the shadow side of wealth* (Toronto: House of Anansi, 2008). This passage is quoted by John Gray in his review "The way of all debt," *New York Review of Books*, April 9, 2009.

11   **an arc from beauty through truth to goodness:** See H. Gardner, "A blessing of influences," in J. Schaler, ed., *Howard Gardner under fire* (Chicago: Open Court Publishing, 2006).

11   **My psychological studies of intelligence:** See H. Gardner, *Frames of mind: The theory of multiple intelligences* (New York: Basic Books, 1983/2011) and *Multiple intelligences: New horizons* (New York: Basic Books, 2006).

11   **My own educational philosophy:** See H. Gardner, *The disciplined mind* (New York: Simon and Schuster, 1999). Reprinted by Penguin in 2000.

12   **According to a recent poll carried out by the Barna group:** See *Christianity Today*, October 24, 2007.

12   **"How strange that technology has brought us . . . ":** D. Kehlmann, *Fame: A novel in nine episodes* (New York: Pantheon, 2010).

14   **Those beholden to biological or economic accounts:** For a similar critique, see A. Wolfe, *The future of liberalism* (New York: Knopf, 2009).

15   **The biological lens:** See D. Buss, *Evolutionary psychology* (Boston: Allyn and Bacon, 2007); D. Dutton, *The art instinct* (New York: Bloomsbury, 2009); M. Konner, *The tangled wing: Biological constraints on the human spirit* (New York: Holt, 2003); S. Pinker, *The blank slate: The modern denial of human nature* (New York: Penguin, 2003); J. Tooby and L. Cosmides, "The psychological foundations of culture," in J. Barkow, L. Cosmides, and J. Tooby, eds., *The adapted mind* (New York: Oxford University Press, 1991); and E. O. Wilson, *Sociobiology* (Cambridge, MA: Harvard University Press, 1975).

15   **The economic lens:** See J. Bhagwati, *In defense of globalization* (New York: Oxford University Press, 2007); R. Epstein, *Principles for a free society* (New York: Basic Books, 2002); M. Friedman, *Capitalism and freedom: Fortieth anniversary edition* (Chicago: University of Chicago Press, 2002); G. Gilder, *The spirit of enterprise* (New York: Touchstone Books, 1985); N. G. Mankiw, *Principles of economics* (Cincinnati: South-Western College Publishing, 2008); and S. Patterson, *The quants: How a new breed of math whizzes conquered Wall Street and almost destroyed it* (New York: Crown, 2010).

16   **Critiques of the market lens:** See P. Krugman, "How did economists get it so wrong?" *New York Times Magazine*, September 6, 2009; R. Reich, *Aftershock* (New York: Knopf, 2010); G. Soros, *The crash of 2008 and what it means* (New York: Public Affairs, 2009); and J. Stiglitz, *Freefall: America, free markets, and the sinking of the world economy* (New York: Norton, 2010).

16   **Malcolm Gladwell's best-known books:** M. Gladwell, *The tipping point: How little things can make a big difference* (New York: Back Bay Books, 2002); *Blink* (New York: Back Bay Books, 2007); and *Outliers: The story of success* (New York: Little, Brown, 2008).

Chapter 2: Truth

20   **For philosophical treatments of truth:** See S. Blackburn, *Truth: A guide* (New York: Oxford University Press, 2007).

21   **Infant's frustration at a simulacrum:** See T. Bower, *Development in infancy* (San Francisco: W. H. Freeman, 1974).

22   **How our senses can be misleading:** See S. Asch, *Social psychology* (New York: Oxford University Press, 1987); R. Burton, *On being certain: Believing you are right even when you're not* (New York: St. Martin's Press, 2009);

B. M. Hood, *SuperSense: Why we believe in the unbelievable* (New York: Harper One, 2009); A. Newberg and M. R. Waldman, *Why we believe what we believe* (New York: Free Press, 2006); and S. Wang and S. Aamodt, "Your brain lies to you," *New York Times*, June 27, 2008.

23   **The nature of different disciplines:** See H. Gardner, *The disciplined mind* (New York: Simon and Schuster, 1999) and *Five minds for the future* (Boston: Harvard Business School Press, 2007).

24   **The origins of Einstein's theories:** See P. Galison, *Einstein's clocks, Poincaré's maps: Empires of time* (New York: Norton, 2004).

25   **Paradigm shifts in scientific thought:** See T. S. Kuhn, *The structure of scientific revolutions* (Chicago: University of Chicago Press, 1970/2009).

26   **"I believe, and still believe . . . ":** B. Morris, "Politics by other means," *The New Republic*, March 22, 2004.

28   **Journalism as a profession in jeopardy:** See J. Fallows, *Breaking the news: How the media undermine American democracy* (New York: Vintage, 1997); H. Gardner, M. Csikszentmihalyi, and W. Damon, *Good work: When excellence and ethics meet* (New York: Basic Books, 2001); H. Gardner, *Responsibility at work* (San Francisco: Jossey-Bass, 2008); and A. Jones, *Losing the news* (New York: Oxford University Press, 2009).

30   **"Were it left to me . . . ":** Thomas Jefferson's remarks were made in a letter to Edward Carrington dated January 10, 1787.

30   **Philosophical treatment of skepticism:** See E. Blumenson, "Mapping the limits of skepticism in law and morals," *Texas Law Review* 74, no. 3 (February 1996): 523–576.

33   **"That's not the way . . . ":** Bush adviser quoted in Jones, *Losing the news*, pp. 219–220.

33   **"He believed that there was, on most stories, something approximating truth . . . ":** This commemoration of David Rosenbaum's quotation is cited in T. Purdum, "Robin Toner, 54, Times Political Reporter" (obituary), *New York Times*, December 13, 2008, p. B9.

34   **"We all know that art is not truth . . . ":** P. Picasso, "Picasso speaks," *The Arts*, May 1923.

35   **William F. Buckley's taunt:** "I'd rather entrust the government of the United States to the first 400 people listed in the Boston telephone directory than to the faculty of Harvard University."

Chapter 3: Beauty

42   **Certain geometric features favored in art works:** See G. Birkhoff, *Aesthetic measure* (Cambridge, MA: Harvard University Press, 1933); and S. Smee, "Is beauty a matter of mathematics?" *Boston Globe*, February 22, 2009.

42 **Alexander Melamid and Vitaly Komar's polling of artistic preferences:** See J. Wypijewski, ed., *Komar and Melamid's guide to art* (Berkeley and Los Angeles: University of California Press, 1999).

44 **Evolutionary approaches to aesthetic preferences:** See E. Dissanayake, *Homo aestheticus: Where art comes from and why* (Seattle: University of Washington Press, 1995); D. Dutton, *The art instinct* (New York: Bloomsbury, 2009); N. Etcoff, *Survival of the prettiest: The science of beauty* (New York: Anchor, 2000); S. Pinker, *The blank slate: The modern denial of human nature* (New York: Penguin, 2003); and "Why music? Biologists are addressing one of humanity's strangest attributes, its all singing, all dancing culture," *Economist*, December 20, 2008.

44 **Biological reactions to works of art:** See I. Biederman and E. Vessel, "Perceptual pleasure and the brain," *American Scientist* (May–June 2006): 249–255.

45 **Cultures valorizing different objects and artifacts:** See G. Robb, *The discovery of France* (New York: Norton, 2007); and O. Pamuk, *Istanbul: Memories and the city* (New York: Vintage, 2007).

46 **Other biologically based accounts:** See D. Dutton, *The art instinct* (New York: Bloomsbury, 2009); and J. Tooby and L. Cosmides, "Does beauty build adapted minds? Toward an evolutionary theory of aesthetics, fiction, and the arts," *SubStance* (University of Wisconsin Press), no. 1/2 (issue 94/95): 6–27.

46 ***Style* versus *idea*:** See A. Schoenberg, *Style and idea: Selected writings* (Berkeley: University of California Press, 1984).

47 **Mirror neurons:** See A. S. Byatt, "Observe the neurons: Between, above, below John Donne," *Times* (London), September 22, 2006.

47 **Tallis's critique of Byatt's claims:** R. Tallis, "License my roving hands: Does neuroscience really have anything to teach us about the pleasures of reading John Donne?" *Times Literary Supplement* (London), April 11, 2008. See also R. Tallis, *The kingdom of infinite space* (New York: Yale University Press, 2009). For another skeptical view of the relevance of neuroscientific findings for an explication of the virtues, see S. Berker, "Can normative conclusions be wrung from neural bases?" Unpublished paper, November 30, 2008, Harvard University.

48 **"We who live . . . ":** L. Fendrich, *Chronicle Review,* July 11, 2008, p. 22.

49 **"Open concept":** See M. Weitz, "The role of theory in aesthetics," *British Journal of Aesthetics* (September 1956).

49 **Features of artistic beauty:** See N. Goodman, *Languages of art* (Indianapolis: Hackett, 1976) and *Ways of worldmaking* (Indianapolis: Hackett, 1978).

50 **Experimental aesthetics:** See D. Berlyne, *Aesthetics and psychobiology* (New York: Appleton-Century Crofts, 1971); C. Martindale, *The clockwork muse: The predictability of artistic change* (New York: Basic Books, 1990); P. Silva, *Exploring the psychology of interest* (New York: Oxford University

Press, 2006); and E. Winner, *Invented worlds: The psychology of the arts* (Cambridge, MA: Harvard University Press, 1982).

51 **"In comparison to the flamboyantly Baroque display . . . ":** J. Adams, *Hallelujah junction* (New York: Farrar, Straus and Giroux, 2008), p. 313.

51 *I will not make any more boring art:* The Baldessari work was originally part of a short film. See also *John Baldessari—Pure Beauty*, Exhibition, New York Metropolitan Museum of Art, Fall 2010.

51 **Conceptual art:** See A. Alberro and J. Stimson, *Conceptual art: A critical anthology* (Cambridge, MA: MIT Press, 2000).

54 **"the sort of magic . . . ":** Arthur Danto quoted in "Sitting with Marina," *New York Times*, May 23, 2010.

59 **Elliott Carter:** See C. Rosen, "Happy birthday, Elliott Carter," *New York Review of Books*, March 12, 2009.

60 **Matthew Barney:** See "His body, himself: Matthew Barney's strange and passionate exploration of gender," in C. Tomkins, *Lives of the artists* (New York: Holt, 2008).

62 **Or that Miró had not decided:** In 1927, Miró declared: "I want to assassinate painting." This remark became the thesis of the 2008 exhibition *Joan Miró: Painting and Anti-Painting, 1927–1937* at New York's Museum of Modern Art.

64 **Economic approach to artistic value:** See D. Galenson, *Painting outside the lines* (Cambridge, MA: Harvard University Press, 2002) and *Artistic capital* (London: Routledge, 2006).

65 **Familiar content of old media presented in the form of new media:** See M. McLuhan, *Understanding media: The extensions of man* (New York: McGraw-Hill, 1964).

65 **Distinctions challenged:** See P. Antonelli, *Design and the elastic mind* (New York: Museum of Modern Art, 2008).

70 **Blurring boundaries:** See P. Galison, Comments on Howard Gardner's lecture on "Truth," Museum of Modern Art, November 25, 2008; W. T. Gowers, "Bridging the cultural divide: Art and mathematics review of conversations across art and science," *Science* 320 (May 16, 2008); R. Kennedy, "Art made at the speed of the Internet: Don't say 'geek,' say 'collaborator,'" *New York Times*, April 19, 2010; M. Leslie, "An artist develops a new image—with aid of bacteria," *Science* 322 (December 19, 2008); and D. Overbye, "Art and science: Virtual and real, under one big roof," *New York Times*, September 23, 2008.

70 **The divisions among disciplines, arts, and crafts:** See Gowers, "Bridging the cultural divide"; Leslie, "An artist develops a new image"; and Overbye, "Art and science."

71 **The museum without walls:** See A. Malraux, *The voices of silence* (Princeton: Princeton University Press, 1978).

73 **"Rather than creating a unique movement language . . . ":** Carla Peterson quoted in C. La Rocco, "Say, just whose choreography is this?" *New York Times*, August 24, 2008, p. 25.

Chapter 4: Goodness

79   **Our moral sense:** See M. Hauser, *Moral minds: The nature of right and wrong* (New York: Harvest, 2007); and R. Wright, *The moral animal* (New York: Vintage, 1995).

80   **Group size:** See R. Dunbar, *How many friends does one person need? Dunbar's number and other evolutionary quirks* (London: Faber and Faber, 2010).

83   **Sense of good and bad in early life:** See P. Bloom, "The moral life of babies," *New York Times Magazine*, May 9, 2010; and J. Kagan, *The second year* (Cambridge, MA: Harvard University Press, 1981).

84   **The ethics of roles:** See H. Gardner, ed., *GoodWork: Theory and practice* (Cambridge, MA, 2010). Available online at http://www.goodworkproject.org/publications/books.htm.

85   **"Just community":** J. Rawls, *A theory of justice* (Cambridge, MA: Harvard University Press, 1970/2005).

87   **Research on "good work":** L. Barendsen and W. Fischman, "The Good-Work Toolkit: From theory to practice," in H. Gardner, ed., *Responsibility at work* (San Francisco: Jossey-Bass, 2007); H. Gardner, *GoodWork: Theory and practice*; and H. Gardner, M. Csikszentmihalyi, and W. Damon, *Good Work: When excellence and ethics meet* (New York: Basic Books, 2001).

88   **In executing the Good Work Project:** See http://www.goodwork project.org and the ten books cited there.

89   **Memes:** See S. Blackmore, *The meme machine* (New York: Oxford University Press, 2000).

92   **Encouraging good work:** See W. Fischman, B. Solomon, D. Greenspan, and H. Gardner, *Making good: How young people cope with moral dilemmas at work* (Cambridge, MA: Harvard University Press, 2004).

93   **Religion and ethical behavior:** See R. Wright, *The evolution of God* (Back Bay Books, 2010).

93   **Attacks on religion:** See R. Dawkins, *The God Delusion* (Mariner Books, 2008); R. Dennett, *Breaking the spell* (New York: Penguin, 2007); S. Harris, *The end of faith* (New York: Norton, 2005); and C. Hitchens, *God is not great* (New York: Twelve Publishers, 2010).

94   **Relation between crime rate and secularism:** See G. S. Paul, "Cross-national correlations of quantifiable societal health with popular religiosity and secularism in the prosperous democracies," *Journal of Religion and Society* 7 (2005).

95   **Moral freedom:** See A. Wolfe, *Moral freedom: The search for virtue in a world of choice* (New York: Norton, 2002).

95   **Tendency toward moderation in religious views:** See Wolfe, *Moral freedom*; M. Mellman, "Another country," op-ed in *New York Times*, September 17, 2008; and R. Putnam and D. Campbell, *American grace: How religion divides and unites us* (New York: Simon and Schuster, 2010).

96   **Study of good work among American youth:** Fischman, Solomon, Greenspan, and Gardner, *Making good.*

96   **thin ethical dossier:** See D. Callahan, *The cheating culture: Why more Americans are doing wrong to get ahead* (New York: Harvest Books, 2004).

97   **"Reflection" sessions:** See W. Fischman and H. Gardner, "Implementing GoodWork programs: Helping students to become ethical workers," Paper No. 59 (2008). Available online at goodworkproject.org.

98   **Postmodern arguments:** See C. Belsey, *Poststructuralism: A very short introduction* (New York: Oxford University Press, 2002); C. Butler, *Postmodernism: A very short introduction* (New York: Oxford, 2003); P. Gay, *Modernism: The lure of heresy from Baudelaire to Beckett and beyond* (New York: Norton, 2007); F. Jameson and S. Fish, *Postmodernism* (Durham: Duke University Press, 1991); G. Josipovici, *Whatever happened to modernism?* (New Haven: Yale University Press, 2010); G. Kitching, *The trouble with theory: The educational costs of postmodernism* (State College: Pennsylvania State University Press, 2008); C. Lemert, *Postmodernism is not what you think* (Malden, MA: Blackwell Publishers, 1997); S. Lukes, *Moral relativism* (New York: Picador, 2008); and J.-F. Lyotard, *The postmodern condition* (Minneapolis: University of Minnesota Press, 1984).

98   **Student cheating:** See E. Ramirez, "Cheating on the rise among high school students," *US News and World Report,* December 2, 2008.

99   **Adolescent moral reasoning:** See L. Kohlberg, "Development of moral character and moral ideology," in M. L. Hoffman and L. Hoffman, eds., *Review of child development research,* Vol. 1 (New York: Russell Sage Foundation, 1964).

100   **The Good Play Project:** See C. James et al., *Young people, ethics, and the new digital media: A synthesis from the Good Play Project* (Cambridge, MA: MIT Press, 2009).

101   **Lori Drew and Megan Meier:** See J. Steinhauer, "Arguments in case involving net and suicide," *New York Times,* November 19, 2008. Available online at http://www.nytimes.com/2008/11/20/us/20myspace.html.

102   **Comparably tragic stories:** See "Suicide of Rutgers freshman tied to webcast," *Los Angeles Times,* October 1, 2010.

102   **The "apparat":** G. Shteyngart, *Super Sad True Love Story* (New York: Random House, 2010).

105   **"Whatsoever is the object . . .":** T. Hobbes, *Leviathan,* Part VI.

Chapter 5: A Promising Start

108   **Alison Gopnik's books:** A. Gopnik, *The philosophical baby* (New York: Farrar Straus and Giroux, 2009); and A. Gopnik, A. Meltzoff, and P. Kuhl, *The scientist in the crib* (New York: Harper, 2000).

108   **the world over:** See H. Gardner, *Developmental psychology* (Boston: Little, Brown, 1982) and *The unschooled mind* (New York: Basic Books, 1991).

110 **Prenatal influences:** See A. Paul, *Origins: How the nine months before birth shape the rest of our lives* (New York: Free Press, 2010).

112 **Creature comforts in monkeys and children:** See H. Harlow, *Learning to love* (New York: J. Aronson, 1978).

112 **once these demands have been met, young children come to desire:** See Maslow's discussion of the hierarchy of needs in A. Maslow, *Toward a psychology of being* (New York: Wiley [1961] 1998).

114 **For a classical view of egocentrism:** See J. Piaget, "Piaget's theory," in P. Mussen, ed., *Handbook of child psychology*, Vol. I (New York: Wiley, 1970).

114 **Theory of mind:** See J. Astington, *The child's discovery of the mind* (Cambridge, MA: Harvard University Press, 1994); A. Leslie, "Pretense and representation: The origins of 'theory of mind,'" *Psychological Review* 94, no. 4 (1987): 412–426; and J. Perner, *Understanding the representational mind* (Cambridge, MA: MIT Press, 1991).

115 **Accepting testimony:** See P. Harris, "Trust," *Developmental Science* 10, no. 1 (2007): 135–138.

116 **Rules of conversation:** See H. P. Grice, *Studies in the way of words* (Cambridge, MA: Harvard University Press, 1991); and J. Searle, *Speech acts: An essay in the philosophy of language* (Cambridge, UK: Cambridge University Press, 1970).

116 **Gravitating toward helpful adults:** See J. Hamlin, K. Wynn, and P. Bloom, "Social evaluation by preverbal infants," *Nature* 450 (November 22, 2007), pp. 557–559. See also P. Bloom, "The moral life of babies," *New York Times Magazine*, May 9, 2010.

116 **Birth of morality:** See J. Kagan, *The second year* (New York: Basic Books, 1981).

117 **Distinguishing the conventional from the moral:** See E. Turiel, *The development of social knowledge* (New York: Cambridge University Press, 2008).

118 **As Lionel Bart's Fagin intones:** Bart is the composer and lyricist of the musical *Oliver!*

120 **Melamid and Kolmar:** See the discussion in Chapter 3 of the present volume as well as E. Dissanayake, *Homo aestheticus: Where art comes from and why* (Seattle: University of Washington Press, 1995); D. Dutton, *The art instinct* (New York: Bloomsbury, 2009); N. Etcoff, *Survival of the prettiest: The science of beauty* (New York: Anchor, 2000); S. Pinker, *The blank slate: The modern denial of human nature* (New York: Penguin, 2003); and "Why music? Biologists are addressing one of humanity's strangest attributes, its all singing, all dancing culture," *Economist*, December 20, 2008.

122 **Pleasurable experiences in children (and adults):** See P. Bloom, *How pleasure works: The new science of why we like what we like* (New York: Norton, 2010).

122 **Children as essentialists:** See Bloom, *How pleasure works*; and S. Gelman, *The essential child* (New York: Oxford University Press, 2005).

123 **once a stick has been anointed a hobby horse:** See Bloom, *How pleasure works.*

125 **The possibility of falsification:** See K. Popper, *The logic of scientific discovery* (London: Routledge [1959] 2002).

126 **Misconceptions held by children:** See Gardner, *The unschooled mind.*

126 **Teaching and learning for understanding:** See H. Gardner, *The disciplined mind* (New York: Simon and Schuster, 1999); and S. Wiske, ed., *Teaching for understanding* (San Francisco: Jossey-Bass, 1997).

127 **mastering STEM culture:** C. P. Snow, *The two cultures and the scientific revolution* (Cambridge, UK: Cambridge University Press, 1960). Delivered as the Reith Lectures in 1959.

128 **Constructive engagement:** See W. Damon, *Greater expectations* (New York: Free Press, 1996). See also D. Meier, *The power of their ideas* (Boston: Beacon Press, 1995).

128 **Shift to "propositional attitudes":** See D. Olson, *The world on paper* (New York: Cambridge University Press, 1996).

130 **Moral development and education:** See W. Damon, *The moral child* (New York: Free Press, 1988) and *Greater expectations* (New York: Free Press, 1996).

134 **Artistic development in children:** See N. Freeman, *Strategies of representation in young children* (New York: Academic Press, 1980); A. Housen, *A review of studies on aesthetic education* (Minneapolis: American Association of Museums, 1996); M. Parsons, *How we understand art* (New York: Cambridge University Press, 1989); and E. Winner, *Invented worlds: A psychology of the arts* (Cambridge, MA: Harvard University Press, 1982).

134 **Artistic development in adolescence:** See H. Gardner, *Artful scribbles: The significance of children's drawings* (New York: Basic Books, 1980).

134 **Formal and informal education:** See Gardner, *The unschooled mind.*

136 **the chance to behold works that have been valued:** See P. Antonelli, *Design and the elastic mind* (New York: Museum of Modern Art, 2008), as well as the discussion of this exhibit in Chapter 3 of the present volume.

137 **Kohlberg's theory:** See L. Kohlberg, *Essays on moral development: The psychology of moral development* (San Francisco: Harper and Row, 1984). See also the summary of related research in E. Turiel, "The development of morality," in W. Damon, ed., *Handbook of child psychology*, Vol. 3 (New York: Wiley, 1998).

137 **in the case of the arts:** See H. Gardner, *The unschooled mind* (New York: Basic Books, 1999) and *The arts and human development* (New York: Basic Books, 1994).

139 **should the young person prove able to resist:** See H. Gardner, *Changing minds* (Boston: Harvard Business School Press, 2004).

144 **Psychologists' views of identity:** See E. Erikson, "Identity and the life cycle," *Psychological Issues* 1, no. 1 (1959).

145 **Young people's use of the new digital media:** See C. James, K. Davis, A. Flores et al., *Young people, ethics, and the new digital media: A synthesis from the GoodPlay project* (Cambridge, MA: MIT Press, 2009).

146 **Good Work sessions:** See H. Gardner, ed., *GoodWork: Theory and practice* (Cambridge, MA, 2010). Available online at http://www.goodworkproject.org/publications/books.htm.

148 **Knowing the good after confronting evil:** See D. Keltner, *Born to be good: The science of a meaningful life* (New York: Norton, 2009); and S. Seider, "Social justice in the suburbs," *Educational Leadership* 66, no. 1 (2008): 54–58.

150 **Confident assertions of truth called into question:** W. Perry, *Forms of ethical and intellectual development in the college years: A scheme* (San Francisco: Jossey-Bass, 1998).

150 **Metacognition:** See J. Dunlovsky and J. Metcalfe, *Metacognition* (Thousand Oaks, CA: Sage, 2008); and D. Kuhn, *Education for thinking* (Cambridge, MA: Harvard University Press, 2008).

153 **Wikipedia:** See J. Giles, "Special report: Internet encyclopedias go head to head," *Nature* 438 (December 15, 2005), pp. 990–991.

153 **Fragmented young persons:** See S. Seider and H. Gardner, "The Fragmented Generation," *Journal of College and Character* 10, no. 4 (2009): 1–4.

Chapter 6: Learning Throughout Life

155 **"The sixth stage shifts . . . ":** W. Shakespeare, *As you like it*, act II, scene vii, verses 157–166.

156 **Piaget's scheme:** See J. Piaget, "Piaget's theory," in P. Mussen, ed., *Handbook of child psychology*, Vol. 1 (New York: Wiley, 1970).

156 **Post-formal thought:** See C. Alexander and E. Langer, eds., *Higher stages of human development* (New York: Oxford University Press, 1990); P. Baltes, U. Lindenberger, and U. Staudinger, "Life span theory in developmental psychology," in R. M. Lerner, ed., *Handbook of child psychology*, Vol. 1 (New York: Wiley, 2006); and M. L. Commons, F. A. Richards, and C. Armon, *Beyond formal operations: Late adolescent and adult cognitive development* (New York: Praeger, 1984).

157 **Systemic thinking after adolescence:** See K. Fischer and T. Bidell, "Dynamic development of action and thought," in W. Damon, ed., *Handbook of child psychology*, Vol. 1 (New York: Wiley, 2006).

158 **Emergent adulthood:** See J. Arnett, *Emerging adulthood* (New York: Oxford University Press, 2006); and R. Henig, "What is it about 20-somethings?" *New York Times Magazine*, August 18, 2010.

158 **"Third stage" of adulthood:** See S. Lawrence-Lightfoot, *The third chapter* (New York: Farrar, Straus and Giroux, 2009).

159 **Women in Islamic settings:** See Ayaan Hirsi Ali, *Nomad: From Islam to America. A personal journey through the clash of civilization* (New York:

Free Press, 2010); and Z. Salbi, *Beyond two worlds: Escape from tyranny. Growing up in the shadow of Saddam* (New York: Gotham Books, 2010).

159 **"Hot" and "cool" societies:** See C. Lévi-Strauss, *Myth and meaning* (London: Routledge, 1999).

160 **Weak and strong ties:** See M. Granovetter, *Getting a job: A study of contacts and careers* (Chicago: University of Chicago Press, 1995).

162 **Plasticity of the nervous system:** See S. Barry, *Fixing my gaze* (New York: Basic Books, 2010); N. Doidge, *The brain that changes itself* (New York: Viking, 2007); and J. Ledoux, *Synaptic self: How our brains become who we are* (New York: Penguin, 2003).

164 **Aging successfully:** See R. Butler, *The longevity revolution* (New York: Public Affairs, 2008); and G. McKhann and M. Albert, *Keeping your brain young* (New York: Wiley, 2002).

164 **Feeling overwhelmed:** See R. Kegan and L. Lahey, *Immunity to change* (Boston: Harvard Business School Press, 2009).

164 **Imperative to synthesize:** See H. Gardner, *Five minds for the future* (Boston: Harvard Business School Press, 2007), ch. 3.

165 **The increasing role of individual agency in the contemporary world:** See J. Hagel, J. S. Brown, and L. Davison, *The power of pull: How small moves, smartly made, can set big things in motion* (New York: Basic Books, 2010).

167 **Artistic trends over time:** See C. Martindale, *The clockwork muse: The predictability of artistic change* (New York: Basic Books, 1990).

168 **Taste and age thirty-nine:** See the work of Robert Sapolsky, described in "Investigations, Open Season," *New Yorker*, March 30, 1998, p. 57.

170 **Moral development after adolescence:** See L. Kohlberg, *Essays on moral development: The psychology of moral development* (San Francisco: Harper and Row, 1984).

171 **Pseudospeciation:** The notion of pseudospeciation has been variously attributed to the biologist Julian Huxley and the psychologist Erik Erikson.

172 **we'd ideally need a constantly changing "Toolkit" for each profession:** L. Barendsen and W. Fischman, "The GoodWork Toolkit: From theory to practice," in H. Gardner, ed., *Responsibility at work* (San Francisco: Jossey-Bass, 2007).

172 **Ethical issues in neuroscience:** See K. Sheridan, E. Zinchenko, and H. Gardner, "Neuroethics in education," in J. Illes, ed., *Neuroethics: Defining the issues in research, practice, and politics* (New York: Oxford University Press, 2005); and H. Gardner, "Quandaries for neuroeducators," *Mind, Brain, and Education* 2, no. 4 (2008): 165–169.

175 **The Matthew Effect:** This term was coined by sociologist Robert K. Merton; see "The Matthew Effect in Science," *Science* 159 (1968): 56–63.

180 **The head of a Muslim family:** See U. Wikan, *Honor and agony: Honor killings in modern-day Europe* (Chicago: University of Chicago Press, 2008).

182 **Fundamentalist thinking:** See H. Gardner, *Changing minds: The art and science of changing our own and other people's mind* (Boston: Harvard Business School Press, 2004).

182 **Ease and difficulties of changing minds:** See Gardner, *Changing minds.*

183 **"Moral imagination":** See R. Wright, *Nonzero* (New York: Vintage, 2001); and *The evolution of God* (New York: Little, Brown, 2009).

183 **Chomsky's caution:** See N. Chomsky, interview conducted by Howard Gardner, Harvard Graduate School of Education, December 11, 2007.

184 **"there is but one truly serious philosophical problem . . . ":** A. Camus, *The myth of Sisyphus and other essays* (New York: Vintage, 1991).

185 **the final years of life:** E. H. Erikson, *Childhood and society* (New York: Norton, 1963).

Conclusion: Looking Ahead

189 **three great chains of being:** See A. O. Lovejoy, *The great chain of being: A study of the origin of an idea* (New York: Harper Torchbooks, 1936).

195 **"We must indeed all hang together . . . ":** This quotation, attributed to Franklin, appears in P. M. Zall's *Ben Franklin, laughing*, which was published in 1908.

196 **Enlightenment ideas:** See E. Cassirer and P. Gay, *The philosophy of the Enlightenment* (Princeton: Princeton University Press, 2009); R. Nisbet, *History of the idea of progress* (Piscataway, NJ: Transaction Press, 1994); and R. R. Palmer, J. Colton, and L. Kramer, *A history of the modern world* (New York: McGraw Hill, 2006).

197 **" . . . human character changed":** Virginia Woolf made this remark in her 1924 essay "Mr. Bennett and Mrs. Brown."

198 **Biological and economic approaches:** For references on these approaches, see under "The biological lens" and "The economic lens" in the endnotes for Chapter 1.

199 **Our questionable rationality:** See, for example, D. Ariely, *Predictably irrational* (New York: Harper Perennial, 2010); R. Burton, *On being certain: Believing you are right even when you're not* (New York: St. Martin's Press, 2009); B. M. Hood, *SuperSense: Why we believe in the unbelievable* (New York: Harper One, 2009); D. Kahneman and A. Tversky, eds., *Choices, values, and frames* (New York: Cambridge University Press, 2000); A. Newberg and M. R. Waldman, *Why we believe what we believe* (New York: Free Press, 2006); and S. Wang and S. Aamodt, "Your brain lies to you," *New York Times*, June 27, 2008.

199 **The financial meltdown of 2008:** See M. Lewis, *The big short: Inside the doomsday machine* (New York: Norton, 2010); R. Lowenstein, *The end of Wall Street* (New York: Penguin, 2010); S. Patterson, *The quants: How a new breed of math whizzes conquered Wall Street and almost destroyed it* (New

York: Crown, 2010); R. Reich, *Aftershock* (New York: Knopf, 2010); and A. R. Sorkin, *Too big to fail* (New York: Viking, 2009).

200   **Freud's statement:** This remark has been credited to Sigmund Freud in letters written to Carl Jung and to Marie Bonaparte. It also appears in Freud's 1930 publication *Civilization and its discontents* (New York: Norton, 1969).

200   **Criticism of economics:** See J. Fox, *The myth of the rational market: A history of risk, reward, and delusion on Wall Street* (New York: Harper Business, 2009); P. Krugman, "How did economists get it so wrong?" *New York Times Magazine*, September 6, 2009; D. Leonhardt, "Theory and morality in the new economy," *New York Times Book Review*, August 23, 2009; S. Marglin, "Why economists are part of the problem," *Chronicle Review*, February 27, 2009; and D. Rushkoff, "Economics is not natural science," August 13, 2009, available online at http://www.edge.org/3rd_culture/rushkoff09/rushkoff09_index.html.

201   **Linking the several sciences:** See E. O. Wilson, *Sociobiology* (Cambridge, MA: Harvard University Press, 1975); and *Consilience: The unity of knowledge* (New York: Vintage, 1999).

202   **Declining interest in the humanities:** See J. Engell and A. Dangerfield, *Saving higher education in the age of money* (Charlottesville: University of Virginia Press, 2005); A. Kronman, *Education's end: Why our colleges and universities have given up on the meaning of life* (New Haven: Yale University Press, 2008); and L. Menand, *The marketplace of ideas* (New York: Norton, 2009).

202   **scientists have laid claim to much of the terrain of this book:** W. Chace, "The decline of the English department," *American Scholar* (Autumn 2009).

204   **Experimental philosophy:** A. Appiah, *Experiments in ethics* (Cambridge, MA: Harvard University Press, 2008).

204   **A famous debate:** See P. Gordon, *Continental divide: Heidegger, Cassirer, Davos* (Cambridge, MA: Harvard University Press, 2010).

Index